Breaker's Mate

On the Wool Track
C. E. W. Bean.

Breaker's Mate

Will Ogilvie in Australia

John Meredith

Kangaroo Press

First published in 1996 by Kangaroo Press Pty Ltd
3 Whitehall Road Kenthurst NSW 2156 Australia
P.O. Box 6125 Dural Delivery Centre NSW 2158
Printed by Australian Print Group, Maryborough, Victoria

ISBN 0 86417 825 5

CONTENTS

PART I: THE ITINERANT BALLADIST

PART II: STRAYS, CLEANSKINS AND SCRUBBERS

PART III: THE HONOUR OF THE STATION

ACKNOWLEDGMENTS

I am happy to have the opportunity to thank the following people who have helped in gathering material for this book:

Catherine Jeffries of Edinburgh, great-grand-daughter of Will H. Ogilvie and owner by inheritance of copyright in the works of Will Ogilvie and of his son George Ogilvie, for permission to publish copyright material, and for cheerfully answering a steady stream of letters asking for information about her family.

The staff of the Mitchell Library, Sydney, especially Jenny Broombead and other librarians in the Original Materials section; Betty Erickson, Archivist of the Iowa State University, USA.;

Mark Cranfield of the National Library of Australia; and Ian Landles of Hawick, Scotland.

People of 'the Lachlan Side' were both generous and enthusiastic in offering assistance and material. In Forbes: Rob Willis and family, Don Scott, Ruth Horsburgh, Ninette Caldwell and Jeanette Hildred; and in Parkes: Isabel Townsend, Nell Beuzeville and Heather Veal all rendered outstanding help.

Marg Muller of Penola, South Australia, was big-hearted in sharing her own research material, as was Bill Cameron of Boggi Bend, Bourke. Others who volunteered assistance were Doug and Maggie Crawford of Malacoota, Stephan Williams, Craig Edgman, Jamie Carlin and R. M. Williams.

I am grateful to the Mitchell Library of New South Wales for permission to use manuscript poems and to quote from letters in the Stephens Papers; to the General Reference Library, State Library of New South Wales, for a negative from the *Sydney Mail*; and to the National Library of Australia for two photos of Will Ogilvie.

For providing the text of the Ogilvie sketches, *The Honour of the Station*, I offer special thanks to the Librarian and staff of the Australian Defence Forces Academy Library in Canberra; to Mrs Margaret Drury and to Chris Woodland.

John Meredith
July 1996

Part I

THE ITINERANT BALLADIST

Introduction

Will Ogilvie came to Australia from Scotland at the end of 1889 and remained in this country during the golden years of Australian literature, the 1890s. When he returned to his homeland after an absence of eleven years he was farewelled as one of our leading bush balladists. In the following piece, he writes his own introduction:

How I Wrote 'Fair Girls and Gray Horses'
by Will H. Ogilvie

Long, long ago, in the broom-witch days, I wrote rhymes; I think I was only seven or eight when lines used to come singing along like the big brown bees in the garden where I played; but I must have been quite fifteen when a local editor — oh! long suffering local editor! — gave me four inches of valuable space — which possibly might have been better employed in the usual way, in the interests of the largest local pumpkin or the ewe with six lambs — for some lines on 'Flodden Field'. Two of the lines were cribbed wholly, but innocently, from Aytoun's 'Lays', and most of the others seem, when read in the bright light of mature criticism, to reflect somebody else; nevertheless they were boldly headed 'Original Poetry', and, as such, were apparently accepted by a credulous countryside.

My pride, as I carefully ran the scissors round those four stanzas, can be imagined, and though I have cut many yards of my verse out of newspapers since then, I have never attained to the thrill of that supreme moment of triumph.

Haunting Rhymes
Somehow, with a new life and new surroundings, came lines that stood alone, as it were, and I woke to find that I could jingle rhymes to my own satisfaction and that of my friends, rhymes that were really my own. Lines still came singing, but they came with the hum of the cicadas at sunset, and the beat of bare hoofs by the moon. I did not take things very seriously, having at that time infinitely more ambition to be a rider of buckjumpers more than a writer of verses; but I rhymed because I had to, and because the lilting phrases worried me until they were written down.

A line or a couplet would come to me, maybe, in a moonlight ride, singing up through the beating hoofs with rhythmical persistence. Thus, one night, I remember, the whole wild Lachlan bush seemed to be chanting of the summer moon, 'Rail high with the lore of a million nights, And the legends of all the years.' For aught I know, the lines may be someone else's that have come singing down the moonlit beaches of forgotten Time; but, anyway, I took them, and wrote them down, and round them the other verses took shape, and in this way the rhyme was written — the rhyme which I have called 'The New Moon'.

Nearly every set of verses in my book was written in this way; a couplet or quatrain came unasked, and round them the other lines fell into place. But always the key lines were the best, and I can pick them out among their neighbours, and remember exactly the hour when they came, and rode by my bridlehand, pleading to be pencilled down. I have often thought since: If only a whole poem would come to one in that way, possibly it would be worth the reading.

My First Poem

It was from far away Broken Hill that I sent my first poem to the Sydney *Bulletin*. 'Beyond the Barrier' was the piece in question, and I watched the Answers to Correspondents column with some anxiety, to read the editorial verdict. When it appeared, it was simply this: 'The optimists are coming along', and my fate was still in the balance. But the verses were accepted and published, and thus I made my first appearance in the famous weekly which for many years printed my bush songs with kindly encouragement, and eventually launched for me my first literary venture.

At this time my verses were almost invariably scribbled upon the backs of old envelopes or on unused backs of letters at odd moments stolen from a busy life of sheep-droving, horse-breaking and mustering. The whole of the piece, 'Fair Girls and Gray Horses', was written on dinner camp, under a gum-tree on the stockroute between Forbes and Bogan Gate, in the intervals of getting up to fling sticks and stones at refractory ewes that would not camp. 'His Gippsland Girl' took shape one summer day on the lignum plains below Goodooga; 'Deserted' was written at a grassgrown Warrego homestead; 'How the Chestnut Horse Came Home' at a station near Mt Gambier, in South Australia.

There was music in everything in those days, sad music or sweet; but always music. And the roaring whips and the beating hoofs and the jangling chains all wrote themselves down in one rhyme or another.

Then friends began to say, 'Why don't you collect in book form?' and the idea took definite form in a letter to *The Bulletin*. The firm named was willing to take the necessary risk, and *Fair Girls and Gray Horses* was issued from their office as the first book of '*The Bulletin* Library', now so well known throughout Australia and New Zealand; thanks, I may say, to books of much more interest and value than mine. *Fair Girls* was most kindly received by the press and public of Australia, and is now in its fourth edition, with a sale of eight thousand copies.

Generous Critics

Surely no new writer of such little worth was ever so tenderly handled by his critics — paper after paper generously offering to the author at once a place in their foremost rank of Australian authors. An occasional reviewer, however, put the writer in his proper place with one sturdy blow; as witness the editor who wrote '*Fair Girls and Gray Horses* is mostly sickly stuff like this' — and then he quoted from a piece which another more kindly critic had just called 'both musical and dramatic'. Even this stern censor had the kindness to say that *Store Cattle from Nelanjie* was not quite so sickly as the rest.

Reviewers, like doctors, frequently disagree on minor points; and it was amusing to observe that some found fault with the volume for its persistent note of melancholy, while others praised it particularly for the absence of that note of sadness so peculiar to Australian poetry.

But nearly all, as I have hinted, were kind after their several fashions, and to the country press in general, and to *The Bulletin* in particular, is owed the fact that the book went far and wide, and gained a favour which, if scarcely deserved, was at least, I may claim, duly appreciated by the author.

The publication of *Fair Girls and Gray Horses* brought forth a number of letters from unknown admirers in all the States. Many of them were written in verse, and what they lack in metrical beauty they certainly supply in warmth and sincerity. There are letters from bushmen, to testify to the truth of 'Gray Horses', and letters from women who have found pleasure in 'Fair Girls' — all generous and flattering. An occasional one comes along which is critical, or even frankly antagonistic, not to say crushing; as in the case of one candid critic, who wrote to *The 'Bulletin*: 'Paterson I like, and Lawson brings the tears to my eyes; but this Ogilvie makes me sick'.

LITERARY THIEVES

I have more than once had the honour paid me of having my verses appropriated entire, and published unblushingly over another man's name. One literary aspirant — his name was Bogue, which, *The Bulletin* wittily remarked, was most probably a misprint for Rogue — copied from *The Bulletin* my verses 'A Scotch Night', and sent them to various papers in Scotland over his own signature. Another bold pirate altered the title and one of the lines in a poem of mine, signed a euphonious nom-de-plume, and dished it up to *The Bulletin* for the second time in six months or so.

The humorous parodist did not pass *Fair Girls and Gray Horses* by; 'Bowmont Water' suffered, and somebody did quite a clever burlesque of 'At the Back of Bourke'.

After the publication of my book I, of course, met many bushmen who had read and liked it, and the bushmen all have a soft place in their hearts for rhymes of their loves and their horses; but a township within a hundred miles of Dubbo first convinced me of my importance in letters! In a local paper, published in the above-mentioned place, I read, with some pride, my lines:

> A weird wild road is the Wallaby Track,
> That is known to the bushmen only,
> Stretching away to the plains out-back
> And the big scrubs lorn and lonely —

and underneath was written:

> 'If you are going on the Wallaby Track, buy a pair of Smithson's boots!'

Then I recognised the fact that I had put my foot upon the lowest rung of the ladder of fame — a foot encased in a Smithson boot!

It was in the same township that I, in riding dress, was swinging round a corner, when I nearly upset a diminutive urchin, who looked up in my face, and aptly quoted:

'Ullo! You in the boots and the long-necked spurs!'

a line which, needless to say, he did not read in Tennyson!

SERIOUS ART

The *Australian Review of Reviews,* in a fair and kindly critique of *Fair Girls and Gray Horses*, said: 'Mr. Ogilvie does not take his art very seriously'. Those words were true in the days when I wrote scraps of verse on old envelopes held against a saddle-flap or a stockyard post, as mere interludes in a life of manual labour; But I think I may deny them now, for the days of horsebreaking and droving are done, the stockwhip is laid aside for the pen, and literature has become, not the handmaid, but the mistress of my life.

It is a long road, and a hard one to travel, as many of us know. Some will drop out by the way, and the laurels are hung too high for most of us to reach; and perhaps there will never again be days so happy as those when, careless and reckless, we wrote lyrics for *Fair Girls and Gray Horses* under the gum-trees, and planned them in night-rides under the stars.[1]

Thus wrote Will Ogilvie about himself, but how did others see him? J. Corrie, writing in the world's oldest magazine, *The Scots Magazine*, December 1958, gives this graphic outline of the young Borderlander:

A handsome, quiet-spoken Scot of medium height and comprehending glance, with a fair moustache and brick-red complexion, deeply sun-tanned; a dusty, modest figure who had little to say when other bushmen were boasting of man-killers they had ridden, but who showed, as soon as he approached a horse, however untameable, that he had little to learn about handling them.

Douglas Stewart wrote of Ogilvie that 'Australia had the best of him', meaning of course, that we got his best years, for all of his twenties were spent in this country. The combination of a talented, well-educated young Scot and the literary ebullience of Australia in the 1890s resulted in a balladist who frequently outshone his *Bulletin* contemporaries. The influences of Sir Walter Scott and Robert Louis Stevenson and the excitement of his new life, working as a jackeroo on Belalie Station gave form and content to galloping rhymes which outdid those of our earlier horseman–poet, Adam Lindsay Gordon.

Of course, like the rest of us, he had his odd little quirks, and not the least of these was a propensity for lying when it suited him. Or, perhaps it might be kinder to say that, at times, he had very convenient lapses of memory!

For instance, in August 1898 he wrote to A. G. Stephens to say he was leaving Forbes for a few months to escape the heat and dust of another

Lachlan-side summer, and intended to camp in the shadows of Mount Kosciusko. This, while Forbes would still be experiencing frosts! And in October, by the middle of spring, he had returned to Forbes!

He only reached as far south as Ulladulla, and as he rode back up the coast, Stephens invited him to spend a few days with the Stephens family in their Hazelbrook cottage. Will accepted with alacrity writing that he had never been there and would welcome the opportunity to make the acquaintance of the Blue Mountains. Yet in July he had written to Stephens *from Hazelbrook* to say he was exploring the Blue Mountains, had lost his horse, and had been the previous day at Leura!

Perhaps his most obvious fib was told in a note to Stephens apologising for not turning up for drinks with *The Bulletin* staff (probably at the nearby Newcastle Hotel) on the day before his farewell dinner. He claimed to have had a sore throat; that he was subject to sore throats; that he tried to send a telegram of apology but the post office was shut! All because he was too shy in company to face up to the ordeal of meeting with a mob of strangers!

But genius goes hand in hand with eccentricity, and of his poetic ability there is no argument. He was sensitive to the rugged beauty of the strange new world in which he found himself on the north-western plains of New South Wales; he was a bold and fearless horseman, humane and compassionate, and he was possessed of understanding and acceptance of human weaknesses in others, as personified by his mateship with the incorrigible Harry Morant, 'The Breaker' of *The Bulletin*. In his two poems about 'The Breaker' this understanding is evident, and the obvious pen portrait of Morant in Ogilvie's short story, 'Only for the Brave' exemplifies this.

Ogilvie wrote with detachment — people and places are rarely identified, though occasionally a river might be named, as in 'Bells Along Macquarie'. One may search in vain through the autobiographical *My Life in the Open* for the word 'I'. The self-effacing young Scot writes about the environment of countries where he worked like the journalist he was, and not as an egotistic self-aggrandising fellow. In fact he involves the reader in the action by constantly referring to the observer in the second person instead of the more obvious first.

Even in the comical 'An 'Orsetralian Alphabet', which obviously describes his personal acquaintance with outlaw buckjumpers, the would-be rider is always described in the second person, not the first. Only in half a dozen poems dedicated to fellow bards does he bring in people's names.

In the poetry of Will Ogilvie there is a certain quality which is missing from the work of his contemporaries. This is what might be termed a 'Gaelic mystique', interwoven as it is with the sometimes harsh Australian landscape. It was the pervading presence of this mystique which led me to assert that he was the author of 'The Death of Ben Hall', long attributed to 'Anon'. This was several years before Nancy Keesing produced proof that the poem had, in fact, been published over the name of Will Ogilvie in *Smith's Weekly* in 1924. It is that same Gaelic quality that adds an air of mystery to the boggy swamp of 'The Fire Queen'.

Evidence of the strong and lasting effect of 'the wide brown land' on the impressionable young Scot is apparent in his continued contributions to Australian journals and newspapers for years after he had returned to his native soil. From Selkirk and from Iowa, during his American sojourn, Ogilvie pieces appeared in *The Bulletin, The Lone Hand* and even in that totally unsuspected outlet, the scurrilous *Smith's Weekly!*

Occasionally Ogilvie has yielded to temptation and used themes that are cliches, even urban myths in bush balladry. Three examples are:

A baby or a girl is left in an unattended sulky or buggy; the horse bolts and the victim is rescued by a combination of an heroic rider and a fast horse.

A fantasy female, or child trapped in the path of stampeding cattle, to be rescued by the same combination as above. Ogilvie uses this theme in 'Linden Lea' and 'Willanjie' — in the latter a very improbable rescue is achieved by sweeping up a prostrate woman by a rider on a galloping horse!

A wild ride on an heroic horse, through black night, a raging storm or a flooded river to fetch a doctor to a selector's ailing wife, a theme overworked by 'Anon', Lawson, Paterson . . . and Will Ogilvie in 'Rainbow in the Yard'. (At least in Ogilvie's case the doctor was sober!)

Far more than has been the case with Lawson and Paterson, Ogilvie's work has entered the oral tradition of Australian folklore and is widely recited by the bushmen of New South Wales. My introduction to him took place in 1952 when I recorded the Lee family at Auburn, a western suburb of Sydney. The Lees came from Hillston in the south-west of the state, and 'Hoopiron' Jack Lee, his brother Colin and a couple of old shearer mates played their accordions, sang and recited bush ballads for me. Two of their favourite pieces were 'Off the Grass', which they had renamed 'Myall King', and 'The Stockyard Liar' which they knew as 'The Liar on the Stockyard Fence'.

This renaming of Ogilvie ballads is commonplace, and I have never heard 'The Riding of the Rebel' called anything else but 'The Outlaw of Glenidol'.

For all of his life Will Ogilvie shunned the use of a typewriter. Using a broad 'J' nib, his small, neat script is even more legible than that of the typewriters used at the turn of the century.

Altogether, over twenty volumes of his works have been published. The inherent musical qualities in his lyrics seem to suggest that they be sung, and in England over fifty pieces have been set to music, mainly in the 'drawing-room art song' genre; in Australia the country-western singers have taken him up and at least ten Ogilvie poems have become popular songs.

And now, a hundred years after many of them were written, the poems of Will Ogilvie are experiencing a strong revival. Along with the regeneration of interest in his work, there is a revival of interest in the man and his life in Australia. He is featured in annual festivals at Penola in South Australia and in Bourke in western New South Wales, and in both places commemorative cairns and plaques have been erected to mark the places where William Henry Ogilvie lived, worked and wrote while in Australia.

CHAPTER 1

Youth!

William Henry Ogilvie was born on 21 August 1869, at Holefield, near Kelso, close to the Scottish border and in the shadow of the Cheviot Hills. His family is a branch of the Ogilvies of Hartwoodshire and Chesters, landowners and farmers since 1600.

His father George Ogilvie, 1826–1904, was born at Woodcot, and at the age of forty married twenty-year-old Agnes Christie Campbell. Agnes had been born at Cawnpore where both her parents were murdered during the Indian Mutiny. Brought to England, she was adopted by her late father's friends.

George brought his bride to a rented farm at Holefield, where they had eight children, several of whom died in infancy. Will was the only one to marry. The children were taught by Miss Herbert, a resident governess, and when he was ten Will was sent as a weekly boarder to Kelso High School for a couple of terms. He was then coached by the Reverend Firth who prepared him for entrance to Fettes College in Edinburgh, Scotland's leading public school.

Aged twelve, he was accepted by Fettes, where he remained for the next seven years. He excelled at running, and was an average sportsman at rugby and cricket. He did well in the classics and won a prize for Latin verse. After leaving Fettes, Will worked for a year on his father's lowland farm as a 'mud student'. When he turned twenty it was decided to send him out to Australia to gain experience in sheep farming. A friend of his father, William Scott, of Lempitlow, near Holefield, arranged for the lad to go to his brother Robert who had a sheep station called Belalie in northern New South Wales. The idea was for Will to work as a jackeroo for a year or so, and when he had 'learned the ropes', to look about for land of his own.[1]

Young Ogilvie sailed out of Belfast on the SS *Arcadia*. He became seasick in the Bay of Biscay, but soon recovered and was able to enjoy the rest of the voyage, arriving in Sydney on 1 November 1889. There was still a long way to go. The first stage of his overland journey was by the Western Mail train to Bourke over the track completed just four years earlier. The night train departed from the Sydney terminal, then situated at Redfern and arrived at Dubbo for breakfast the following morning.

The breakfast menu in the Dubbo Railway Refreshment Rooms remained unaltered for years. It was a hearty meal consisting of eggs and thick rashers of bacon with sausages; toast was laid on, butter plentiful, and there was a bottle of Worcestershire sauce on every table. The meal was rounded off with big pots of tea, or coffee made with full cream milk.

Then the Western Mail continued on to Bourke, while, with much ringing of hand-bells and whistling of engines, branch-line trains departed for Coonamble and Merrygoen.

The journey over the western plains during the 503-mile trip must have fascinated the young Scotsman — the vast expanse of the plains, the occasional sighting of kangaroos, emus and roving dingoes and the lack of fences, and then, after travelling for hours without signs of habitation, a scattering of houses and the big sign at the little station proclaiming, NEVERTIRE!

Probably the traveller would have stopped overnight in a Bourke hotel before continuing the journey in a Cobb & Co coach. This service ran between Bourke and Cunnamulla, via Enngonia and Barringun. Belalie Station was about a hundred miles north of Bourke, situated between the Mitchell Highway and the Warrego River.

Will must have decided that the owners of such a large property would be wealthy, and so dressed in his best clothes to meet them. The Scott family were greatly amused when the new jackeroo alighted from the coach wearing a frock coat and top hat, and with an English hunting saddle over his arm. The saddle aroused the most interest, as it lacked the thigh pads which were a feature of the Australian stock saddle.

During the evening meal, the Scott children warned him of the many venomous snakes in the area — so much so that he was not unduly scared when he turned back his bedding to disclose an artistically arranged stockwhip! Next morning they gathered to watch him mount the frisky stock horse allotted him, but Will soon showed that he had little to learn about horsemanship.[2]

CHAPTER 2

The Belalie Jackeroo

At Belalie Ogilvie became friendly with Benuko, the storekeeper, whom he described as 'one of the best' — a great teller of tales, who died of consumption not long after Will's arrival.

It was at Belalie too, that he is said to have found the inspiration for perhaps his best known verse, 'Fair Girls and Gray Horses'. Robert Scott's daughter, Lynette, and the grey horse Loyal Heart provided the inspiration to the poem. 'To all Fair Girls! For the sake of one, whose bright blue eyes were awhile my star', and 'To all Gray Horses! Fill up again, for the sake of a gray horse dear to me', give a clear indication of the importance of both to the poet.[1]

In her book *Kings in Grass Castles* Mary Durack refers to the connection between the grey horse and the poet. While working on Belalie, Ogilvie bought a grey horse from a pound. Later a traveller identified the brand '7PD' and recognised the horse Pannick, which had been stolen from Patsy Durack's property Thylungra. Many, many years later, Ogilvie wrote from Scotland, 'I have ridden many hundreds of horses in Australia, America and over here hunting, and in the Remount Department in the Great War, but there was never a horse like Loyal Heart. His old grey tail is here as I write — memento of many a glorious ride. I begin to think that when I am dead, they will find 7PD engraven on my heart.'[2]

He soon settled down to station work, although he must have found the sudden change from Scottish winter weather to the subtropical summer climate at the Queensland border somewhat trying. His younger brothers were attending Fettes College, and during a fit of nostalgia for his *alma mater*, Will sent them a letter which took the form of an unusual poem — his first to be written in Australia.

Not many years had passed since Longfellow published his great narrative poem 'The Song of Hiawatha', and it was quite the fashion in Britain to write parodies on it, one of the best known being, perhaps, Lewis Carroll's 'Hiawatha's Photographing', a send-up of both Longfellow and photographers. Will's versified letter to his brothers was yet another 'Hiawatha' parody.

FLOREAS FETTESIA

I am writing from Australia,
From the land of gold and gum-trees,
Writing to my younger brothers
In the land of fight and five-balls,
In the land where snowy five-balls
Leap away above the side walls
To the thieving roofs and stay there.

Here we hunt the brown opossum
From his home among the tree-tops,
In the moonlight from the tree-tops
Drop him with the double barrel;
Take his skin as prize and trophy,
Weave it into rugs for winter
For our friends in far-off Scotland.
Here we mount our steed at morning,
In the golden south-land morning,
Gallop out among the ranges,
Follow from the rocky ranges
Where the kangaroo, the brusher,
Leads the chase across the hollows,
Spur the good horse up beside him,
Stun him with the stirrup iron —
Make his skin a wrap for winter.

Here we canter to the muster,
When the sun has scarcely painted
Half the shadowed east with crimson,
Canter to the shearing muster,
Bringing home the sheep, the jumbuck
From his haunts among the tea-trees;
Bring him to the cruel shearers;
Take the silver fleece from off him —
All his woolly glory off him;
Pack it up in bales and send it,
Send it to the land of sunset,
In the steamships to Old England;
By the pound the dealer buys it,
Giving us a paltry ninepence,
Nothing more a pound than ninepence.

So we toil or take our pleasure
In the sun-land, in Australia,
In the very great Australia,
But we sometimes grow aweary,
And our hearts are sore within us
For the good old days in Scotland
For the merry days at Fettes.[3]

and so on for several more homesick verses.

At home Will had ridden to the hunt whenever he could borrow a horse; now he was being paid to do what he most enjoyed — riding a horse! For a twenty-year-old, bursting out of his skin with good health and animal spirits, the new life was almost unbearably exciting. Later, he was to erupt into lyrical prose when describing the joyful experience of running in the morning horses:

It is early morning on the plains below the Queensland border, after the warm, semi-tropical night. In the east there is a ruby flush in the sky, every moment widening with the day; the long barley grass dripping with dew brushes boot and stirrup, and the scent of the eucalyptus steals to the very heart. The quaint, twisted stems of the gum trees look even quainter, more bizarre than ever in the dim light, and there is no beauty, as the Englishman's eye is trained to beauty, but only this strange, weird bewitching charm that is hard to realise or express. Suddenly from the vine trees a burst of warbling melody — the magpies calling to the dawn — and round and round your horse's feet flutters the black wagtail, the 'shepherd's companion' of the Bush, flying on ahead, then waiting or fluttering back, as though to lead you on to the unexplored beauties of the plains. A sweep to the right and your horse's feet are muffled in the soft, red sand as you ride up through the ridge; on either side the vines and supplejacks trail green branches to the ground; here and there a quandong or a native cherry stands like a trim bush in the grounds of some country house. Higher still and we are among the pines; here and there a dripping branch touches cheek or hand with the cool touch of a woman on a fevered brow, and thrills us with that magic of the Bush. From bough to bough the spiders have spun their silken threads, making broad targets on which the rising sun makes many an inner white and gold with his swift arrows. On the ridge-top you rein your horse and look back over the green plain to the river; far away among the timber gleam the silver homestead roofs; through the lignum bushes under the sandhill the horses are feeding out into the swamp, snatching up the three-foot barley grass in great mouthfuls, and ringing merry peals from the horse-bells as they go.

You move your horse from the pine trees out into the open space on the crown of the hill, then, clear of the trees, let the heavy stock-whip fall; fourteen feet from keeper to cracker it lies out along the sand, and the roar of it fills the air and dies away along the ridges to the north like a muttered thunder in the hills.

Down on the plain there is a scramble among the horses; tossing manes and sweeping tails, they rush up together. From every side they gather, trotting, galloping in, bays, browns and chestnuts, a grey, a creamy, and another grey; then, as if swung by one impulse, they lower their heads and gallop down the track to the stockyard in a cloud of dust, plunging, bucking as they go, and chasing one another in wanton play. Your own horse bites on the bit, and then, rearing straight up, makes a plunging buck forward, and taking rein from your willing hand, is down through the bushes like a flash of light, shaking the cold drops from the pine trees as he passes, and every now and again throwing his lean head to his knee, asking mutely for leave to overtake the flying mob. And there is no real beauty about the horse paddock in the early morning, only a strange fascination that appeals to horse and man, and makes a man restless when he is away from it — the weird, unaccountable witchery of the Bush.[4]

Later, he again celebrated this exhilarating moment in an equally stirring set of verses:

AFTER THE HORSES

Have they ever waked you early
    While the shadows lingered yet,
Ere the grey light gathered fairly
    And the drowsy stars had set?
Have you heard the wagtails chirrup,
    Felt the dawn wind creeping cold?
Till your foot was in the stirrup
    And the whole world changed to gold!

Ah, the joy of daybreak riding!
    How it makes the warm blood start,
With a good horse striding, striding
    To the music of your heart!
And the morning's welcome olden
    With the magpies all astir,
When the long wet grasses golden
    Wipe the dry blood from the spur!

How they gather from their feeding
    In the white mists far and near,
Take the track with Sunflower leading
    And old Possum in the rear!
How the bare hoofs rattle under!
    For the Cowrie fillies know
When they hear the snake-plait thunder
    It is time for them to go.

Ah! the joy of it, ye riders!
   When the old grey horse takes hold
Through the bushes where the spiders
   Spin their bushy threads of gold!
Down the box-flat where the grasses
   Drip in silver with the dew,
And the last brown shadow passes
   As the fairy Day steps through!

On the sandhill hear them muster!
   Cross the roadway see them swing!
In the lignums how they cluster!
   Down the netting how they string!
Rolling fat yet lithe and limber,
   Shoulders creamed with sweat and foam,
Head them at the river timber —
   Rush them up the flat for home!

Gone forever yon glad hour is:
   When the sunrise floods the plain,
I shall never run the Cowries
   Down the blue-grass flats again.
Drop the slip-rails in their places,
   Take the saddle from the grey;
Foamy shoulders, white-starred faces
   Fade, and fade, and fade away.

       ★ ★ ★ ★

But if you have fought the forces
   Of the Drought and Dust and Sun,
If you've ever tailed the horses
   On a far-out Western run,
If you've ever heard them neighing
   As they gathered to the whip,
You will understand me saying
   I would let a fortune slip

Just to take the old malacca
   From its place upon the wall,
With its foot of silken cracker
   And its yard of greenhide fall,
And be down those watercourses
   Where the ten-foot lignums are,
Bringing up the station horses
   On a reefing R S bar!

The 'R S bar' referred to was, of course, the registered brand of Robert Scott of Belalie; 'the old grey horse' in the fourth stanza was Will's own beloved Loyal Heart. In after-years, when the poet had returned to Scotland and the old mount had to be put down, a lock of his silvery gray tail hair was sent to Will, when it was commemorated in a nostalgic reverie, 'Loyal Heart's Tail'.

Ogilvie retained happy memories of his adventures at Belalie where everything was new and fresh, and life and work both were a wonderful experience. Sixty years later, he reminisced in a letter to Michael Mallon of Sharon Station:

I remember Tom Allen's hotel very well, indeed — half way between Belalie and Barringun. I can tell you two stories that keep that old Pub in my mind.

A friend of mine and I rode up to Barringun one day from Belalie as we often did. When we were about to return home, we suddenly found that my friend's mare was dead lame and we were puzzling over what we should do, when a man we knew who had a farm close to Barringun, said if we would leave the mare with him, he would lead her to his home and look after her, and my friend could ride his old grey horse home to Belalie. This was all right, so we said good-bye to everybody and got on the horses. My friend galloped off and I followed more slowly. I never saw him again till Tom Allen's where I saw the grey tied up to the horse rail.

I went in and found my friend there who explained that the horse had pulled so hard that he could not hold him and had just had to let him gallop all the way, only stopping him with difficulty at the Pub. He said his arms were aching and his hands blistered and he refused to ride the horse any further. So, I said I would ride him the rest of the way, which I did. But what a horse, no mouth at all. You might as well have pulled at a railway engine. He raced right up to the horse paddock gate and looked like jumping it or going straight through it, but with a great pull, I managed to stop him in time. My friend came up on my horse, and we then walked them and got safely home, but my arms ached for many hours afterwards.

That is one story connected with Tom Allen's Pub, and here is another: I bought a big strong bay horse once. He was a very good one and I thought a lot of him. He was very quiet and well behaved and a good hack, but one day a man told me he knew my horse and that he was a famous buck jumper well known in Queensland. I did not believe him and went on riding him and he went on carrying me quietly and never out of temper.

Then one day two friends and I, on horse back, pulled up to Tom Allen's Pub to have a drink. We tied our horses to the rail where already another horse was standing. This belonged to a teamster who was in the house when we went in. Suddenly, there was a scuffle outside and we ran out and found a kicking match going on among the horses. The stranger's horse pulled back and broke his bridle and galloped off. He said 'Lend me one of your horses and I'll soon get him'. I said 'Take mine' and he put my reins over the yellow horse's head and jumped on him and galloped off, driving the spurs into him. The horse put his head down and with a 'tree-mend-ous' buck, threw the fellow a yard or two away. When he was picked up, his leg was broken and he lay in that Pub for some weeks.

I rode that horse for some time afterwards, but he was just as quiet as ever. However, after seeing that buck — the biggest I ever saw — I thought it best to get rid of him, so I sold him. And that is my second story.[5]

While he was working on Belalie, Will Ogilvie carved his initials and the date, 'W.H.O. 1890', on a slab table in the Irrara hut. Mr Bligh Ridge, an uncle of Bill Cameron of Bourke, remembered seeing the table with its inscription and said it was later burnt for firewood![6] This wanton destruction is a sad comment upon the philosophy of certain bush louts: 'If it moves, shoot it; if it doesn't, chop it down'. To which regretfully might be added: 'If it's already down, burn it!

There was more to living at Belalie than shooting possums, hunting 'roos or riding over to Tom Allen's pub for a beer. Working as a jackeroo meant spending many hours on horseback, which Will loved, but also involved backbreaking work in great heat handling sheep. The merinos were much heavier than the Border Leicesters at Holefield and they came in thousands rather than in scores. His first Christmas Day was spent swathed in sweat as he played 'woolly billiards' with uncooperative sheep. One job he was given was counting a mob of about 6000 sheep. He had learned to count them in threes as they were driven through a gateway, or between hurdles especially erected for the job, as they were on this occasion. He started off — 'Three, six, nine, twelve . . .' and at one hundred called out 'Tally!' to the boy beside him who then cut a notch in his tally-stick while Will started again:- 'Three, six. . .' All went well until he came to the last few hundred, when disaster struck. The hurdles at one side of the gap gave way and the remaining mob gushed over the flattened fence in glorious confusion. Will was devastated. Too tired even to raise a swear! 'What's the tally?' came the boss's voice behind him. 'Six thousand two hundred,' called the boy. 'We'll call it six thousand three hundred,' said the boss. 'That's near enough.' [7]

Will's son George Ogilvie tells of another incident that occurred soon after his father's arrival at Belalie:

When my father came to live in the bush he was to learn its joys and perils the hard way. The fiery heat of a December sun, the droughts and bush fires. The tropical rain which, when it did come, turned the dry dust to slimy mud and the creeks into torrents. Even finding one's way across the bush had to be learnt in a land where the sun shone in the north and the very stars were different. He had not been long in Australia before he had navigation trouble.

He was riding home one evening with a stable hand and having been all day in the saddle, looking forward to getting home, when his companion told him he was going home another way to look in on a pal. 'You'll be home in half an hour,' he said, 'just keep straight ahead keeping the sun half left'.

Dad rode on confidently through the bush, content that he would soon be home. After a couple of miles he started to pick up familiar landmarks and even caught sight of the homestead. It had been a tiring day and he was looking forward to his tucker so he tightened his reins and made a beeline for home. This led him through an area of Umbrella Mulga where he had to pick his way through the shade of the trees. The Mulga was more dense than he had expected and he could no longer see the sun. He was not following a beaten track and was beginning to worry about his navigation when he came on hoof marks and they were going his way. His spirits rose when he realised that if he was careful and kept his eyes on the trail he was bound to be home in no time.

He felt even better when he observed that the hoof prints were fresh and that there were quite distinctly tracks of two horses and — dash it — surely that rotten log is familiar — and now there are three tracks. Then the penny dropped. He had been riding in a circle following his own track. He pulled himself together. He was a horseman. Was there any reason to believe that an Australian horse was any different than another horse on its way home after a long day? He dropped his rein and gave his horse its head and was out in the sunlight in five minutes and into the station yard in ten.[8]

Ogilvie remained at Belalie for a couple of years, working first as a jackeroo and later as an overseer. After moving down to South Australia for a further two years, he celebrated his return to northern New South Wales with a jibe at the occupation of jackerooing, published in *The Bulletin* over his nom-de-plume of Glenrowan.

JACKAROOINATION

Home and luxury eschewing,
He must needs go Jackarooing.

* * *

In a Queensland summer stewing,
Next I found him Jack-a-rueing.

* * *

Drink and gambling his undoin',
There I left him Jack-a-ruin.

* * *

Although he had not at this stage submitted them for publication, Ogilvie wrote, or drafted, at least six poems while at Belalie. 'Kings of the Earth' was one of his earliest efforts, and it was followed by 'The Riding of the Rebel' (perhaps better known as 'The Outlaw of Glenidol'), 'Deserted' (which was suggested by an old homestead at Leila Springs); 'A Draft from Tringadee', 'Habet' and 'The Song of Songs'.

The evocative 'How the Fire-Queen Crossed the Swamp' was to be written later at Maaoupe, but was suggested by a swamp below Belalie. When it appeared in *The Bulletin*, in July 1896 its title was 'How the Fire-King Crossed the Swamp', but for inclusion in *Fair Girls and Gray Horses* the gender of the waggon name was altered.

CHAPTER 3

Bound For South Australia

It has been written that Ogilvie had: 'A bush voice more authentic than those of Paterson who smelled strongly of station 'big houses' and 'picnic races', and Lawson who learned about the bush mostly in city bars'.[1]

Ogilvie had lived and experienced everything he wrote, and, since he kept no diary, we must turn to his poems to discover details about his life in the Australian bush. In later years he told his children about his first big droving trip, from somewhere up near the Queensland border to Adelaide. After his death an old map of New South Wales was discovered among his papers, with the following places underlined in pencil: Barringun, Enngonia, Fords Bridge, Louth, Wilcannia and Menindee; Broken Hill and Silverton also were marked. Probably, with the exception of the last-mentioned two, this indicated the route of the droving trip. The stock consisted of about 130 horses, both broken and unbroken.

As the drovers passed through the Coorong, on the coast of South Australia, the young Scotsman was again inspired by what he described as the glamour of the bush, and he wrote:

It is sunset on the Coorong, the ribbon of blue water that divides the Ninety-mile Desert from the sea on the coast of South Australia below Adelaide. Behind the low sandhills the sun is going down in a regal crimson splendour; the water takes a peculiar greenish purple tint beside us, fading away into crimson and gold between the brown of the sand hummocks and the dark green of the mallee scrub on the desert side.

Great flocks of wild-fowl sweep and settle again, with strange, discordant cries, and the white beach gleams with a ghastly pallor that will heighten under the summer moon. It is all ghostly and strange and unreal, with a weird — almost repellent — witchery, and yet, once seen it is never forgotten; and so it is that over here in Scotland, among the most beautiful scenery in the world, one would give a king's ransom to hear the sudden whistle of the black duck's wing and the little whisper of the wave on the sand.[2]

As they neared Adelaide the poet's lofty thoughts were jerked back to reality when an unexpected noise caused the mob of horses to bolt. Ogilvie, riding in the lead, had no chance of holding them and was forced to dig in his spurs and ride for his very life. Later, he recorded the event in a poem:

THE ROAD TO ADELAIDE

The Coorong lay beside us as placid as a pond;
    The horses ran before us, and who so gay as we,
With mallee to the right of us, a desert waste beyond,
    And sandhills to the left of us, and after that the sea?

A hundred head and over, and half of them unbroken,
    They filled the open country and they kept us wide awake;
For they were wild and nervy, and by the self-same token
    There were many rogues among them who were ready for a break.

On the trodden sand beneath us one could hear the bare hoofs drumming,
    The ever-present challenge that the big mob made;
Half a league ahead of us you might have heard us coming
    As we swung along the Coorong on the road to Adelaide.

Soon we met the lanes again, and through a town we battled;
    I was riding Parasite and steadying the lead;
A youngster kicked an empty tin; among their feet it rattled;
    And off they went, a hundred head, in terrified stampede.

No threat of whip could stop them and, maddened in their fright,
    The whole mob swept upon me in a narrow crowded lane;
I galloped on before them with the spurs in Parasite,
    And did a mile at racing pace before I breathed again.

The chestnut was a blood one, and if somewhat past his prime
    Was full of pluck and stamina and more than passing fleet;
He could throw behind the furlongs pretty fast at any time,
    And now he went the faster for the thunder of their feet.

From fence to fence they shouldered; no room to stand aside;
    Wild-eyed, with streaming forelocks, they kept their level line;
There was one only answer: to ply the spurs and ride
    And leave the rest to fortune and that gallant horse of mine.

We won to open country with a length or two to spare;
    The outlaws spread and steadied and returned to sober sense.
'Twas an easy job to wheel them with the other riders there,
    And calm the beating hearts of them and hold them on a fence.

I've backed a few good buckers and preserved a cheerful smile;
I've ridden over fences and have never been afraid;
But I wasn't quite so happy when I rode that flying mile
The day our mob went crazy on the road to Adelaide.

After the horses had been delivered, Ogilvie made his way back east to the Penola district where he got a job on Maaoupe Station as an overseer, at £3 a week. Maaoupe was owned by a cousin of Robert and William Scott, so it was very likely he carried a letter of introduction from the owner of Belalie. Two letters to his mother, descriptive of life at Maaoupe have survived; the paragraph describing the crop of flowers grown from seed she had sent him suggests he had been at Maaoupe already for some time.

Dec. 22nd   Maaoupe
1892   Penola
                                                       South Australia

My dearest Mother

We finished shearing yesterday and have now got all our men payed off, and when we have got the sheep fixed up in their proper paddocks we shall be able to rest on our oars for a time and watch the grass grow and the thistles flourish, and clean out the waterholes etc. etc.

I enclose you a cutting referring to the cricket match at Mt Gambier in which I took part — taken from a local paper. I also enclose a Poem 'On Clansman's Grave' which I hope you will like.

I am so glad to hear that Uncle Frank is now better after his serious illness.

Our shearing was long drawn out owing to the wet weather, but it is an ill wind that blows nobody good! And as I got 3£ a week, I clear 21£ for the job.

There was a young fellow out here a couple of days ago who could play tennis, and he and I had a couple of sets which I won after good games, so my right hand still retains its cunning — I am glad to say.

Our wool is nearly all away now by rail to Kingston, and from there it is shipped direct to London to the sales there where I hope for the credit of the Maaoupe brand, it will bring a good price — thistles and all.

I was out hunting this afternoon, but only got 1 hare, but we had the young dogs today and not the regular pack, which accounts for it.

I am sorry that Loe has not been able to go down South this year as I know she enjoys the trip immensely. — She enclosed me a letter from Ellie Robson to her saying they had met Paton in their continental wanderings, she evidently thinks a lot of him too — I suppose he is grown a goodlooking man now.

I had not time to get photographed at Mt Gambier as I had intended, and anyway I expect the money is better in my pocket than employed in putting my ugly phiz. on paper, — but I know you won't think so.

A long day today & I am tired so you will excuse a scrap this time, darling.

> From Your loving Son,
> W. H. Ogilvie [3]

Will Ogilvie demonstrated on several occasion that he was careful with his money, and though he uses lack of time as his excuse for not having his photo taken at Mount Gambier, obviously he considered the exercise a waste of hard-earned cash. Yet an advertisement in the *Border Watch* at that time offers portraits for only five shillings a dozen, at Watson's Studios.

Dec 3rd [year not given, but 1893]   Maaoupe
                                                             Penola
                                                             South Australia

My Dearest Mother,

Here we are again in the Christmas month, and rapidly getting near to that festive season.

Our shearing has got on grandly this last week it having been fine every day of the week. We have now shorn about 20,000 sheep and have another 16,000 to do yet, we will probably finish next Tuesday week if all goes well. We are all well into the swing of the work now and everything goes smoothly and well.

I have some nice samples of merino wool which I am sending to father either this mail or next.

I am afraid when the English buyers put their hands into our bales in London they will draw them out again pretty quick as the thistles are like bayonet points right through all the wool.

I think I have mentioned before to you how over-run this place is with the Scotch thistles, and I see this year a fresh crop is coming up thicker than ever. Yarding up the sheep into the shed is very hard as you are afraid to touch them — they are just like porcupines — and every time one passes you he leaves from 1 to 20 thistle points in legs, arm or hands. Our hands and bodies are really sore with them; but still we will soon get over this, and enjoy a well-earned spell at Christmas time.

I was out with the pack today for a hunt — we do not shear on Saturday afternoon, you know — but the dogs were too fat and as it was very warm in the sun they would not run well, and consequently we only killed one hare, though we certainly had a merry gallop or two after some others.

The seeds you sent me some months ago grew very well here and I get many 'buttonholes' given me made out of them — larkspur predominating, I think.

There have been some splendid gooseberries in our garden and we have had many a good tart out of them, a delicacy which is quite a fancy with me now.

There is some promise of fruit but not a great deal, though I believe the mulberries are magnificent in both quality and quantity.

You will excuse a short scrawl this time as my time is limited in this time of rush and hurry. I have always my counts of sheep shorn and other figures connected with the shed to make up at night — so that I have but little time for writing. But even this very short note will let you know that I am as usual in excellent health & heart.

> With kind love to them all
> I am your affect. son
> Will H. Ogilvie

Will probably arrived at Maaoupe Station about the middle of 1892; certainly he was there for two shearing seasons, which start there about the beginning of November. It was here he made the acquaintance of a young Englishman named Gordon Tidy who was tutor to the owner's children at Maaoupe. Both men had received a classical education and both were aspiring poets. They formed a firm friendship which endured for the rest of their lives. It is thought that Tidy encouraged Ogilvie to send some of his work to the local newspaper, the *Mount Gambier Border Watch*.

Over the pen-name of Glenrowan, Will Ogilvie's first poem in the *Border Watch*, and his first to be published in Australia, was 'Kings of the Earth'. Filled with the thunder of galloping stock horses it carries a stirring recurrent stanza:

> We are heathen who worship the idol
> We keep for our honour and pride,
> If we're slaves of the saddle and bridle
> We are Kings of the Earth when we ride.

This debut was on 22 April 1893. Glenrowan's poems continued to appear at intervals during that year, the fourteenth and final piece being 'The Mission of the Pines' which was dated December 1893 but which did not appear until 3 January 1894, just before he left South Australia.[4]

Earning £3 a week at Maaoupe, Ogilvie apparently was working as an overseer, or perhaps 'boss of the board' in the shearing shed, a job he had already filled while at Belalie. Early in the New Year, mounted on his beloved grey gelding, Loyal Heart, the intrepid young Scotsman set out for Broken Hill, where he remained for several months. There is no record of what he did or where he spent his time, but most likely it would have involved station work or horse-breaking.

In the Introduction, Will describes how, from Broken Hill, he wrote to *The Bulletin*, enclosing with his letter the poem titled 'Beyond the Barrier'. After an anxious wait, there was an encouraging line in the 'Answers to Correspondents' column, and in the following issue — over his soon to be well known pen-name of Glenrowan — there appeared the forerunner of the hundreds of his verses to be accepted by 'The Bushman's Bible'. Occasionally

Glenrowan's work appeared on page three, under the masthead, as a full-page spread, illustrated and hand-lettered. The date of his first *Bulletin* acceptance was 21 April 1894.

Ogilvie then left the Broken Hill district and, still riding alone, set out for Bourke. The road was eastward to Wilcannia to cross the Darling River via the high-level bridge. Here he encountered that strange phenomenon, the Darling in full flood, although there had been no local rainfall. The Darling gathers its waters from the confluence of the Paroo, Warrego, Culgoa and Barwon Rivers which have their sources in south-eastern Queensland.

The first sign that the Darling is 'coming down' is a great wall of debris, the flood-wrack, being pushed along by a massive wall of water, succinctly described by Henry Lawson in his 'A Word to Texas Jack':

> You must swim the roarin' Darling
> When the flood is at its height,
> Bearin' down the stock and stations
> To the Great Australian Bight.

as well as thousands of bobbing empty beer and wine bottles.

As he gazed upon the mass of yellow-brown turbulent water surging by, Will put down his impressions in a poem which, with its ever-changing forms and moods, reflects those of the meandering inland waterway:

THE MARCH OF THE FLOOD

> There's a whisper away on the Queensland side
> Of the Barwon a banker, the Warrego wide
> Spread from range to red range; of the siege of a town.
> Of farms that are wasted and cattle that drown,
> Of a trackless road and a bridgeless sea,
> And grey miles measured from tree to tree —
> And the people gather at gate and rail
> For the latest news by the Darling mail.
>
> Through all the merry daylight
>   Long leagues behind her fall
> Till golden turns to grey light
>   And wedding-robe to pall;
> Above her rolling thunder
>   The shrieking parrots fly,
> And the bush-world waits to wonder
>   When the Darling mail goes by!

Through all the night she spurns the ground,
   Her headlights shame the stars,
The rolling dust-cloud wraps her round
   From ledge to leading bars;
And like some half-roused sleeper
   Stands each gaunt-armed gum aghast,
And the shadows gather deeper
   When the Darling mail goes past.

She takes the fearsome message down
   By reach and point and bend,
And camp and farm and river town
   Will hail her as a friend;
For comes she not as horsemen ride
   Who ride a race to win?
What wonder if they crowd beside
   When the Darling mail comes in!

And close behind is the fierce Flood King:
   In the pride of his strength he comes
Where the tangled masses of drift-weed swing
   Like dead men up in the gums;
He sings the paean of curbless might,
   The song of a broken chain,
And he rides himself in the foremost fight
   With the scourge of a loose-held rein.

He throws an arm to the Southward now,
   Now an arm to the golden West,
And the circled lives to the bidding bow
   And are lost on his tawny breast;
And day by day as he thunders by
   There is ground to be captive led,
And night by night where the lowlands lie
   Are the wings of his army spread.

There's never the stem of a bank-fed tree
   For the touch of his hand too tall,
And he leaves his brand for the world to see
   On the hut and the homestead wall;
There's never a star in the midnight sky
   Or a sunbeam crossing the morn
But has heard the boast of his battle-cry
   And the threat of his bugle-horn.

And down where the Queen of the river lies girt with her garland of green
The toilers have heard it and tremble, whose wealth is the life of the Queen;
In the hush of the evening they hear his low beat on the shield of the shore,
And stand to the dam and the earthwork; they know it his challenge of yore!

And the stockmen ride out in the dawnlight by billabong, runner and creek,
To gather the sheep and the cattle wherever his war-notes speak;
And the blood will be red on the rower, the sun will be low in the west,
Before they have left them in safety to camp on the red hill's crest.

And so shall we live and suffer so long as the big rains come
With their ruin and wreck for many, their danger and death for some,
Till we go from the Culgoa and Darling to camp on a drier shore
Where the Warrego out in his war-paint shall harry our homes no more!

With acceptance by *The Bulletin* — and more importantly, by its new literary
editor, A. G. Stephens, Will Ogilvie, alias Glenrowan, became the third name
in *The Bulletin* triumvirate of bush balladists, the other two being of course A.
B. Paterson, writing under the pen-name of The Banjo, and Henry Lawson,
who always wrote under his real name.

CHAPTER 4

On the Lachlan Side

Although he described his marathon ride as being from Broken Hill to Bourke, it is likely that having got so far, Ogilvie would have continued northward to renew acquaintances with the Scott family of Belalie. From here he rode out to the west, where, evidently by prior arrangement, he took charge of the Brindingabba shearing shed. Here it was that he wrote what is possibly his best-loved poem, 'From the Gulf'.

He would know by now that shearing in Australia starts off in Queensland and northern New South Wales in mid-to-late winter and moves southward with the seasons, and doubtless, like the shearers, he had lined up a series of jobs as 'boss of the board', for which he was well experienced. 'Northward to the Sheds' is another poem written about this period. There is a remarkable similarity between this piece and one which was written at a later date by West Australian balladist Jack Sorenson, titled 'Call of the North'. Although most sheds had converted to machine shearing by 1894, Ogilvie's poem takes a backward look at shearing with the blades — the B-Bows or hand shears — while Sorenson describes a machine shed. Both poems were intended to be sung, as indicated by the provision of a repeated chorus. Clearly Sorenson's poem has been based on the earlier one by Ogilvie:

NORTHWARD TO THE SHEDS

There's a whisper from the regions out beyond the Barwon banks;
There's a gathering of the legions and a forming of the ranks;
There's a murmur coming nearer with the signs that never fail.
And it's time for every sheerer to be out upon the trail.
They must leave their girls behind them and their empty glasses, too,
For there's plenty left to mind them when they cross the dry Barcoo;
There'll be kissing, there'll be sorrow such as only sweethearts know,
But before the noon tomorrow they'll be singing as they go —

For the Western creeks are calling,
And the idle days are done,
With the snowy fleeces falling
And the Queensland sheds begun!

There is shortening of the bridle, there is tightening of the girth,
There is fondling of the idol that they love the best on earth;
Northward from the Lachlan River and the sun-dried Castlereagh,
Outward to the Never-Never ride the ringers on their way.
From the green bends of the Murray they have run their horses in,
For there's haste and there is hurry when the Queensland sheds begin;
On the Bogan they are bridling, they are saddling on the Bland;
There is plunging and there's sidling — for the colts don't understand

That the Western creeks are calling
And the idle days are done,
With the snowy fleeces falling
And the Queensland sheds begun!

They will camp below the station, they'll be cutting peg and pole,
Rearing tents for occupation till the calling of the roll;
And it's time the nags were driven, and it's time to strap the pack,
For there's never license given to the laggards on the track.
Hark the music of the battle! It is time to bare our swords;
Do you hear the rush and rattle as they tramp along the boards?
They are past the pen-doors picking light-wooled weaners one by one;
I can hear the shear-blades clicking and I know the fight's begun!

Having made the claim that Sorenson's poem is based on Ogilvie's, it is, I suppose, only fair to produce the evidence and let the reader be the judge:

CALL OF THE NORTH
by Jack Sorenson

Oh the western wind is blowing, so there's rain and storm in store,
And the teams have long been going down the road to Glendalough,
To where tropic sun is gleaming, and the fragrant wind blows free,
I've awakened from my dreaming and the North is calling me.

Chorus:
Oh the steam is in the boiler, in the engine room below,
While upon the board each toiler waits to hear the whistle blow,
'Cause the shearing is beginning and my heart is fancy free,
And the friction wheels are spinning, yes the North is calling me

From the southwards to the northwards, where the long brown tracks wind down,
All my mates are pacing forwards, to the wilderness from town,
Gone by stony hill and hollow, to where I now fain would be,
Where they lead my feet must follow, for the north is calling me.

What's this news I have been hearing, tidings strange to me indeed,
Picture me and my mates shearing, with the ringer in the lead,
Straining camel teams are swaying from the Junction to the sea,
Why so long am I delaying, when the North is calling me?

And so northward I am going, for I cannot linger here,
For the starting whistle's blowing, and the guns are into gear,
And to be there I am yearning, I would hail the sheds with glee,
And the friction wheels are turning, and the North is calling me.

Ogilvie is known to have worked in sheds in the Cunnamulla, Coonamble and Condobolin districts as 'boss of the board' and between times went droving in southern Queensland and north-western New South Wales. He also took on horse-breaking in the Lachlan Valley and Central West regions of New South Wales.

Always those unsought phrases kept coming into his mind, and always he found time to scribble them down on any available scrap of paper. And always, he wrote of his experiences — new and wonderful experiences: daybreak on the Queensland border; sunset on the Coorong, and moonlight on the Macquarie River; the carolling of magpies in the morning, the fussing of wagtails — dew-spangled cobwebs and the thrilling thundering of the station horses as they galloped up to the stockyard. He was now in his mid-twenties and joyously living life to the fullest. In his own words: 'There was music in everything in those days — sad music or sweet, but always music, and the roaring whips and beating hoofs and the jingling chains all wrote themselves down in one rhyme or another'.[1]

Gradually, during 1895 and 1896 he began more and more to frequent the areas around the three western rivers, the Macquarie, the Lachlan and the Bogan. He was inspired by the beauty of the first-mentioned to burst into lyric prose:

It is night upon Macquarie — a clear, starry and moonlight night. The footsore cattle are camped on the rising ground by the river, and in the weird stillness you are keeping the midnight watch. In the scrub a nightowl chants his melancholy note, 'Mopoke! Mopoke! Mopoke!' then there is silence, a heavy silence that is weird in the extreme.

It is these long night-watches in the dead silence that turn a man in on himself as it were, on himself and the Bush, these two only, until the Bush seems to become wedded to his heart, and his heart to the Bush, till the bush at night, with its weird cries and its still more weird hush, become an actual part of himself.

Another log on the fire! And away up the river a curlew calls querulously; a pitiful, wailing cry is the curlew's, voicing all that is lone and lost and hopeless

in the world, and many a watcher in the still Australian night has heard the echo
of that wailing cry in his own heart.

But grim, lonely and oppressing at times as the Bush night is, it still has that
peculiar witchery of its own that will never be found in the gladdest nights of
nightingale and guitar; that spell that brings the drover and the traveller back
again and again to worship at the shrine of its silent beauty; that charm that
chains the true bushman to his love though half the world lies between.[2]

The love he felt for the Macquarie found expression again, this time in
verse and about shearers and the girls they left behind them:

BELLS ALONG MACQUARIE

When the summer days grow long
    And the grass is turning brown,
South and Eastward with a song
    Come the shearers riding down;
South and Eastward from the battle,
    With the lights of love to lead:
Listen! how the chain-rings rattle
    As the hobbled horses feed.
Homeward from the westward foray
    Through the whispering gum-trees tall...
Hark! the bells along Macquarie
    When the dark begins to fall

Jangling bells along Macquarie
    When the dark begins to fall.
When the sheep are shorn out west
    And the harvest days begin,
To their riot or their rest
    Come the shearers riding in;
You can see the tent-roofs whiten
    In the oak-shade down the bends,
You can see the camp fires brighten
    Like the faces of old friends;
And the girls! — ah, world-old story!
    Wait with listening hearts to hear
How the bells along Macquarie
    Tell of sun-browned lovers near
Tinkling bells along Macquarie
    Tell of sun-browned lovers near!

Where the courtly sunflowers bend
    And the river breezes roam,
Where the rose and ivy blend
    Round the casements of her home,
Far to Southward waits a lover,
    Shading eyes along the track
Tearful eyes would fain discover
    One false sweetheart riding back:
But — it is the world-old story
    Soon her breaking heart will tell
That there sounds along Macquarie
    For herself no jingling bell
Never more along Macquarie
    Sounds for her a jingling bell!

Still North by West the shearers ride
    And still red camp-fires burn,
And white tents star Macquarie side
    To mark their gay return;
And the suns go down in splendour,
    And the river oak-trees sway
To the whisper low and tender
    Of the winds at close of day.
And nights of moonlight hoary
    And dawns of silver dew
Hear the bells along Macquarie
    In the gold grass tinkling through
Lilting bells along Macquarie
    In the gold grass tinkling through!

Ogilvie has stated his whereabouts when certain poems were written, and this helps to trace his movements during the mid-1890s. For instance, 'Deserted' is about an abandoned homestead on the Warrego near Belalie and was published in mid-June of 1894. 'From the Gulf' was written when he was in charge of the shed at Brindingabba, near the Queensland border in December the following year, and 'His Gippsland Girl', about the same period, near Goodooga.

According to Miles Franklin, 1894 and 1895 were drought years, and Ogilvie's experiences during this time of hardship has been given as the reason for him not taking up land in Australia.[3] Finding plenty of work in the Lachlan Valley, he decided to make this area the centre of his activities.

Two events took place in 1896 which were to strongly influence Ogilvie — Gordon Tidy, his friend from Maaoupe Station in South Australia, moved to join Will on the Lachlan, and he met Harry Morant. On arrival, Tidy secured employment as tutor to two daughters of Ernest Sharpe of Goimbla Station. The two girls, Ruby, born 1883, and Sybil, born 1885, lived with their mother in Forbes.

When the girls no longer needed his tuition, Tidy became editor of the Parkes newspaper, then called the *Western Champion*. He and Ogilvie remained friends after they returned to their respective native lands, whence they kept up a correspondence, always addressing each other by their *Bulletin* pen-names of Glenrowan and Mousquetaire. Back in England, Tidy studied for the Church, was ordained and finally died in a Home for Retired Clergy at Tiverton in Devon.

In April 1896 Will got work at Nelungaloo Station, and there he made the acquaintance of the horse-breaker, Harry Harbord Morant. The pair shared two interests: writing bush poetry for *The Bulletin* and the ability to ride any horse just about anywhere. As is well-known, Morant wrote under the pen-name of The Breaker.

Tidy's poetry, although published, was pedantic and lacked imagination; The Breaker's was often lacklustre, and neither could measure up to Ogilvie, whose swinging verses were imbued with a Gaelic mystique which set them above those of all of his contemporaries, frequently surpassing even The Banjo and Henry Lawson.

The three poets joined forces with Reg Lackey, son of the owner of Nelungaloo Station, and after weekend drinking sessions the quartet got up to all sorts of high-spirited pranks, such as playing polo in the main street of Forbes, and using a couple of butchers' carts for chariot races around Parkes! Frequently after Sunday afternoon revels, they would adjourn to the *Parkes Champion* newspaper offices where they would work all night helping Tidy to produce Monday morning's paper.

While he was at Nelungaloo Ogilvie wrote 'The Stockyard Liar' which, after publication in *The Bulletin* became highly popular with bushmen reciters, who frequently changed the title to 'The Liar on the Stockyard Fence'. The 'Liar' in the poem was Percy Weston of the firm Percy Weston & Seaborne, stock and station agents in Parkes.[4] In a letter to his friend Alexander Irvine in 1907, Ogilvie writes:

You will enjoy being back in the old office — rather I fancy it is a new office, isn't it? Since the days when I and Regie used to sit on the table swinging our spurred feet and listening to Percy Weston telling us how he used to 'ride 'em to a finish' when he was our age!

Ogilvie continued to drift from station to station in the Lachlan district, and worked for a time for S. L. West on Botfield Station, between Trundle and Bogan Gate. West, who also owned the Bogan Gate hotel, was the father of ten attractive daughters, and Will fell in love with one of them. His adoration was unrequited. Miss Rose West saw no happy future as the spouse of an itinerant horse-breaker and, on 24 April 1898 married a Mr H. Hernfield of Granville. Ogilvie's heartbreak found expression in this poem which appeared in *The Bulletin* on 4 June following:

THE ROSE OUT OF REACH

A red rose grew on a southward wall,
There was never a rose on the tree so tall;
Though roses twined at my lingering feet,
Roses and roses, scented sweet,
And roses bent to my love-lit eyes,
Roses flaming in wanton guise,
And roses swung at my shoulder height,
Damask and crimson and golden and white,
With a curse for all and a frown for each
I longed for the rose beyond my reach.

The gold sun shone in the summer days,
The wee buds opened a hundred ways;
Winds of the morning, whispering sweet,
Tossed the blown roses down at my feet,
Dainty petals for lover's tread,
Ruby and ivory —brown and dead!
But morning to nooning, noon to night,
One rose only glowed in my sight
Silently, all too rapt for speech,
I worshiped the rose beyond my reach.

I stormed her tower on the southward wall
To drop fatigued from the bastions tall;
Thorns made sport of me, red as the rose
A hundred wounds ran blood at their blows;
The soft little roses red and white
Changed to the bitterest foes in spite,
Scourged my face with their stinging wands,
Mocked my toil and my bleeding hands
Till I learned at last what they strove to teach:
The great red rose was beyond my reach.

And so I watched in the autumn days;
'Summer is dead,' so I mused agaze;

'The cold mists creep when the night is nigh,
Day after day the roses die.
Storms of winter will gather soon,
Frosts will follow the coming moon
Here if I wait where the blooms are cast
My love will drop to my arms at last! . . .
But wild winds laden with death for each
Blew the red petals beyond my reach.

CHAPTER 5

The Bogan Gate Polo Club

Nelungaloo Station, where Ogilvie met Morant, was owned by the Lackey family and was situated about halfway between Parkes and Bogan Gate. After leaving the station, Morant rented a paddock near the Bushman's Mine where he broke-in horses for the townspeople of Parkes.

The Breaker taught Will and a few others to play polo, and they joined forces with local enthusiasts to form a club. Organising a working bee, members cleaned up a large natural clearing known locally as The Little Plains, and converted it into a polo field. Situated on the Trundle road, it was conveniently close to the Bogan Gate hotel, owned by Simeon Levi West of Botfield Station, and officially titled The Selector's Arms Hotel'.

After the club had played a few chukkas among themselves, somebody had the bright idea of forming two teams, to consist of the 'Sterling' — migrant, or 'imported' players — and the 'Currency Lads', all Australian-born. Then they announced a grand international match: Great Britain versus Australia.

Local oral tradition and the rural press of the day have preserved the names and status of the teams which were as follows:

The Australians: Captain, Victor Foy of Mordialloc Station; Bert Balcombe of Coradgerie Station; Arthur Pike, Stock and Station Agent in Trundle; and Will Black, storekeeper of Bogan Gate.

The Great Britain Team: Captain, Harry Morant, representing England; 'Swinglebar' (Ogilvie, playing under an alias) for Caledonia; Paddy Ryan and Ed McDonald for Ireland. Paddy Ryan was trainer and jockey for West of Botfields, and later married one of the West daughters; of Ed McDonald, nothing appears to have been recorded, particularly the reason for his playing for Ireland.

The match received a lot of publicity, both before and after the event, in the country newspapers; it was further commemorated in verse by Will Ogilvie in his poem 'The Glory of the Game' and by Banjo Paterson in 'The Geebung Polo Club'. Over his pen name of Glenrowan, Will sent his effort to the *Windsor and Richmond Gazette*, in which paper it occupied one-and-a-half columns of the front page on Saturday, 6 February 1897, the match having been played in December of the preceding year.

For the Honour of Old England
And
THE GLORY OF THE GAME
(A Viracious* History of International Polo)

On Saturdays and Sundays, many polo men of late
Had mustered up for practice near the pub at Bogan Gate,
They have ridden many ponies, and have broken many a stick,
Till the men are all in practice, and the ponies all in 'nick'.

Till at length they tired of playing with teams described as 'scratch',
And their scientific playing seemed to justify a match,
Which should the population of this sleepy land excite,
And yield the sporting public both amusement and delight.

And so it was decided that two picked teams should be sent
To play against each other, and that they should represent
Great Britain and Australia — so eager for the fray,
Each player rode to Bogan Gate on the appointed day.

Thus four 'imported' players on their ponies came to play
For the honour of Old England on the polo ground that day;
Whilst long-necked spurs were burnished for the sake of British fame —
For 'England, Home, and Beauty' — and the glory of the game.

And there were four Australians, upon the other hand,
Went out to bravely battle for their Sunny Southern Land;
And, on well-conditioned ponies, they meant to die or do
For the land of 'junk and damper', and the giddy kangaroo.

There Foy from Mordialloc on his pony sat alert;
And Balcombe, of Coradgerie — they mostly call him 'Bert'!
Whilst Pike and Black were with 'em all eager for the fray,
They were out upon the warpath of the Britishers that day.

And there came the minstrel 'Swinglebar', who Caledonia sent;
And 'The Breaker' gave the polo team its English element;
Whilst 'Ould Oireland' sent McDonald, and Paddy Ryan, too —
All keen upon the scalping of the bounding kangaroo!

Victor Foy, 'the Native's skipper', wore upon his manly breast,
Embroidered by fair fingers, the back-country squatters' crest —
An emblem to make bushmen's hearts with wild delight to stir:
'A CRIMSON RABBIT, — RAMPANT, 'NEATH A SPRIG O' BATHURST BURR'!

---

* 'Viracious': Will's son George Ogilvie interpreted this word as 'vicarious' but plainly
it is meant to be 'veracious', or truthful.

And a wandering photographer, in search of Art and Fame,
Was prancing round adjacent ere they started on the game;
And he brought his snap shot camera to the polo field along,
And photoed all the heroes here immortalised in song.

Then the umpire slung the ball in, and the scrimmages began,
And Australians rode their ponies as but Australians can;
The Britishers found out how hard, at times, 'twas to resist
A rushing horseman with a swinging mallet in his fist.

Bert Balcombe of Coradgery came swift careering by,
Whilst 'Ride him off!' and 'Take it on!' and 'Old man, mind your eye!'
Were frequent cries; and eager men that afternoon were oft
Reminded of the 'playing rules' by umpire Harry Croft.

Now the bold Australian players had quite made up their minds
To dock the British lion's tail, or ride their ponies blind;
Whilst the Englishmen had settled, as was very soon revealed
That they'd carry off the honours — or be carried off the field.

And the game waxed wild and willing, but when half the game was done,
The Britishers were foremost; with a lead of two to one;
And the sharp bright spurs were crimson, and the ponies wet with foam,
When the lads who played for Britain waded in to fight for 'Home'.

Then somehow, in a scrimmage, a face and stick got linked,
And the timber broke in pieces, though 'The Breaker' never winked;
The mallet went to hospital, whilst 'The Breaker' bathed in gore,
Went sailing through the scrimmages more fiercely than before.

And still the game waxed keener, till the steeds began to roll,
And 'England, Home and Beauty' added yet another goal;
Whilst Balcombe of Coradgery, kept up the cracking pace,
And Pike and Ed McDonald battled bravely face to face.

Whilst 'Swinglebar' on Sweep-the-board, a champion nag to 'stay',
Did yoeman service, now and then, by getting in the way;
And, in a gallant gallop, to the occasion rose,
And stopped with a 'backhander' the rush of Britain's foes.

Then Pike — whose brilliant, forward play deserved a better fate,
Met Paddy Ryan's mallet with the whole of Paddy's weight;
And underneath the 'green and white' the blood began to creep —
Such blow had sent another head an hour or so to sleep.

Though Pike but slightly shook his ears, and gripped his pony's rein,
And drove into the throbbing flanks the blood-stained spurs again,
But all in vain, for yard by yard the English horsemen bored,
And yet again, between the flags, Britannia's skipper scored.

And when the game was over, and when the play was done,
The umpire gave the verdict that the English team had won,
And the good old British lion knocked out the kangaroo,
For scores, when final time was called, just stood 'four goals to two'.

Then the victors cheered the vanquished and all gaily sought the pub,
And drank the toast of 'Polo' and the 'Mordialloc' Club;
To each Australian member, and to every British boy,
And filled a final bumper for their patron saint, St. Foy.

Glenrowan

Probably the name of the club was the 'Bogan Gate' or even the 'B.G.' Club, which Paterson playfully punned to 'Geebung'. Popular tradition in the Lachlan district has it his poem is based upon the same match:

THE GEEBUNG POLO CLUB

It was somewhere up the country, in a land of rock and scrub,
That they formed an institution called the Geebung Polo Club.
They were long and wiry natives from the rugged mountain side,
And the horse was never saddled that the Geebungs couldn't ride;
But their style of playing polo was irregular and rash
They had mighty little science, but a mighty lot of dash:
And they played on mountain ponies that were muscular and strong,
Though their coats were quite unpolished, and their manes and tails were long.
And they used to train those ponies wheeling cattle in the scrub;
They were demons, were the members of the Geebung Polo Club.

It was somewhere down the country, in a city's smoke and steam,
That a polo club existed, called 'The Cuff and Collar Team'
As a social institution 'twas a marvellous success,
For the members were distinguished by exclusiveness and dress.
They had natty little ponies that were nice, and smooth, and sleek,
For their cultivated owners only rode 'em once a week.
So they started up the country in pursuit of sport and fame,
For they meant to show the Geebungs how they ought to play the game;
And they took their valets with them — just to give their boots a rub
Ere they started operations on the Geebung Polo Club.

Now my readers can imagine how the contest ebbed and flowed,
When the Geebung boys got going it was time to clear the road;
And the game was so terrific that ere half the time was gone
A spectator's leg was broken — just from merely looking on.
For they waddied one another till the plain was strewn with dead,
While the score was kept so even that they neither got ahead.
And the Cuff and Collar Captain, when he tumbled off to die
Was the last surviving player — so the game was called a tie.

Then the Captain of the Geebungs raised him slowly from the ground,
Though his wounds were mostly mortal, yet he fiercely gazed around;
There was no one to oppose him — all the rest were in a trance,
So he scrambled on his pony for his last expiring chance,
For he meant to make an effort to get victory to his side;
So he struck at goal — and missed it — then he tumbled off and died.

*   *   *   *

By the old Campaspe River, where the breezes shake the grass,
There's a row of little gravestones that the stockmen never pass,
For they bear a rude inscription saying, 'Stranger, drop a tear,
For the Cuff and Collar players and the Geebung boys lie here.'
And on misty moonlit evenings, while the dingoes howl around,
You can see their shadows flitting down that phantom polo ground;
You can hear the loud collisions as the flying players meet,
And the rattle of the mallets, and the rush of ponies' feet,
Till the terrified spectator rides like blazes to the pub
He's been haunted by the spectres of the Geebung Polo Club.

The Banjo

Victor Foy of Mordialloc Station was not only captain of the Bogan Gate Club, but apparently also the patron, which office he supported with a liberal purse in the pub after a match. Later in 1897, Ogilvie and Morant spent some time at Mordialloc as the guests of the Foys, prior to the Foys' departure on a cruise to England. On their sailing, Ogilvie wrote a tribute to their generosity, which was published in the *Parkes Champion Post*:

GOOD OLD VICTOR FOY

Come gather round you Trundle boys
    Join in this toast with me;
We'll drink success to Victor Foy,
    Wherever he may be.
If he were here among us,

His company we'd enjoy,
For the brightest star in Trundle
Was good old Victor Foy.

He has gone upon a pleasure trip,
Some foreign lands to see;
We hope he may enjoy himself
When far across the sea;
And until he returns again,
Good health may he enjoy,
Is the unanimous wish from Trundle
To good old Victor Foy.

Left behind are his selections,
His sheep and cattle too,
To scenes dear and familiar
He has bid a brief adieu;
Given up his single freedom
He tastes bliss without alloy
And a second star in Trundle
Will be Mrs Victor Foy.

He has been a good employer
As a boss he 'can't be beat!'
Ever generous to travellers
In providing such with meat;
He'd help along the working man
His chances ne'er destroy;
None more generous were in Trundle,
Than good old Victor Foy.

But the time will soon pass over,
In eighteen months or more,
We will expect our good old Vic
To scenes bright as of yore.
And when his face again we see,
Each heart will thrill with joy
To welcome back to Trundle
Mr and Mrs Foy. [1]

Victor Foy, one of the Sydney 'Mark Foys' family, gentleman farmer, viniculturist and vintner, and 'Patron Saint' of the Bogan Gate Polo Club has been described as 'the ever exuberant Prankster of the district'. The story is told that in 1893, in the newly opened Trundle School of Arts Hall, a dance was in progress, with music being supplied by a solitary concertina. Victor Foy brought an untimely end to proceedings by rushing into the hall armed with a pair of B-bow shears and, before the startled musician could prevent it, cut the concertina in two![2]

Foy does not appear to have been a vindictive man, and it is likely that this was an 'act', worked out with the musician beforehand, using an instrument which had reached the end of its useful life.

CHAPTER 6

Breaker's Mate

When Ogilvie met Harry Morant at Nellungaloo they became good mates — they worked together, went droving, broke horses, wrote bush verses for *The Bulletin*, played polo and got gloriously drunk together. Theirs was a strange friendship, because Morant had a propensity to engender in people immediate feelings of fear and disgust. Although Morant may not have fully reciprocated the young Scotsman's overtures of friendship, and possibly just looked on him as a drinking companion who was good for a touch of an occasional quid or two, Ogilvie always overlooked his mate's darker aspects of character and cultivated his friendship to the extent of writing at least half a dozen poems addressed to him. Probably Glenrowan was the only true mate The Breaker possessed.

During the 1890s, the legendary period of Australian literature, The Breaker's verses were as well known and as popular as those of The Banjo and Glenrowan. Bushmen readers of *The Bulletin* read, learned and recited such ballads as 'West by North Again', 'Who's Riding Old Harlequin Now' and 'Since the Country Carried Sheep'.

Morant's fearless steeplechase riding and his innate ability to 'lift' a horse over a hurdle had won him fame among the horseracing fraternity of Sydney and Melbourne, as well as in the bigger country towns, and he was frequently offered mounts and booked to ride in big races.

On one such occasion Ogilvie celebrated the booking in a verse titled 'When The Breaker Goes South', which has been taken by some people to refer to Morant being bound for South Africa, but the piece was written three years before the Boer War began! In December 1896 Glenrowan sent four poems to *The Bulletin*, namely: 'Leila', 'When The Breaker Goes South', 'Forty Miles for a Kiss' and 'The Men That Blazed the Track'.

Three of the poems were published during January 1897, and on 15 February Ogilvie signed a *Bulletin* receipt for the sum of £2.6s., being payment for the four titles. 'The Breaker' poem was never published, for one good reason. It was libellous! In recent years *The Bulletin* had experienced two costly libel suits and was guarding against a recurrence.

WHEN THE BREAKER IS BOOKED FOR THE SOUTH

He will leave when his ticket is tendered
A bundle of debts, I'm afraid —
Accounts that were many times rendered
And bills that will never be paid;
Whilst the tailor and riding-boot maker
Will stand with their thumbs in their mouth
With a three-cornered curse at The Breaker
When The Breaker is booked for the South.[1]

It is possible that Morant's engagement was for Melbourne, and that Ogilvie went south with his mate, and an incident experienced while there was the inspiration for a curious poem.

Most likely the occasion was when Victor Foy, of Mordialloc Station, took one of his racehorses down to run in Melbourne. His brother-in-law Tom Flanagan owned a pub in Melbourne, and it is possible that, with Ogilvie as strapper and Morant for his jockey, the trio stopped at the Flanagan hostelry, where Will encountered 'The Waster'.

Foy was an exuberant character with many interests and his ten-roomed homestead was designed to cater for these. There was a billiard room, a photographic darkroom, an aviary for his Japanese pheasants and, somewhere near at hand, a winery and cellars. Not a man to do things by halves, Victor Foy had planted a ten-acre (four hectare) vineyard and employed a French wine-maker, M. Nerac from Bordeaux, to produce his vintages. Mordialloc also produced wool, wheat, cattle and thoroughbred horses. With S. L. West, he bred racehorses and maintained a stud on a property at Nelungaloo, which he called The Monastery. Morant and Ogilvie would have been much in demand there as trainers and breakers.

Many stories were current regarding mad-cap Foy's exploits in the district. One was that after the Parkes Show, he and Morant were drinking on the balcony of the Tattersalls Hotel, when he bet Breaker he could not jump from the balcony onto the roof of a refreshment marquee next door — and lost his five bob.

Written on what appear to be pages torn from an autograph album, pasted onto a foolscap sheet, 'The Waster', subheaded '(For The Bulletin)', is accompanied by four other Ogilvie pieces all of which were published in 1896.[2] Evidently the piece was rejected, as it did not appear in *The Bulletin* during that period. An amazing aspect of 'The Waster' is Ogilvie's description of the invasion of Australia by the Japanese Imperial Army some forty years before they attempted just that! Was it an instance of Gaelic second-sight that he could forecast what might have happened had not the 'yellow flood' been halted in the Owen Stanleys of Papua-New Guinea? An interesting device in this piece is the poet's use of the incremental interrogative as a means of dramatically creating a rising sense of urgency as the career of The Waster rolls on to its inexorable conclusion.

THE WASTER (FOR THE BULLETIN)

The waster leans throughout the day
Against a pub 'darn Carlton way'
And, idly watching passing trams
Awaits the racin' telegrams;
While, ever and anon will fly
This question to the passer-by —
'Wot won the 'Urdle?'

He haunts his glorious racin' clubs
And frowsy private bars of pubs,
Where Wires are posted from the course;
He argues endlessly of horse;
The racing argot of the south
Drops from his foolish gaping mouth
'Garn! Positand — wot's it done?
Stiffened the moke before it run —
Backin' the field at ten to one —
Wot won the 'Urdle??'

The myriad hosts of Asian blood
Rise in a threatening yellow flood;
The news comes of invading fleets
The papers issue scare-head sheets —
'The Coming War.... The First Shot Fired!'
The waster scans them bored and tired.
Sucking his everlasting fag;
'There ain't no sportin' in this rag.
Nothink but blanky scares and croaks!
Suppose them Japs is murderin' folks
Well, wot's the 'urry.... I say blokes
Wot won the 'Urdle???'

Swift outposts from our tiny fleet
Come in with news of dire defeat,
Reflecting on his latest bet

The waster sucks his cigarette
And lounges through the clamouring throng
To ask the newsman: —' 'Ere, wot's wrong?
Them last results ain't come along
Wot's stopped the postin' of 'em up?
Did Shyster get the Ascot Cup?
Wot won the 'Urdle????'

A trooper from our beaten host
Rides in to gasp that all is lost:
'The armies crushed, the Asian brown
Is marching upon Melbourne Town!!
The waster starts and drops his butt:
'Gorstrewth! Suppose the pubs get shut!'
Then lounging to the panting scout:
'Say, mister, wot results is out?
Darn't want no guts abart the fray!
Lor' blime ain't it Saturday?
I seen yer come darn Caulfield way,
Wot won the 'Urdle?????'

The brown hordes reach at last their goal;
The waster swells their human toll.
His soul soars upward through the skies
Till Heaven's walls before him rise.
All heedless of the ruling Fates
The waster scans the Golden Gates,
Sucking a ghostly cigarette:
'Them last results ain't posted yet!'
And when the Angel of the Tomb,
Draws near to seal the waster's doom
He hears that lost soul's accent strange
As soon as he comes into range
Across the Universe 'Say 'Ange,
Wot won the 'Urdle??????'

(Augustus Blowfly. Vic.)

In his book *The Poetry of Breaker Morant* David McNicoll prints an error
which has gained some public credence: that Morant 'was encouraged by Will
Ogilvie to send some of his verse to *The Bulletin*...' The subtitle of McNicoll's
book reads: 'From *The Bulletin* 1891–1903', and Ogilvie's first contribution to
that journal was made in April 1894.

Toward the end of 1896, while Morant was away from the Lachlan, Ogilvie sent him a photo of himself with an inscription on the back:

'Glenrowan' to 'The Breaker'

By our mutual love of a horse and a stiff fence
In the days when the splinters flew up from the rails,
   In spite of the slight disagreement the diff'rence
Of drinking 'gin-soda' and 'lime juice' entails,
   By our mutual love of a laughing-eyed maiden
In spite of a quibbling o'er brown eyes & gray
   By sympathy born of our debts overladen
In spite of our settling in different ways
   By the same firm belief that the world's ways are pleasant,
The same disregard of the money we spend
   This photograph now in the place of a present
I hope you'll accept as the face of a <u>friend</u>!

Morant, four years Ogilvie's senior, apparently did not appreciate the friendly gesture, and soon after receiving the autographed photo gave it away to Henry Lawson, who added to the inscription: 'This is the youngest and best photo of W. H. Ogilvie, with his holograph poem to Harry Morant. Rcd. from 'The Breaker', H. Morant Jan 1897.' [3]

Morant spent part of 1897 on the Hawkesbury River. In March he was staying with R. H. Forrester of Richmond when he tried in vain to get a berth on the SS *Oronsay*. Later that year he spent some months at Penrith, when he had a number of poems published in the *Nepean Times*. In December he had a bad fall which was reported in the same paper on the 11th:

On Saturday afternoon Mr. Harry Morant ('The Breaker') mounted a brown mare belonging to Mr Tom Dobson in the Nepean Times yard. The animal reared right over on the top of 'The Breaker' who was at once taken inside and attended to by Dr Barber. On Friday he got out again, and, though somewhat weak, is pretty right.

For several years, up to early in 1898, Ogilvie and Morant had worked together in the Lachlan district as stockmen, horse-breakers and drovers. Years later, after Morant's execution in South Africa, Ogilvie wrote a ballad reminiscing about the time when the two mad-caps raced a wild one-hurdle steeplechase for a one pound bet. Morant won and Will paid over his quid with a laugh, albeit, being a canny Scot, the laugh may have had a hollow ring to it. One can imagine, had the situation been reversed, Morant saying laughingly, 'Well, that's a quid I owe you, mate!'

HARRY MORANT

Harry Morant was a friend I had
   In the years long passed away,
A chivalrous, wild and reckless lad,
   A knight born out of his day.

Full of romance and void of fears,
   With a love of the world's applause,
He should have been one of the cavaliers
   Who fought in King Charles's cause.

He loved a girl, and he loved a horse,
   And he never let down a friend,
And reckless he was, but he rode his course
   With courage up to the end.

'Breaker Morant' was the name he earned,
   For no bucking horse could throw
This Englishman who had lived and learned
   As much as the bushmen know.

Many a mile have we crossed together,
   Out where the great plains lie,
To the clink of bit and the creak of leather
   Harry Morant and I.

Time and again we would challenge Fate
   With some wild and reckless 'dare',
Shoving some green colt over a gate
   As though with a neck to spare.

At times in a wilder mood than most
   We would face them at naked wire,
Trusting the sight of a gidyea post
   Would lift them a half-foot higher.

And once we galloped a steeplechase
   For a bet — 'twas a short half-mile
With one jump only, the stiffest place
   In a fence of the old bush style.

A barrier built of blue-gum rails
   As thick as a big man's thigh,
And mortised into the posts — no nails
   Unbreakable, four foot high.

Since both our horses were young and green
    And had never jumped or raced,
Were we men who had tired of this earthly scene
    We could scarce have been better placed.

'Off' cried 'The Breaker', and off we went
    And he stole a length of lead.
Over the neck of the grey I bent
    And we charged the fence full speed.

The brown horse slowed and tried to swerve,
    But his rider with master hand
And flaming courage and iron nerve
    Made him lift and leap and land.

He rapped it hard with every foot
    And was nearly down on his nose;
Then I spurred the grey and followed suit
    And, praise to the gods — he rose!

He carried a splinter with both his knees
    And a hind leg left some skin,
But we caught them up at the wilga trees
    Sitting down for the short run-in.

The grey was game and he carried on
    But the brown had a bit to spare;
The post was passed; my pound was gone,
    And a laugh was all my share.

'The Breaker' is sleeping in some far place
    Where the Boer War heroes lie,
And we'll meet no more in a steeplechase —
    Harry Morant and I.

While, on the surface, Ogilvie accepted the shortcomings of his mate as those inherent in any man, he continued in later life to mull over Morant's inability to come to terms with his complex personality. 'The Ballad of Devil-May-Care', written six months after Morant's death, and a short story titled 'Only for the Brave', published eleven years later, both appear to have been based on The Breaker. The poem excuses his drunkenness; the story suggests a way out. As in other pieces, Ogilvie shows in the yarn that he is well aware of the dark side to his mate's character.

While 'Bob Bartlett', the protagonist of the story, is obviously based on Morant, Ogilvie has disguised him by making him into a squatter. Handsome, with polished manners in company, gifted with an outstanding singing voice, Bartlett is a welcome guest when sober. At other times he is a hopeless and disgusting drunkard. A lovely girl promises to marry him if he can foreswear the grog for a year, but after a couple of months of sobriety he breaks out again. In the middle of a drunken spree, engaged in outrageous behaviour outside a bush pub, he is confronted by his horrified sweetheart. Later that night, in a fit of remorse, he blows out his brains with a revolver, having sent a farewell note to the heroine. The story appeared in the *Town and Country Journal* for 3 December 1913.

But Ogilvie's writing in the short story genre cannot compare with his verse, and 'Only for the Brave' lacks the smooth-flowing lyricism which characterises his poetry. This is not so in the sketches from real life that make up *The Honour of the Station*, published in England in 1914. These twenty-two stories cover the entire range of human emotions, and are comparable with the work of those other great story-writers of the 1890s, Paterson, Lawson and Baynton. Published for the first time in Australia, they comprise Part III of this book.

CHAPTER 7

A Tarnished Hero?

Since the release of the film *Breaker Morant*, Harry Harbord Morant has been the subject of adulation by singers and musicians of the folk revival and elevated to the status of a folk hero, but many of his peers did not hold him in such high esteem.

His poems and bush ballads had some standing with readers of *The Bulletin* and country newspapers, but they lacked the emotional depth possessed by the work of such men as Lawson, Ogilvie and Paterson. Whilst they regularly ran his poems, *The Bulletin* never published a volume of his work as they did for most of their outstanding balladists. Walter Stone wrote of him: 'Sometimes a man finds a permanent niche on the foothills of Parnassus, not because of the real merit of his work, but because of some dramatic incident in his life or death. So it was with Harry Harbord Morant.' [1]

Early in 1896 Breaker met Ogilvie at Nelungaloo Station and the two men worked together on several locations in the Lachlan Valley, and they became good mates despite their widely differing personalities. The reason their friendship endured was probably due in great part to the Scotsman's tolerance and levelheadedness.

Harry Morant was possessed of a strange, complex make-up. People were both attracted to and frightened and repelled by him. When drunk, he has been described as a filthy, loathsome animal; sober, he could present a polished, urbane manner that won instant acceptance anywhere and in any society. Yet always hovering in the background was that dark, threatening shadow which ultimately would lead to his downfall.

He openly sponged on his mates, recklessly borrowing money which he had no intention of repaying; he put up at country pubs, then rode off leaving his bill unpaid and often had no title to the horse he rode.

Ogilvie once described him as 'A man who would do anything for a friend — generous to a fault. If he had money it was yours as well as his, and as he seldom had any, yours was his if he could get it'.

Morant had the ability to engender fear in people. When he worked on Ducabrook Station, one of the men had made Morris Hawkins, the owner's son, a bugle from a bullock's horn, which he prized. It disappeared, to be eventually found rigged up as a smoker's stand near Morant's bed. 'I left it there', said young Morris. There is no doubt he and his brother Bill were scared of Morant, one of whose habits was to take the last of the black tea from the pots up to his tent in a kitchen jug. When finished he just threw the jug out of his tent and it was the boys' job to go and get it. Morris remembered, 'We always made sure he was well away.'[2] During the early part of 1897 Breaker was staying at the Exchange Hotel in Parkes. At weekends he would meet and play polo with Ogilvie. After the game they would pick up their mutual friend Gordon Tidy, editor of the *Western Champion* newspaper. They would get gloriously drunk together, then repair with Tidy to his office to help him get out Monday's edition.

In March Morant went to stay with R. H. Forrester at Richmond, on the Hawkesbury River, from where he journeyed down to Sydney to make several unsuccessful attempts to get a job as deck hand on the SS *Oronsay*, in order to work his passage to London. The cheapest single fare at the time was £25, apparently an impossible sum for a man of his dissolute lifestyle to accumulate.

Later that year he moved to Penrith and had verses published in the *Nepean Times* in October, November and December 1897 and in January 1898. During the spring of '98 he rode in several races in Sydney, where he was injured in a fall. Ogilvie wrote to A. G. Stephens, literary editor of *The Bulletin* on 8 July: '[Had a letter in] Breaker's characteristic scrawl — send him the enclosed "ode". It may cheer his wintry hours "in bandages." '[3] And again on 23 July: 'You can tell Breaker I can't be down tomorrow, if you see him again. I shall see him some day later on. Hope he'll be a success over the fences.'

Then something out of the ordinary seems to have happened to Ogilvie. In August he wrote to Stephens from Young: 'I'm steering south to Summer somewhere in the shade of Kosciusko if possible — sick of the backblock summers — Heaven knows I love the Bush but her hand at times is over warm.'

Now in August, the Lachlan Valley would still be experiencing frosts, and since he returned to Forbes in October, as summer was approaching, the reason for his journey was patently false. What was he running away from? It was four months since his 'Rose out of reach' had spurned him and became Mrs. H. Hernfield of Granville; and two months since the poem 'A Rose Out of Reach' had appeared in *The Bulletin*. Perhaps one of his wild mates, Reg Lackey or Harry Morant, had involved him in some escapade, the consequences of which he hoped to avoid.

In his letter Ogilvie went on to state: 'I enclose a little piece I've done jogging along the road — wrote it down in an hour of casual inspiration! "Post equitem sedet Atra Cura".' His Latin line translates as 'black care behind the horseman sits', suggesting some worrying reason for his southern excursion.

Then, from Forbes, on 6 November he asks Stephens, somewhat peevishly: 'Any word of Breaker lately?'

But Will Ogilvie was never to see Breaker Morant again and there was no further news of his former mate until Frederick Cutlack described him as turning up at Paringa Station, on the Murray River in South Australia in 'late summer' in 1899, probably towards the end of February.[4]

Breaker Morant left the haunts of his friends and disappeared for over three months. Did that dark side of his character draw him away to engage in some illicit activity, and then to lose himself in the back country?

On the cover of his book *The Breaker*, Kit Denton proclaimed: 'The Life of Breaker Morant — Poet, Horseman, Mercenary . . . Murderer?' Murderer? The author suggests that if the whereabouts of Harry Morant during the latter part of 1898 and early 1899 could be ascertained, some light might be thrown on the identity of the man who committed four shocking murders in South Queensland in December 1898.

Breaker disappeared in December, and at the same time a mysterious young man turned up in South Queensland who said his name was Thomas Day . . . a man whose description closely matched that of Morant. Day's fellow worker, butcher Bob King, described Day as looking about thirty years old and weighing thirteen to fourteen stone (about eighty-five kilograms). He said the new man was strong and experienced in handling carcases and positioning them for skinning; he immediately took an intense dislike to Day. Clarke, their employer, agreed with King that he did not like the look of Day and said he would get another man as soon as he could. Sergeant Arrell of Gatton added that Day was five feet nine inches tall (175 centimetres), had a scruffy beard of recent growth, but thought he appeared to be in his early twenties.

Morant was described as being thirty-three years old, the same height as Day, with brown hair and blue eyes. Stephens saw him as a broad, short, nuggetty man with a forty-four inch (one hundred and twelve centimetres) chest and a stout pair of capable arms. Breaker appeared to Banjo Paterson as a bronzed, clean-shaven man of thirty, well set up. So it would have been possible for one man to pass as the other.

Further, Morant was experienced in slaughtering cattle, he carried a revolver, and in a letter to Banjo Paterson from Enngonia in late 1895, he reveals a somewhat sadistic streak when he describes the slaughter of a heifer, using the weapon:

There are a few scrubbers (cleanskins) yet remaining in an adjoining ten-mile block. The country is fairly dense brigalow and gidgee and it's not the easiest thing in the world to get them — in fact we cannot get them, so whenever we want beef here we go out and shoot or rip — do you know the latter performance? — and butcher some cheap beef off the beast's hide. Last week my mate and I went beef hunting. We were riding colts and had but four revolver cartridges. Four bullets failed to drop the cleanskin heifer we selected, and I got alongside the heifer to knife her. She turned and charged in her tracks, and the colt not being up to the game, his bowels came out instead of the heifer's, whilst I was hurled headlong. The colt went off (died that night, poor brute!) and I just managed to put a tree between me and the heifer as she charged. After one or two narrow squeaks I managed to hamstring her and the cuddy's misfortune was avenged.[5]

The man who called himself Thomas Day met the Gatton butcher Arthur George Clarke on the road and, after a conversation, Clarke gave him a job assisting in the slaughter yard, looking after the rendering down coppers and transporting the meat to the shop in Gatton. Day said he had worked for a man named Wilson in Wagga Wagga, had come from Sydney to Brisbane by boat, arriving on 6 December and carried his swag across to Gatton, taking ten days to cover the distance.

Four days after the young swagman had left Brisbane, Alfred Hill, a fifteen-year old youth was riding his pony to visit his uncle at Redbank Plains. Shortly before he reached the village of Oxley he was decoyed off the road and murdered. Both he and his pony were shot through the head, and near the bodies were found a .380 bullet and a spent cartridge of the same calibre. It was suspected by police that a man named Wilson had shot the boy to conceal an unnatural offence, and then had sold or given his revolver to a swagman. Wilson was arrested and charged with the murder, but later the charge was dropped. By the time the Royal Commission into the maladministration of the CIB was held in September 1899, it was considered that the murder had been committed by the swagman, and that the swagman was Thomas Day.

Ten days after Day's arrival at Gatton, the town was shocked by news of another murder, perpetrated during the evening of Boxing Day.

On that night in 1898, a young man named Michael Murphy, aged 29, and his two sisters Norah, 27 and Ellen aged 18, left their home to drive by horse and sulky into Gatton, about ten kilometres distant, to attend a dance. Arriving at the hall soon after nine o'clock, they found the function had been cancelled. Turning around they headed back towards their home. But they never arrived there.

Next morning a worried mother sent her son-in-law William McNeill to enquire for them. Halfway to town he noticed wheel tracks leading off the road, through sliprails into a bushy paddock. Recognising the track because of a wobbly left wheel on the sulky, he followed it. In the middle of the paddock he found the three Murphys and the horse lying dead. Michael and the horse had both been shot in the head by a .380 gun; the two girls had been raped and clubbed to death. Just as there had been at Oxley, a spent .380 cartridge case was found near the bodies.

The Gatton uniformed police, Sergeant William Arrell and Acting Sergeant

Toomey, were out of their depth in handling a crime of this magnitude and the CIB were called in. The detectives suspected Richard Burgess, not long out of prison where he had served a sentence for attempted rape. After several weeks of investigation he was able to prove he had been at least fifty kilometres distant on the night of the murders.

Meanwhile Sergeant Arrell had been getting reports that a person resembling Thomas Day had been seen in the vicinity of the sliprails leading into Moran's paddock — the scene of the murders on the fatal evening. When interviewed, Day insisted that on the night in question he had had his tea at seven o'clock then went to bed and read a book. Acting Sergeant Toomey searched the hut in which Day slept and made a list of his scanty possessions. They consisted of two each of trousers, singlets, shirts and jumpers, a pair of boots, a wide-brimmed soft felt hat, a blanket and a couple of swag straps. He had none of the usual baggage of a swagman, such as billy, frying pan, water bag, tucker bag or other camp gear.

The book he was reading was *Rienzi* by Lord Bulwer Lytton, a colourful historical romance about a fourteenth century Roman tribune who sought to become a dictator and was violently murdered. On promise to take out a subscription when he got his wages, Day had been allowed to borrow from the School of Arts library.

Thomas Day was a strange, aloof, unsociable sort of man. When he was not at work he would lie on the bed in his hut and read. After dark, he would go for a walk along the Tent road as far as the sliprails, wearing his wide-brimmed felt hat pulled down over his eyes, and had been seen by several people lurking about the spot. Later, by the light of a lantern, he would read in bed until ready for sleep. He always slept fully clothed and with his boots on, with the door and window open, as though prepared for some nocturnal disturbance.

The senior detective of the CIB was so strongly convinced of Burgess' guilt that he ignored evidence against Day and was incensed when he discovered the Gatton police were carrying out an investigation on their own initiative. They were ordered to leave Day strictly alone, in spite of the fact that Clarke and many of the townspeople suspected him.

Sergeant Toomey, Clarke and Bob King all noticed bloodstains on Day's jumper on the day after the Murphy murders. He explained them as having come from the meat he had handled that morning. He spent some time next day washing out the stains, using both soap and washing soda to remove them. Then, having received his wages, he went into Gatton, where he paid a quarter's subscription to the girl who looked after the library. He also bought a razor and shaved off all his whiskers except for a moustache.

After the murders, Clarke went in fear of Day, convinced that, given the opportunity, he would throw him into one of the boilers. This fear was shared by Mrs Clarke, who added to her husband's apprehension by suggesting Day would probably brain him with a waddy first. Relations between Day and his employer became strained, and a few days later he gave Clarke one week's notice. Then perhaps he heard about the Magisterial Inquiry into the murders which was being organised, for he became impatient to get away.

He began to abuse Clarke, and then to swear at his children, and became so objectionable Clarke was forced to sack him and pay a week's wages in lieu of notice. After he had cleared his departure with Sergeant Arrell, Day left by train for Toowoomba, then a day or two later passed through Gatton on the way back to Brisbane, where he disappeared.

He vanished by enlisting in the Militia and going into army camp, giving his place of birth as Cunnamulla. A few weeks later he deserted and vanished again, this time for good. Nothing further was ever heard of Thomas Day other than, in later years, there arose an oral tradition that he went to the Boer War and was killed in Africa. Subsequent enquiries by the army showed that no Thomas Day had been born in Cunnamulla, nor had anybody named Day lived there.

So, who was this strange young swagman who came from nowhere, disappeared into the blue, and who had a taste for classic English literature? The Gibney brothers, James and Desmond, in their book *The Gatton Mystery*, after failing to identify him summed up their chapter on Thomas Day with the following paragraph:

Who was this introspective and unsociable man who called himself Thomas Day? What was his real name and where did he come from? What sort of a man was he — this youthful swagman who was fond of reading? What ultimately became of him after he left Gatton in 1899? The answer to all these questions is 'Regrettably we do not know.' [6]

Author and poet Merv Lilley has his own ideas about the identity of Thomas Day. In his book *Gatton Man*, Lilley makes an even more amazing claim: that Thomas Day was, in fact, his father!

A travelling tea salesman, Bill Lilley sometimes used the alias Thomas Wilson and, without producing any proof, Merv Lilley states that his dad also assumed the name of Thomas Day and was the Gatton murderer. Then he further complicates an already complicated plot by asserting that his father of many names worked as an offsider for Breaker Morant at Blue Nobby Station on the Queensland–New South Wales border.[7]

Thomas Day left Gatton two weeks after the Murphy murders, and deserted from the militia in Brisbane three or four weeks later. A month later, Harry Morant reappeared on the lower Murray. It was at Paringa Station, a remote place in South Australia, not far from Renmark and close to where the borders of the three states conjoin. Frederick Cutlack writes:

To a boy of twelve, such as myself then, the adventures of attending the arrival on the farther river-bank of a mob of a hundred or more cattle, to be crossed by swimming over the broad river to the Paringa shore, then driven outback, and later mustered and brought into the frontage — these doings filled unforgettably wonderful days.

It was on one such occasion that The Breaker appeared in the late summer of 1898-99.[8]

If Morant was seeking a place where he would not be recognised as Thomas Day, he chose well. The lease of Paringa was owned by two young Englishmen who lived elsewhere and rented the homestead to Mr and Mrs Cutlack and their twelve-year-old son, Frederick. The only others on the place were a couple of Irish stockmen. Breaker was given a job as stockman on Paringa and was there when news of the Boer War reached them in October 1899.

As Thomas Day did in Brisbane, Harry Morant saw the opportunity for anonymity in an army camp and, further, the means to leave Australia by means of a free passage to South Africa as the first stage of his return to England.

Young Fred Cutlack remembered Breaker's departure:

Morant was not with us for long. After the Boer War broke out in October 1899 there was a morning when for the last time he boiled his quart-pot on the river-bank while he and others waited to catch the down-river steamer for railhead to Adelaide, and he gave me that quart-pot as a parting gesture.[9]

CHAPTER 8

The Boer War Ballads

Like all wars, the Boer War disrupted many lives and at least three of these were writers. In South Africa, a brilliant young author named Olive Schreiner had, after eleven years work, brought to completion a major feminist work titled *Musings on Woman and Labour*. In 1899 she was living in Johannesburg when, to relieve severe asthma attacks, she had to move down to a lower altitude. While she was absent the war broke out. Subsequently she was interned, and during her absence her home was looted and her papers burned, including the manuscript of her book. She rewrote the first chapter only, and this was published as *Woman and Labour*, a pioneering work on the feminist cause, but the balance of the book was lost to the world.

Harry Morant, 'The Breaker', met his inglorious end in South Africa, terminating what might have developed into a successful career as one of Australia's bush poets; and the relationship Will Ogilvie had established with *The Bulletin* as one of its leading contributors was destroyed.

The Bulletin opposed the Boer War. Co-founder and editor J. F. Archibald claimed it was being waged for the benefit of British shareholders in South African goldmines. It was not a popular stance, and circulation dropped as a result. Caught up in the wave of patriotic fervour, many *Bulletin* contributors declined to submit their work to what had become known as 'The Bushman's Bible'. One of these was Will Ogilvie — Australian poet at heart, but British to the core by nature.

After an interval of some fifteen months Will at last had news of the whereabouts of The Breaker, who was about to sail with the South Australian Contingent of the Bush Carbineers. Writing to Stephens from Parkes on 25 January 1900, he tells of his next address then continues:

I've got a few poems on the war-contingent subject — no use sending them to the misguided paper with which you are associated so contemplate pamphlet form by some Sydney publisher. Are you averse to this?

Your candid opinion please; of course the stuff is not good — its jumps — very jingo — also jingle, but I had to get it off my chest and now feel better, but isn't there money in it at the present enthusiastic crisis. Of course I'm apologetic to you, but inwardly really a little proud of it, tho' it's no good as literature.

Please advise instanter and
   Believe me
      Your Will Ogilvie.

(News item — H. Morant 'Breaker' leaves with S.A. Contingent.)

> Whatever they may say
> You're a fighter all the way
>   (Goodbye, Breaker!)
> Let us put your faults behind
> Let us put your better qualities before,
> For we're glad to hear you've signed —
> And we'll drink the red night blind
> To another bulldog fighter for the War!
>
> Whoever may deny,
> You're a plucky sort, say I,
>   (Good luck, Breaker!)
> We have seen you go ahead
> In the rattling polo-rally and the hunt,
> So we'll hope you dodge the lead
> And we'll fill the wine cup red
> To another reckless devil for the front.
>   W.H.O

'N.B. Publish this if you care to.' [1]

This letter with its included poem was followed by another on the matter of the war poems, written from Condobolin on 3 February, in which, among other topics, Ogilvie writes:

I'm collecting the war-jingle to send to you — the verses in last Sydney Mail are part of it. I did not think you had any objection to my sending verse elsewhere so long as it was *paid* for, but since your last letter I see your business intentions and promise not to transgress again. I should much rather have *you* make profit out of my writing than anyone else, seeing how much I owe you as a mentor and friend.'[2]

Ogilvie's promise to Stephens not to transgress again must have been lightly given. The piece referred to as having been published in the *Sydney Mail* was titled 'The Overlander's Farewell to His Mates'; it had already been published by *The Bulletin* in the poet's book *Fair Girls and Gray Horses* as 'L'Envoi — To the Overlanders'. This, no doubt, was the reason for Stephens' objection to the piece appearing in a rival journal. But on the same day that Ogilvie wrote his letter, namely 3 February, the second of his three 'War Poems' appeared in the *Sydney Mail!*

The *Sydney Mail* was a weekly tabloid journal which featured a pictorial supplement, printed on glazed art paper and with high quality black-and-white illustrations and photographs. They made a big feature of the Boer War, and each of the Ogilvie poems was given a full-page spread with both photographs and drawings. Nothing came of his proposal to publish his war poems as a booklet, and they appear to have been limited to the three published in the *Sydney Mail*.

THE OVERLANDER'S FAREWELL TO HIS MATES

Take this farewell from one must leave
    The rowel and the rein
Before the blue Canoblas weave
    Their snow-white hoods again;
Before the winter suns have kissed
    The lips of Autumn dead,
Before they call the next year's list
    At Nocoleche shed:
Before the pines on Lightning Ridge
    Have bowed to six new moons,
Before the floods to Tarrion Bridge
    Back up the dry lagoons.
In vain the luring West-wind sighs
    For Home's across the sea,
And Northward round the Leeuwin lies
    The next long trip for me!

In leisure and in labour
    We've faced the world afield,
With saddle for a sabre
    And brave heart for a shield;
We've fought the long dry weather,
    We've heard the wild floods wake,
We've battled through together
    For the old game's royal sake.

We have heard the tug-chains ring in the swamps
    When the thundering whipstrokes fall;
We have watched the stars on the droving camps
    Come out by the gum-trees tall;
We have lingered long by the low slip-rails
    Where maybe a light love waits,
When the shadows creep and the red sun sails
    Low down by the stockyard gates;

We have stirred perhaps by the lone watch-fires
　　The ashes of old regret,
The loves unwon and the lost desires,
　　And the hopes that are hard to forget.

The tracks we've travelled over
　　Were hungry tracks and hard;
Long days we've played the rover,
　　Dark nights we've kept our guard;
But chained in silver glories
　　The Bush our hearts has stirred,
And told the starlight stories
　　And no-one else has heard.

The gray-white dawns will wake you and the gold noons watch you pass
Behind the roving Queensland mobs knee-deep in Nebine grass;
You will cross the old tracks Nor'ward, you will run the old roads West,
And I shall follow with my heart dream-droving with the rest;
And often in the sleepless nights I'll listen as I lie
To the hobble chains clink-clinking and the horse-bells rippling by,
I shall hear the brave hoofs beating, I shall see the moving steers
And the red glow of the camp-fires as they flame across the years;
And my heart will fill with longing just to ride for once again
In the forefront of the battle where the men who fight are Men;
And when beyond the Ocean we are pledging toasts in wine,
I shall give 'The Overlanders' in that far-off land of mine.

The Brave West! Here's toward her!
　　The 'plant's' gone out before;
Their heads are to the Border
　　But I'll go out no more;
We've fought the long dry weather;
　　We've faced the blinding wet;
And we were mates together
　　And I shall not forget!

SO LONG! OLD MATES!
Being a Farewell to the Bush Contingent

You have gathered from the camp-fires and the far-back station huts,
To the calling of the bugles over-sea;
We have tried you at the timber, we have proved you at the butts,
And we brand you as the thing you claim to be.
You are bushmen of the bushmen and your steeds are bridle-wise,

And if your leaders learn to lead you light
You will show the Transvaal rebels when the Mauser bullet flies
That the back-block boys are not afraid to fight.

Pass across the gangway, to the bugle call!
(Five hundred miles behind you are the dusty stockyard rails)
Spurred and booted, bushmen all,
For the honour of the Empire and the pride of New South Wales.

You have taken down the slip rails, set the mustered cattle free,
You have put the snaffle bridles on your best,
You have kissed a sobbing sweetheart by the moonlit wilga tree,
You are riding from the north and from the West.
And the empty creeks are calling as you take the bridle-track
And the gaunt brown gums are clutching at your heart,
And your lips are curled with laughter that may bring no jesting back
And the tears are on your faces as you part.

Pass along the gangway, to the bugle call!
(Miles and miles behind you are the gum trees and the creek)
Spurred and booted, bushmen all,
We will charge in heart beside you when the snapping rifles speak!

You have left the half-turned furrow, you have slung the golden lode,
You have chosen for the blood-red fields of War
Sunburnt stockmen from the mallee, hard-faced drovers from the road —
And behind you there's another thousand more!
Oh! Comrades of the camp-fire, merry muster-mates of mine!
You the restless rovers with the stars to guide!
You will teach them in the Transvaal when they wheel you into line
How to shoot and — don't forget it! — how to ride!

Pass along the gangway, to the bugle call!
(Two hundred miles behind you are the weeping myall trees)
Spurred and booted, bushmen all,
For the succour of the Empire and her banner over seas!

You are teamsters from the Tarrion, you are boys from Inverell;
You are here and there a scion of a squatter king;
You are comrades, if need be, charging down the slopes of Hell
With loose reins and touching stirrups all a-ring!
You are bushmen of the bushmen, you are out to win or fall
(How we'll cheer you down the harbour when she sails!)
They have picked you from the best men in the station hut and Hall
The chosen and the pride of New South Wales.

Pass across the gangway, to the bugle call!
(Miles and miles behind you are your weeping Western girls)
Spurred and booted, bushmen all,
Fighters till the old Flag on Pretoria unfurls!

In your ranks are dressed the outlaws of an older land than yours;
They have learned to love the Bushland, let them go!
For the shame and for the lost love, for the sorrow that endures,
You will take them heel to heel against the foe!
By the blood of fighting fathers running fiery in their veins,
By the honoured names they once were proud to bear,
They will take the foremost places when the foam is on the reins,
They will charge among your best men over there!

Pass them down the gangway, to the bugle call!
(Far and far behind them are the sins of all the years)
Spurred and booted, bushmen all,
For the brave old Flag of England they will follow through their tears

Hands across the gangway! And your hands are rough and scarred
With the labour of the axes and the rope.
Aye! Your hands are brown and blistered, and your brows are lined and hard;
But your hearts, oh! rugged bushmen are our Hope!
When we hear by lonely watch-fires, when we read by scorching suns,
How the bushmen cleared the trenches for the Line,
How they rode their fiery walers to the muzzles of the guns,
We shall proudly tell them, 'These were mates of mine!'

Pass along the gangway, to the bugle call!
(Far and far behind you are the bridle tracks at home)
Spurred and booted, bushmen all,
As you fought your foes of drought-time fight your foes across the foam!

The third poem, was published on 2 June 1900. Like the other two, it was given a full-page spread, and was illustrated by Fred Leist, Ogilvie's favourite horse artist. On one occasion, when writing to Stephens about illustrations for some poems, he stated, 'What ever you do, don't let Norman Lindsay do them; he can't draw horses! Give them to Fred Leist'.

A LENGTH IN THE LEAD

The last bell is ringing,
The riders are up,
The gay jackets stringing,
The start of the cup;

The wind in our faces,
The roar at our back,
The struggle for places,
The turn of the track,
The morning sun glittering
On rider and steed,
The strain on the bit-ring —
A length in the lead!

A length in the lead!
'Tis the joy of the breed!
The aim of the horseman, the triumph of speed;
The last fence — and over! A length in the lead!

The east sky is brightening
And Day's at her birth,
What shortening and tightening
Of stirrup and girth!
The wild mob is lifting
Grey dust on the plain,
The stockman is shifting
Short hold on the rein;
O'er swampland and ridgy
He holds them for speed,
And wheels in the gidgee
A length in the lead!

A length in the lead!
'Tis the pride of the breed!
Tho' brave hearts are broken and sobbing sides bleed,
The goal of the stockman's a length in the lead!

The picket-rope's idle,
The Squadron's afar;
A hand to the bridle,
A foot to the bar;
On lone Modder River
The bugle's obeyed
By men who will never
Ride back to parade.
But willing fore loopers
Wherever the need,
We trust to our troopers
A length in the lead!

A length in the lead!
'Tis the boast of the breed!
Tho' saddles be empty and heroes may bleed,
'Australia for ever! A length in the lead!'

Ogilvie never saw The Breaker again after Morant went to Sydney during the second half of 1898, nor did he hear news of him until, in January, 1900 he saw an announcement in a newspaper that Morant was about to sail for South Africa with the Second South Australian Mounted Rifles.

A little over a year later, on 3 February 1901, Ogilvie also said goodbye to Australia and sailed for home. He was living in the old family home, Holefield, in Kelso when he heard that his old horse-breaking mate had been sentenced to death by court martial and executed by firing squad on 27 February 1902.

Both Gordon Tidy, (Mousquetaire) and Will Ogilvie, (Glenrowan) wrote memorial poems for their fellow poet. Ogilvie's, titled 'To the Memory of One Dead' was sent to an old mate, Archie McLean of Boona West, above Condobolin, who in December 1910 donated the manuscript to the Mitchell Library.[3] In later years, Archie McLean became manager of Anna Creek Station in South Australia for Sidney Kidman, and in the early 1920s gave the youthful R. M. Williams his first job.

TO THE MEMORY OF ONE DEAD

This is the real epitaph of poor old Breaker Morant; and the sort he would have liked us to write above his grave. — W. H. Ogilvie.

When the horses broke for the stony ridge
    How his face would set in a grin,
As he shortened his hold of the brown colt's head
    And hammered the long-necks in!
And he drew his whip on the racing wing
    And was lost in the mulga trees,
His 'Get to the lead of the cattle, mate!'
    Came cheerily back on the breeze.

He went to fight in a foreign land,
    And I know that he only went,
To fight with the cares that were creeping close,
    And stealing his heart's content.
He went to fight with a foreign foe
    And he fought them gallant and grey,
T'would be, 'Get to the lead of the cattle, boys!'
    As the scared Boers broke away.
                X X X X X

They laid him low in a coward's grave,
    Somewhere out on the grey Karoo,
(Yet I know one mate would have called him brave
    And a woman who thought him true!)
And his hopes were spread like a scattered mob,
    But his pride was a crippled steed
It was 'Get to the lead of those cattle, there!
    <u>But he never got to the lead</u>!

CHAPTER 9

Ben Hall Legends

Ogilvie most certainly heard stories of Ben Hall's exploits during the years he spent working in the Forbes–Parkes area, and while droving through the district. His three poems about the bushranger are remarkable for the period of time over which they were written and for their diversity of form.

'Ben Hall's Stirrup Irons' appeared on the Red Page of *The Bulletin* for 3 December 1898, given as an example in a discussion headed 'Title Deeds of an Australian Poet', which was not concerned with real estate, but was about the Australian content of work by the *Bulletin* poets. Red Page editor, A. G. Stephens had this to say of the piece:

Ogilvie tried his pen at sonnets a little time since, and the best (and irregular) result (now first printed) heads this page. It shows the vision, and the power of picturing his vision in words, which are poetically among his most fascinating attributes. Of a thousand persons who saw the 'lithe young squatter' probably five hundred failed to note the anti-climax of rusty stirrups to gleaming gear — so blind are many of us, though seeing.

And of the possible five hundred who noted, and queried, and heard the story, possibly one hundred appreciated the romance, and possibly a dozen felt it fully. And there was just one who felt, and whose brain instantaneously crystallised emotion into words surely almost as vivid as itself —

> 'The lifeless form bound to the saddle-gear,
> The blood-drops falling on the stirrup-bars.'

Vision — emotion — and the phrase which leaps to concentrate emotion: these are the Poet's prerogatives.

BEN HALL'S STIRRUP IRONS

A lithe young squatter passes in the dust.
His buckles gleaming and his bars aglance;
But laden with long years of old romance
The quaint old stirrups covered with red rust!
The troops are scattered, and the dark days dead

When robber bands made wild the Lachlan side;
No hunted outlaws to the mountains ride,
A thousand pounds of blood-fee on their head;
And only these quaint stirrups hand us down
The thrilling story no one halts to hear
Of long wild rides below the trusted stars,
And that last mournful journey to the town —
    The lifeless form bound to the saddle-gear,
    The blood-drops falling on the stirrup-bars.

The 'lithe young squatter' was Reg Lackey, son of the owner of Nelungaloo
Station and one of Will Ogilvie's best mates.[1]

Some years afterward Reg Lackey wrote to an old friend in the Parkes
district, Mr George Gunn, and stated in his letter: 'I have the stirrup irons that
Ben Hall was using when he was shot. I believe I am right in saying that
Inspector Stephenson, who was in charge of Forbes police at the time, gave
them to my father.'[2]

In a letter to Alexander Irvine of Narromine, in 1912, Ogilvie reminisced
on his friendship with Lackey:

I was specially glad to hear of Regie Lackey who never writes to me now, or
very seldom.

It is impossible to think of Australia without thinking of Regie, for we rode
and raced and drafted sheep and drank whisky & played polo and did many wild
and unprintable things together for several years, and never was a better mate
than he, or a cheerier. For R. had a sense of humour — that rare gift, and he was
in the world to enjoy it & so was I. I loved Regie . . .[3]

'The Saplings', an elegy, is not about just any saplings, but concerns the
clump of eucalypts, still standing, and now big, grown trees, which marks the
site of Ben Hall's last camp, at which he was ambushed and shot down by
police. Hall, aged twenty-seven, was killed at daybreak on 5 May 1865 at a spot
near the Billabong or Goobang Creek, about twenty kilometres west of Forbes.

In his letter to George Gunn regarding the provenance of the stirrup irons,
Reg Lackey, writing from Bribie Island, Queensland, goes on to state:

I was a very small child when my father bought 'Blowclear', which he later
named Nelungaloo. I spent the best days of my life there and on the adjoining
property, 'Brolgan', which belonged to my grandfather.

Hall was shot on South Blowclear, which belonged to Johnny Strickland,
from whom my father purchased it, and it became an outstation of Nelungaloo.
It was virgin country, and when he ringbarked it father left the clump of box
seedlings where Hall was shot. Many were riddled with bullets, and many more
had been cut down by souvenir hunters to obtain the bullets.

There are limestone caves about half a mile from Nelungaloo homestead which Hall used to frequent. In the main entrance to the caves there was a stone with the initials, 'B.H.' inscribed thereon, also a hole which looked like a bullet mould. In later years this stone disappeared and was probably taken also by souvenir hunters.[4]

Reginald Lackey left the Forbes district in 1908, and except for a hurried visit in 1915, never returned. He travelled overseas and visited his old mate, Will Ogilvie at Selkirk. He died in 1957.

The elegy about the clump of box saplings was first published in *The Lone Hand* for 1 October 1917, sixteen years after Ogilvie had gone back to his borderland home.

THE SAPLINGS

Where the hungry oak scrub changes
　　To the lush green Lachlan grass,
On a flat by the Gunning Ranges
　　Where only the wild things pass,
Stands a sapling clump a-quiver
　　With the dread of a dead year's call
As it rings to the Lachlan River —
　　'In the Queen's name — stand, Ben Hall!'

When skies from The Gap to Weddin
　　Are drowned in a sunset flood,
Then the silent saplings redden
　　As if with a tint of blood;
When winds of the dawn blow over
　　Their wail is a human cry,
And stirring the trefoil clover
　　A phantom foot goes by.

You may stand by the saplings dreaming
　　And see, where the shadows creep,
The flame of his camp-fire gleaming
　　Like a little star on the steep;
You may hear — though he never heard it
　　The click of a bolt withdrawn:
A twig as a night-bird stirred it?
　　Or, vengeance waiting the dawn?

You may see through the still dark dimly,
　　What the hunted did not see —
The circle crouching grimly,

The carbine crossing the knee —
What wonder the saplings shiver,
  When the whimpering bush winds call
To the ghosts of the Lachlan River
  On the last of your camps, Ben Hall!

The third Ben Hall piece takes the form of a narrative ballad, cast in five-line stanzas, and has an interesting story attached to it. During the 1950s it was found in a *Bill Bowyang Old Bush Recitations* booklet, attributed to 'Anon'. and was noteworthy because of scrambled type in the first stanza, which read:

Ben Hall was out on the Lachlan side
And a hundred more were ready to ride
Wherever a rumour led.
With a thousand pounds on his head;
A score of troopers were scattered wide.

When Nancy Keesing and Douglas Stewart were collecting material for their work *Old Bush Songs*, they corrected the opening lines and included the ballad in their book. Not long after publication, a reader from Western Australia sent Nancy Keesing a page torn out of a scrapbook. It contained the Ben Hall ballad set in an illustration by Stan Cross, and printed over the name of Will Ogilvie. Nancy Keesing established that the cutting came from 27 September 1924 edition of *Smith's Weekly*. One of Ogilvie's finest ballads, it is remarkable that it was published so long after he had left Australia.

THE DEATH OF BEN HALL

Ben Hall was out on the Lachlan side
  With a thousand pounds on his head;
A score of troopers were scattered wide,
And a hundred more were ready to ride
  Wherever a rumour led.

They had followed his track from the Weddin heights,
  And north by the Weelong yards;
Through dazzling days and moonlit nights
They had sought him over their rifle sights,
  With their hands on their trigger-guards.

The outlaw stole like a hunted fox
  Through the scrub and stunted heath,
And peered like a hawk from his eyrie rocks
Through the waving boughs of the sapling box
  On the troopers riding beneath.

His clothes were rent by the clutching thorn,
      And his blistered feet were bare;
Ragged and torn, with his beard unshorn,
He hid in the woods like a beast forlorn,
      With a padded path to his lair.

But every night when the white stars rose
      He crossed by the Gunning Plain
To a stockman's hut where the Gunning flows,
And struck on the door three swift light blows,
      And a hand unhooked the chain.

And the outlaw followed the lone path back
      With food for another day;
And the kindly darkness covered his track,
And the shadows swallowed him deep and black,
      Where the starlight melted away.

But his friend had read of the Big Reward,
      And his soul was stirred with greed;
He fastened his door and window-board,
He saddled his horse and crossed the ford,
      And spurred to the town with speed.

You may ride at a man's or a maid's behest
      When honour or true love call,
And steel your heart to the worst or best,
But the ride that is ta'en on a traitor's quest
      Is the bitterest ride of all.

A hot wind blew from the Lachlan bank
      And a curse on its shoulder came;
The pine trees frowned at him, rank on rank;
The sun on a gathering storm-cloud sank
      And flushed his cheek with shame.

He reined at the Court; and the tale began
      That the rifles alone should end;
Sergeant and trooper laid their plan
To draw the net on a hunted man
      At the treacherous word of a friend.
                  ★ ★ ★ ★
False was the hand that raised the chain
      And false was the whispered word:
'The troopers have turned to the south again,

You may dare to camp on the Gunning Plain.'
    And the weary outlaw heard.

He walked from the hut but a quarter-mile,
    Where a clump of saplings stood,
In a sea of grass like a lonely isle;
And the moon came up in a little while
    LIKE SILVER STEEPED IN BLOOD

Ben Hall lay down on the dew-wet ground
    By the side of his tiny fire;
And a night-breeze woke, and he heard no sound
As the troopers drew their cordon round —
    And the traitor earned his hire.

And nothing they saw in the dim grey light,
    But the little glow in the trees;
And they crouched in the tall gold grass all night,
Each one ready to shoot at sight,
    With his rifle cocked on his knees.

When the shadows broke and the Dawn's white sword
    Swung over the mountain wall,
And a little wind blew over the ford,
A sergeant sprang to his feet and roared:
    'IN THE NAME OF THE QUEEN, BEN HALL!'

Haggard, the outlaw leapt from his bed
    With his lean arms held on high.
'FIRE!' And the word was scarcely said
When the mountains rang to a rain of lead
    And the dawn went drifting by.
          *   *   *   *

They kept their word and they paid his pay
    Where a clean man's hand would shrink;
And that was the traitor's master-day
As he stood by the bar on his homeward way
    And called on the crowd to drink

He banned no creed and he barred no class,
    And he called to his friends by name;
But the worst would shake his head and pass,
And none would drink from the bloodstained glass
    And the goblet red with shame.

> And I know when I hear the last grim call
> And my mortal hour is spent,
> When the light is hid and the curtains fall
> I would rather sleep with the dead Ben Hall
> Than go where that traitor went.

There is another Ben Hall legend that Ogilvie could not have missed hearing while he was in the Lachlan Valley. The story goes that 'Mrs Coobang Mick' was pregnant to Ben Hall, and that this situation and not the reward was the real reason for the betrayal. It says further, that when Mrs Coobang Mick heard the gunfire, she jumped out of bed and ran to the door, screaming 'That's Ben! They've shot poor Ben!' Later she was taken to Forbes to formally identify the body. When the covering blanket was pulled back and she saw the mangled corpse with its thirty-two bullet wounds she was deeply shocked. So much so, that when her little brown baby was born its body was blotched with a corresponding number of white stigmata — one for each bullet wound. In later years the lad was taken around the country shows to be exhibited in a tent as 'The Leopard Boy'.

When Ogilvie set out on Loyal Heart to ride from Forbes down to Ulladulla on the South Coast, he wrote to Stephens from Young, to say: 'Have just come through the Grenfell country — full of the old romance of Gardiner, Hall & Co. If only I'm not too lazy I'm going to write up 'The Wraiths of Weddin' to some purpose...' [5]

That was in August, 1898. A search of the Sydney journals and of a number of rural newspapers has failed to locate the promised piece under that title, but the phrase does appear in another poem, 'A Queen of Yore', written during that trip and published in *The Bulletin* six months later.

The title is inept, suggesting as it does a broken-down old mare — 'A Song of the Lachlan River' would have been more fitting. Probably 'wraiths of Weddin' was the inspired phrase that entered his mind, but when, later, he sat down to work up the poem, the imagery absorbed during several days of wandering up the river took over. The result was a six stanza tribute to the Lachlan, with the fourth verse being all that remained to acknowledge the presence of the spirits of the bushranging gang:

> She sees no barricaded roofs, no loopholed station wall,
> No foaming steed with flying hoofs to bring the word 'Ben Hall!'
> She sees no reckless robbers stoop behind their ambush stone,
> No coach-and-four, no escort troop; — but, very lorn and lone,
> Watches the sunsets redden along the mountainside
> Where round the spurs of Weddin the wraiths of Weddin ride.

CHAPTER 10

Going Home

In June 1897 Ogilvie wrote to A. G. Stephens, editor of *The Bulletin's* Red Page to ask about the cost of having a volume of his verses published. It was the first of a series of letters written to Stephens during the ensuing ten years and in it he wrote: 'as I shall be leaving this country in a month or two for Scotland, I should like to publish before I go'. But it was to be another three-and-a-half years before he took this step.

Ogilvie was under the impression he would have to pay for the printing of the proposed books, and thought he might be able to pay for 500 copies. Apparently Stephens informed Ogilvie that *The Bulletin* would be prepared to publish a collection of his work, and would do so at their own risk. From that time on, until *Fair Girls and Gray Horses* was published in November 1898, Ogilvie bombarded Stephens with enquiries and fussed about like an expectant father!

He kept up a stream of letters, demanding to know, week by week, when the books would be available, and almost up to the day it went to press he was sending in suggestions and alterations to poems. He need not have worried about the book's reception, because the first edition was sold out in three months, with a second, enlarged edition being released in February 1899. There was a new edition every year for the next seven years, and up to 1960 the book had sold over 65,000 copies — not a bad effort for a young Scotsman who wrote Australian bush ballads!

At last, in November 1900, in another letter to Stephens, Ogilvie states his firm intention to leave Australia:

I almost took the male cow by the antlers the other day and booked a berth on the *Ophir* with a friend of mine who is up anchor for Bowmont Water at end of this week but rather short notice of his leaving prevented me from going. However, I am selling off my quadrupeds and after a final flutter at Forbes Picnic Races next week I mean to get away as soon as possible.[1]

In the same letter he 'put on the bite' for ten or twenty pounds as an advance *on Fair Girls and Gray Horses* 'if it could be worked!'

Having finalised his rural affairs, Ogilvie came to Sydney in the middle of

January 1901, and took up residence in a room at Randwick, just a block away from the racecourse. Meanwhile two of his literary friends, Louise Mack and Victor Daley, started a subscription list for a farewell dinner, which was held at the prestigious Hotel Australia on 28 January 1901. Will's son, George Ogilvie, stated that there were about eighty guests present, but there are only 21 signatures on the souvenir menu. [2]

Sydney's leading artists of the day got together to produce the unique souvenir menu which carried the imprint: 'The composition done in Esteem for Will H. Ogilvie by *The Bulletin* Newspaper Company ... Printed for the Love of Poetry by H. T. Dunn & Co, Artistic Printers, Queen's Place, Sydney.'

The cream paper was completely overprinted with the texts of Ogilvie poems in faint green ink, with the contents in black, superimposed in the manner of an ancient palimpsest. The artists and one photographer involved were: Thea Proctor, front cover; Charles Kerry, portrait; 'Hop', a cartoon; D. H. Souter, cartoon (without a cat!); a facsimile autograph unpublished poem by Ogilvie, 'The Reiver's Heart', while the back cover featured 'Fair Girls and Gray Horses' illustrated by Ogilvie's favourite horse artist, Fred Leist. Those who autographed the Mitchell Library copy were:

Will H. Ogilvie	Louise Mack
Roderic Quinn	Albert Dorrington
Victor J. Daley	D. H. Souter
Julian Ashton	Agnes Janson
Chris Brennan	Tom Roberts
A.B. Paterson	Nelson Illingworth
Laurence Campbell	A. R .Gorius Thomas
Fred Leist	B. Kerry (Mrs. Charles?)
A. G. Stephens	Rose Scott
William MacLeod	Germaine G. Spicer(?)

Virtually a Who's Who of Australian art, literature and music!

The chairman and toast-master, William MacLeod, managing director of *The Bulletin*, proposed four toasts, namely: 'Literature', 'Our Poet and Guest', 'The Allied Arts', and 'Fair Girls and Gray Horses' (not forgetting Dark Girls and Black Horses)'.

The menu is in itself an interesting study of the cuisine offered by Sydney's leading hotel in 1901 — Australian with just a touch of French!

Consommé Tortue Clair.   Cream Asparagus
Fried Fillets of Black Bream, Sauce Valois.
Haunch Venison, Sauce Groseilles.   Braised Ham, Sauce Madère.
Braised Lamb Cutlets and Green Peas.   Pâté a la Financière.
Salmis Duckling, Rouennaise.

Loin Mutton, Purée Lentilles.   Sirloin Beef au jus.
Chicken and Bacon au Cresson.

Mayonnaise Salmon, Green.

Celery demi-glacé.   French Beans.   Baked Pumpkin.
Cucumber Maitre d'Hotel.   Baked, Boiled and Mashed Potatoes.

Frankfort Pudding.   Passion-Fruit Custard.   Assorted Cakes.
Compôte Apricots.

Vanilla Ice Cream.   Albert Sandwiches.

Café

Unfortunately the wine list was not included with the menu.

Queen Victoria had died a week prior to the Ogilvie farewell dinner, and in the days following the send-off all newspapers were full of details of the innumerable church services being held in memory of 'The Widow of Windsor'. All other news items were relegated to small paragraphs on back pages, including reports of the departure of one of our leading poets. George Ogilvie summarised the newspaper accounts:

The Sydney Morning Herald reported:
'The health of the guest was entrusted to Victor Daley who claimed for Ogilvie the occupancy of the highest rung in the ladder of Australian poetry. Ogilvie's response was modest — he could ride a horse with the best, play polo in the streets of Forbes with 'The Breaker', court the pretty girls of the Lachlan night in and night out — but he could not venture to thank that enthusiastic gathering for their kindly recognition of his work.' The Sydney Truth referred to Will as a 'youngish Scotchman, who versifies ideally and orates nervously'. The Sydney Daily Telegraph reported that Will's oratory was 'hardly on the level with his lyrics'.[3]

Another example of this fear of making public utterances was when, having been invited by Stephens to join The Bulletin staff for drinks a day or so before the send-off, Will wrote declining the invitation, making the lamest of excuses that he couldn't attend 'due to having a sore throat!'

Prior to leaving Australia, Ogilvie received an official invitation to attend the opening of the first Federal Parliament in the Exhibition Buildings in Melbourne, and to meet their Royal Highnesses the Duke and Duchess of York, in May of that year — an engagement which would really have put his nervousness to the test.

Ogilvy sailed in the Persic on 3 February 1901, travelling by the White Star Line, via 'The Cape'. At Capetown, he found time to make a quick survey of South African agricultural and pastoral methods, which later provided a chapter of his book My Life in the Open. And during the voyage he wrote nine nonsense poems for the ship's newspaper, such as:

> Now the Persic Star is finished
> With the finish of the cruise
> And in future you poor people
> Must be satisfied with news
> In The Times and in The Standard
> And such paltry little rags
> Instead of Persic cable-grams
> Flashed out on White Star flags;
> And if our log was heavy,
> And our interviews were tough,
> And our little jokes were ghastly,
> And our poems doubtful stuff
> Will you just this once be kindly
> To the editorial train,
> If we promise on our honour
> That it won't occur again.

Australia was gone, but by no means forgotten — Will Ogilvie continued to write Australian bush ballads for many years to come.

Back in Scotland after an absence of twelve years, he spent the next two years on his parents' farm, Holefield, near Kelso, where he devoted his time to writing borderland verse and sending it to the London periodicals. A collection of the best of these was published by Elkin Matthews in London as part of a series of booklets of British poets.

During this time Ogilvie maintained a continuous correspondence with A. G. Stephens, sending him occasional Australian pieces for *The Bulletin*, and in a letter dated April 1902 he discusses poems for inclusion in 'the new book'. This was *Hearts of Gold*, published *by The Bulletin* in 1903, with several later editions coming from Angus & Robertson.

In December 1903 Will left Holefield and moved to 7 Gillespie Crescent, Edinburgh, from where he wrote to Stephens to say how excitedly he was expecting the first copies of the new work. On January 4 1904 he wrote from Holefield to confirm the safe arrival of the first three copies, and this was the last letter Stephens was to receive from Ogilvie from Scotland.

CHAPTER 11

An American Sojourn

Will's father, George Ogilvie died in 1904, and though Will could have taken over the tenancy of the Holefield farm, his interests were drawn in another direction. A neighbour named John Clay had gone to America where he had built up a fortune from the cattle trade. Learning that the Iowa State Agricultural College needed a person to lecture on agricultural journalism and to edit technical bulletins, he endowed a Chair of Agricultural Journalism, recommended Will for the position, then wrote to the Ogilvies suggesting that Will or his brother George might apply for the position.

Will won the appointment and began his lectures in 1905. He embraced the new lifestyle with the same enthusiasm he had displayed on his arrival in Australia sixteen years earlier. In his first letter to A. G. Stephens from America, he states, *inter alia:*

But I am no longer a shiftless, drifting rhymer; but a business man at the head of quite an important department. Shortly, I am engaged at a salary of many hundreds of dollars — it don't look so much in pounds but is about £400 a year — to edit the Bulletins of the Iowa Experimental Agricultural College. So I am Bulletin Editor before you! There is a vile conspiracy on foot even to make me a Professor of Agricultural Literature, but I hope to stave off the evil day for some time to come.

I have only been in the country a fortnight and about a week here. Besides my work I have to wrestle with such problems as ten plates at dinner, baths at the barber's shops, no boots cleaned in your house etc etc.

The food is weird altogether, and since I came here I have eaten enough corn to win the Melbourne Cup.

It is a wonderful country. A fellow won't write many verses here, I should say. Judging from the kind which appears in the local paper there is no time to devote to cultivating the art. American provincial verse seems built quick like American houses, reputations and other things.

If I can go the pace I'll stay here for a bit but the place does not look healthy for a dreamer! [1]

He went the pace, and although sometimes out of his depth, struggled on manfully. Six months later, in April 1905, he wrote to Stephens:

Have you ever been in Iowa? The country is flat as Back o' Bourke and more uninteresting. This is a great college with about 1500 students, men and women, and over a hundred teachers of every language, economy and technique under the sun. Any hints on Journalism will be thankfully received; I don't know much about it myself but am supposed to teach young America how to write. Ye Gods![2]

The degree of success he achieved may be gauged from a passage in a letter from one of his old students, L. E. Treeger to K. R. Marvin of Iowa State College in 1956: 'I recall that I was somewhat disappointed in the way Mr. Ogilvie operated as it was very similar to the conduct of those classes in English which I had attended each of my four years' [3]

By June 1905 Will was battling to keep up with his students and wrote to the long-suffering Stephens begging him to buy any books he could lay his hands on that dealt with the topic of agricultural journalism, most particularly on the subject of preparing articles for the press.

The semester must have ended in June, for in July he was off on a borrowed horse to visit Denver in Colorado and to take a look at the Rocky Mountains. He found that the life of the American cowboy did not measure up to that of the Australian stockman, and later was to write that they had little to say and appeared to live on beans! On the topic of Iowa girls, he wrote that 'They are pretty fair but I have seen bonnier both in Scotland and N.S.W.; but they dress to kill and are great style. (N.B. I'm still a bachelor.)'

A little later he informed Stephens that he had just received a cheque for $101 for an account of his Western trip, and added, 'Thus do we combine pleasure and profit when we go to Colorado for a holiday!' He had lost no time in adjusting to the American go-getter lifestyle!

Ogilvie continued to write to Stephens, almost on a monthly basis — letters which were partly business and partly of a personal nature for he had come to look upon *The Bulletin*'s Red Page editor as a sort of father-confessor cum business manager. Apparently in June 1905 Victor Daley had fallen on hard times and suffered from an illness. His mates started a subscription list to help him along and Stephens asked Will if he would put in. His reply and subsequent remarks reveal an odd quirk of personality. Among other topics he wrote:

In the matter of good old Daley of course you can count on me. I should like to have him know that he has my sympathy — and I'd like him to know that it is practical sympathy & not talk.

At the end of September there will be something coming to me from my books, it will be anything between £5 and £20 & will not be less than £5 I trust. Be it £5, £10 or £20, give it over to the Daley fund on my behalf, or if you don't want to wait till then cannot you pay over £5 or £7 on my behalf now and charge it against my account, that saves me sending it from here? I admire Daley immensely, seven times seven as a poet, and seven times more as a brave Bohemian and a good rebel. I hope to hear of his speedy recovery to health.[4]

But three weeks later, the thought of losing so much money was too much for him and he advised Stephens:

About my offer regarding Daley. If the money is not urgently required don't be shy about sending it to me for I'm always wanting money even on my now quite decent salary. If the books pan out at anything at the end of this month, I may as well have it for drink money as Daley or any one else, but it is all there for any brother writer who really needs it.[5]

So much for his 'seven times seven' regards!

During another break from his academic life Ogilvie made a short trip east to Chicago, the centre for the U.S.A. canned meat industry. Greatly impressed, he wrote a 3000 word article for *The Bulletin* to describe what he found there: the freighting of the livestock; the vast saleyards from which the cattle were driven across to the slaughter-yards, from whence the meat went into the canneries. Used to the Australian way, where cattle were auctioned at the saleyards, then driven hundreds of miles to the meatworks, he felt that the Chicago stockyards ought to carry a sign over the gates, stating — 'Abandon hope all ye who enter here!' The article was held over and does not appear to have been published, for in October 1905 he asks Stephens, 'What became of my Chicago Stockyards article?'

In mid-January 1906 he read news of Daley's death, and immediately wrote to Stephens enclosing an 'In Memoriam' poem for Daley:

Jan 15th 1906

Dear S.

Have just seen in paper cable of Daley's death. Am very, very sorry. With him is buried the only true poet heart in Australia. He, like many others, will be more appreciated years after his death than he is today.

I send these simple few lines that just wrote themselves when I read of his death. They would be better un-sent had they been ground out to catch the popular ear and make 10/-. They were not. They are spontaneous & wrote themselves.

In haste
Your sincere
Will H. Ogilvie

In Memory of Victor Daley — The Fairy's Friend.

Gone is the sparkle of wine in the glass,
    The garland is withered, the laughter is fled;
The feet of the fairies are stopped in the grass
    —Victor Daley is dead.

When the 'little folk' meet by the red rowan tree
   The dance shall be stayed in the ring on the plot
While they twine in his green Irish isle of the sea
   The wreath we forgot.

Will H. Ogilvie.[6]

In the middle of May 1906, he wrote to tell Stephens that he would, in a fortnight's time, 'shake the dust of Iowa from off my shoes'. He added that after eleven years in the Australian bush, he found academic life too narrow and enclosing. By the third week in June he was again writing from the family home at Holefield.

CHAPTER 12

In Double Harness

The reason Will Ogilvie gave to Stephens for his leaving America was not the whole truth. There was something else — a girl. Will's son George relates how, shortly before leaving for America, Will rode to the hunt with the Jedforest hounds. He noticed a girl riding sidesaddle on a nice-looking horse who hurdled a hedge in front of him, and he was immediately struck by the way in which she handled her mount.

He found out from a friend that she was Madge Scott-Anderson, the daughter of the Master of Hounds, and one good reason for wanting to return to Scotland was a desire to have another day's hunting with the Jedforest pack. In later years Madge described what happened when that day arrived:

When hounds ran out of scent on Primside top, huntsman Shore made a forward cast; the field clattered down the road to the valley while my father and I turned off to canter over the springy turf then pulling up to listen — yes, sounds of the chase were being wafted to our ears from the valley below, would we go? Wait a bit, yes there again — hounds giving tongue in chase comes clearly but also from a further distance. They had crossed the valley and we were left hopelessly out of the fun on the very edge of what we knew as the 'Duke's Leicestershire' — grass country.

'We went on, hoping they might take a turn towards us until we reached a formidable obstacle, a dry stane dyke where a big gap had been roughly filled in by loose stones full of fearsome spikes. My father's young horse refused and shied away and he called a warning to me 'Ride this carefully, Madgie'. Nimble Ninepence collected herself, crept up the jagged stones carefully and leaped, taking a considerable drop on the further side in perfect style.

Then there appeared out of nowhere a young fellow in mufti, riding with an easy seat and quiet confidence, gave my father's horse the lead he needed while I felt unaccountably happy tho' hopelessly lost out of the hunt. I learnt afterwards that the young stranger was Will Ogilvie, newly home from Australia, and three years later the bells rang out from Jedburgh Parish Church for our wedding on 24th June 1908.[1]

Will and Madge spent the first winter of their married life in a leased cottage in Bowden. While he could not afford a horse of his own, he rode some of his father–in–law's horses over the jumps in several local shows, where he won great acclaim for his skill.

Later he heard that the Free Kirk manse at Ashkirk was to let, so he leased, and later purchased the house, in which he and Madge lived happily for the rest of their days in what Will termed 'Double Harness'.

In a letter to an old mate in Australia, Alec Irvine of Narromine, written in 1910, Will wrote about his married happiness and his sixteen-month-old daughter Wendy. He also informed Irvine that he had just received a copy of an Australian book for review, C. E. W. Bean's *On the Wool Track*, which he highly regarded. Among other topics he wrote:

This is my birthday [21 August] — I'm forty-one if the testimony of my parents is to be relied upon, but I can't say that I feel as old as that. I am always fit, hard, and well.

My thoughts have been very much in the back country lately, for after your letter came a book which I have been asked to review for the Glasgow Herald. It is called On the Wool Track and is the best descriptive work on the Bush I have so far read.

One gets so much silly clap-trap written about our back country by tourists who have stayed a week or less on a sheep station that it is refreshing to find a writer who really knows the Bush as you and I have known it. I shall be able to review his work favourably as you may imagine.

Now, you'll want to hear about myself and family. Well, I was married two years ago on June 24th and I have a dear wee girl just 16 months old, the sweetest little thing you ever saw. She is a delight to us both, and at a very interesting age just now, just beginning to try to talk and walk. I wish you could see her. I do wish you could peep in on us and see me as a family man.

As to work I have made writing my whole profession. I have worked up a good connection with the magazines in prose and verse and I am kept pretty busy and am fairly well paid. Still it takes me all my time to keep things going, as of course one is expected to live rather more showily here than we could do in Australia.

I have lately invested in a pony and trap and I have a very nice stable. I don't get much riding now, but appreciate it still when I can get it.

I get The Bulletin even unto this day and still find it interesting but if I may say so, without being considered as putting in a word for myself, I think the verse has considerably fallen off since the days when 'Banjo', 'The Breaker', 'Curlew', etc., wrote their ringing bush rhymes in it. Some of the town men are clever on politics, etc., but there isn't a bush bard worth his tucker!

I dare say you are very happy at your work. You are blessed with an appreciative soul that takes to itself those gifts of the great wonderful mysterious Bush which are only revealed to a chosen few' [2]

Later on, Ogilvie's two children, Wendy and George, loved to hear their dad telling stories about his Australian adventures. A particular favourite was the evergreen yarn about that character, famous in Australian folklore, Dirty Dick, the illiterate boundary rider. The yarn, in its many variations has often been recorded in print, and it is a point of interest that C. E. W. Bean included it in the book which Will reviewed for the *Glasgow Herald*. Following are three versions of this Australian classic. The first, and possibly the best version, is that recounted by Rolf Boldrewood in his book *A Sydney-Side Saxon*:

I heard a story about these two men, the stockman and the hut-keeper that lived there, that wasn't bad in its way. A surveyor happened to call at the place, and both of them were out — the stockman after cattle, and the hut-keeper over at the next station. He expected to get something to eat, and to be shown the way. He didn't manage either, as the place was so filthy dirty that he couldn't touch anything. He happened to know their names, and, being a bit of a card, he wrote on the door with a piece of chalk

'Dick and Bob, of Yalco-green,
Are the dirtiest pair that ever were seen.'

'Dirty Dick', as he was called, came home an hour or two afterwards, and saw by the horse-tracks that a white man had been to the hut. He also saw the writing on the door. Now at this time he was expecting the master on one of his half-yearly visits. He couldn't read, neither could Bob. He began to think, indeed to be fully sure, that his master had come, and gone away again for a day or two to a neighbouring station, and that the strange letters on the door were about his making a muster and getting all the herd 'on camp' without loss of them. Such an order meant sending word round to all the neighbours, as of course a single pair, even if Bob left the hut to itself and went with them, could not do much by themselves with two thousand head of cattle.

After thinking it over for nearly an hour, it struck him that the only way to get at the sense of this writing was to carry it bodily to the nearest home station, where there would be sure to be some one who could read and write.

Dick was a strong wiry fellow, though soap and water wasn't much in his line, so he prises the door off its hinges — they were only wooden (there was mighty little iron about a station in those days) — bark and green hide, slabs let into grooves above and below, did most of it — claps it onto his back and starts off at a dog trot to do the twelve miles to the next station.

A hardwood slab door weighs a goodish deal, as anyone may find out that has to lump it a hundred yards. However, Dick was pretty tough, and as fit as regular exercise and beef and damper could make him. So he did the twelve miles in three hours or thereabouts, and trots in with his door on his back up to the men's hut of Mr Lowe's home station.

When the cook saw him take the door off his back, and put it up against the kitchen, while he wiped his forehead with a big yellow silk handkerchief (the sort they used to work up for crackers* in those days), he thought Dick had gone

---

* Cracker: The silken tassle at the tip of a stockwhip that makes the noise.

out of his mind, and started to run over to the house. But Dick muzzled him and gave him a volley or two, just to show he was sensible like.

'What blamed foolishness are you up to? Is the cove at home?'

'He's over at the house, but what do you mean by roofin' over yer back with twenty feet of hardwood like that? Are yer afraid of hailstorms or is it too hot for yer, or what is it? Have yer had a keg up on the quiet?'

'You tell Mr Lowe that Yalco-green Dick wants to see him, and don't stand chattering and opening yer head like a laughing jackass. He'll know when he sees me. I'm not off my chump, no more than you are, and I haven't smelt spirits since last Christmas.'

'And then you went in a docker, eh, Dick? But here's the master coming, and You can pitch Your own Yarn to him.'

'Well, Dick', said Mr. Lowe — a good-natured gentleman he was, 'cattle all right? Not branded any of my calves lately? I suppose you are out of tea and sugar. I can lend you some till the drays come up.'

'Taint nothing o' that sort, Mr Lowe', says Dick, grinning. 'As to the calves, I'm a few short myself, as I think that half-caste chap of yours must have cuffed. But I want you to read this here writin' if you'll be good enough. Ye see I'm expectin' the master, and I don't know the day he'll be here.' As he says this he lifts the door up, and holds it before Mr. Lowe.

'Is it anything about the master, sir, or when the cattle's to be drafted? I'm short of horses too, now Whitefoot's gone lame.'

Mr Lowe casts his eye over the bit of poetry, and all but burst out laughing in Dick's anxious face. He stopped himself however.

'It isn't anything about the cattle, Dick', he says, 'I am very sorry you have had the long walk over for nothing.'

'Walk be dashed!' says Dick; 'a few miles is neither here nor there. I'm just as well pleased it ain't a general muster. Who wrote it, and wot does he say?'

'It was Mr. Langley, the surveyor, and this is what he wrote, and the whole female population (Mr Lowe was a married man) had gathered up to hear the fun. Then Mr Lowe read it out —

'Dick and Bob, of Yalco-green,
Are the dirtiest pair that ever were seen.'

'Well, I'm blowed!' says Dick, 'and to think of my carrying the bloomin' thing every step of the way here for that. It's twelve mile, sir, every inch of it. I'm jiggered if I carry it back again though, if the blessed hut never has a door again. There'll be a dray coming over some day.'

'And I'll see that it gets back safe', said Mr. Lowe, after every one had done laughing. 'It's an interesting document though. If I could I would have a photo taken of it.'

In *On the Wool Track* C. E. W. Bean was more concise in his telling of the tale, in which Dirty Dick has changed his name to Slimy Sam:

There is a story of one of the hands on a certain run who, on account of his personal habits, was known as Slimy Sam. He lived in a hut near the track. One day he came back to it, and found writing on the door. It struck Sam that this might be an important message. Unfortunately he could not read; so he took the door off its hinges, carried it five miles to an hotel along the road, and had the message read. It was: 'Slimy Sam, of Mumblebone, was the dirtiest beggar ever known.'

George Ogilvie tells of how he and his sister Wendy would climb on their dad's knee and pester him to tell them stories about his Australian adventures, and this was their favourite. It is odd that in this version, related by a poet, the rhyme has been lost and replaced by a line of prose. This is how George tells it in his book, *Balladist of Borders and Bush*:

There was the story of Dirty Dick. 'The dirtiest man I ever met', as Dad called him, lived in a boundary rider's hut. His job was to inspect and maintain mile upon mile of wire fencing stretching across the bush. He had a couple of horses in a paddock and a 60 mile stretch to patrol. His hut was a simple wooden shack with a tin roof. It was furnished with a wooden bunk, a table whose legs stood in four tobacco tins filled with kerosene to keep the ants at bay, and a chair.

The table was strategically positioned so that, when Dick had finished eating, he could, with a backward motion of his arms plunge the knife and fork into the wall behind him ready for the next meal. A tin plate lay permanently ready to receive the next damper. Upon the only shelf on the wall, tea, sugar, flour, baking-powder and arsenic. The arsenic was kept for dingoes. The tin had no label, nor was one deemed necessary as Dick had never learned to read or write. This defect in his education mattered little as a rule but there is an exception to every rule.

One evening Dick returned home to find there had been visitors in his absence. He noticed the tracks of horses as he approached his hut, and the billy had been used.

What was more, some one had pencilled some writing on the door. Clearly some of the lads from the station had left a message for him. A message from the manager? Something urgent perhaps? He studied the hieroglyphics again and swore. There was only one thing for it. He lifted the door off its hinges and carried it to his neighbour's hut fifteen miles away. The message read: 'Dick is a dirty old bastard'.

The Ogilvies' daughter Wendy was born on 19 April 1909, and their son George on 2 March 1912. As he had written to Alex Irvine, Will worked hard and consistently at his profession to such extent that he earned a living and supported his family solely through his writing.

He contributed to almost all the British periodicals, including regular features in London *Punch* for many years. At intervals he had collections of his poems and prose published in book form, including four titles in Australia — *Fair Girls and Gray Horses* (1898), *Hearts of Gold* (1903), *The Australian*, (1916) and, many years later, in 1946, a collection of war poems titled *From Sunset to Dawn*.

Of his two books of prose, the autobiographical *My Life in the Open* (1908) contains an Australian section, while *For the Honour of the Station* (1914) is a collection of sketches of outback station life.

Ogilvie loved horses — they featured in most of his Australian ballads — and back at home he continued to be fascinated by them, and to write about equine events in the show ring and at the hunt. He was appointed official Bard of the Buccleuch Hunt and his love of a good gallop is reflected in four volumes of Scottish horse poems: *Galloping Shoes* (1922), *Scattered Scarlet* (1923), *Over the Grass* (1925), and *A Handful of Leather* (1928). In 1931 a selection from these books was published under the title of *Collected Sporting Verse*.

For many years he continued to write occasional bush ballads for the Australian journals — probably inspired by visits from his old Australian mates, who, if visiting Europe or Britain, frequently made the pilgrimage up to Selkirk on the borders.

In 1958 or 1959 he was persuaded, rather reluctantly, to read a dozen of his poems into a tape recorder for the Hazel de Berg collection in the National Library of Australia. In 1952 and again in 1982 Thelma and R. M. Williams edited and self-published an anthology of his verses — mainly the Australian ones — under the title of *A Saddle for a Throne*.

Will Ogilvie died at the age of ninety-three, on 30 January 1962. He was one of the three great *Bulletin* bush ballad writers of the 1890s, when Lawson, Paterson and Ogilvie were the names on everyone's lips, and the one who outlived all of his Australian peers. He was cremated and his ashes scattered over his beloved Hill Road to Roberton, now the site of a memorial cairn. A replica of this cairn has been erected at Bourke, New South Wales, a gift from the people of Scotland.

Charles Kerry portrait of Will H. Ogilvie taken soon after his arrival in Australia.

Belalie Station, north of Bourke, NSW, in 1885. Ogilvie's first job each morning was to bring up the work horses which may be seen in the stockyard. (Photo: Don Scott)

Ogilvie's notes describe how he wrote 'Fair Girls and Gray Horses' during a dinner camp on this travelling stock reserve, while droving a mob of sheep between Bogan Gate and Forbes. The poem was published in *The Bulletin* on 19 December 1896.

Robert Scott, owner of Belalie Station, gave Will Ogilvie his first job in Australia, jackerooing on Belalie. Taken in 1885. (Photo: Don Scott, Forbes)

The clump of box saplings on Nelungaloo Station where Ben Hall was shot by police in 1865, and which was specially preserved by Reg Lackey's father when the paddock of virgin scrub was being ringbarked for clearing.

In

Memory Of

BEN HALL

SHOT 5TH MAY 1865

AGED 27 YEARS

Ben Hall's grave in the Forbes cemetery is still cared for by local people 130 years after his death!

OUT ON THE PLAINS.—A TYPICAL STOCK RIDER.

THE RAW MATERIAL OF THE BUSH BRIGADE.

Assuredly this photo is of Ogilvie hamming it up for the camera. Published over his poem 'The Overlander's Farewell to His Mates' in the *Sydney Mail*, 30 January 1900. (Negative supplied by General Reference Library, State Library of NSW)

In February 1900 Ogilvie wrote to A. G. Stephens that he was having his photo taken 'à cheval and au pied'. Probably this is the one 'on foot'. (Photo: National Library of Australia).

'The Little Plains', a natural clearing near the old Bogan Gate pub, 'The Selector's Arms'. It was cleaned up and made into a polo field by Morant, Ogilvie, Victor Foy and friends. This was the venue of the great 'International Polo Match', celebrated in verse by both Ogilvie and Paterson.

Frontispiece for *My Life in the Open*, published in 1908. Photo probably taken in America.

Will and Madge with Baby Wendy, April 1909.

Cartoon of Ogilvie drawn by G. N. Hetherington for *The Bulletin* in 1908.

In 1949 Will and Madge were visited at Ashkirk by son George and his wife Jean, with children Anne, Kit, Tom, Rosemary and collie Biddie. It must have been a tight fit in the caravan!

Will Ogilvie in middle age at Ashkirk. (Photo: National Library of Australia)

Will and Madge, fiftieth wedding anniversary 1958.

CHAPTER 13

Pilgrims and Critics

Will Ogilvie was a prolific writer, but he maintained a style of detachment, rarely allowing self to intrude into his lyrics. A shy man, he shunned publicity and hated making speeches. So, while his poems became immensely popular with country people, the man who wrote them remained somewhat of a mystery.

After Ogilvie had settled down, back in his native land, his fans and fellow poets, if they happened to be in England, often paid him a visit at Selkirk. Several visitors have written about their experience, and each contributes something to a composite picture of the retiring Scotsman whose name was, and still is, a household word in the Australian outback.

The first visitor who has left us an account of his visit was that remarkable French writer and Australian settler, Paul Wenz. Born three days before Ogilvie, on 18 August 1869, Wenz came from a wealthy Protestant French family. He came to Australia in 1892 to set up a wool-buying agency, worked as a jackeroo to gain experience, then purchased rich grazing land on the Lachlan, between Forbes and Cowra.

During the 1914-18 war, Wenz worked as a liaison officer for the French Red Cross and visited Ogilvie early in 1919. He wrote an entertaining account of this visit, which was published in an unidentified paper on 16 May 1919 and reprinted in the *Western Champion* newspaper in Parkes two weeks later. An accompanying photo shows Wenz seated in an armchair with Ogilvie standing behind him. The reason for this odd pose was that as Wenz was about two metres tall, Will would only have come up to the giant's shoulder!

AUSTRALIA IN SCOTALND
A YARN WITH OGILVIE
by Paul Wenz

One day I wrote from London to W. H. Ogilvie, and told him I was going to 'blow in', as I wanted to meet him. He answered by inviting me to come to his place, Kirklea, on the Borders of Scotland. Who says Scotchmen have no tact?

At St. Pancreas Station, I asked for a ticket to a spot called Hawick. I could spell the name as soon as I saw it written; but it took me some time to get at the right pronunciation which is something like 'Hoick'. I had been warned that the average English aboriginal does not know this place; he might Give me a ticket for Harwich, or Howick, or even Hike.

At 6 p.m. I landed on the Scottish border at . . . well at that place. Hawick is a manufacturing town which makes stockings and poisons, with its dyes, by a river called the Teviot. It was getting dark when I arrived. I could see little of the river, and less of the town; but was able, nevertheless, to recognise at once that the Cockney spoken in Hawick was not the same as that current in London.

First Impressions

A Ford took me up a big hill, and down the other side. The road went between stone 'dykes' and fences. I could barely make out the fields. Clumps of trees and now and then, the light of a house appeared in the darkness. After a few miles, we passed through a village called Ashkirk, a little further on the Ford stopped in front of a small church, and close by was the gate of Kirklea.

W. H. Ogilvie and I met in the garden, and shook hands in the dark, so the first impression was not a bad one for either of us. Will and his wife soon made me feel at home, and I knew from the first that my stay at Kirklea was going to be an enjoyable one.

Smell Gum Leaves

Memory, in spite of Pelmanism, is a most wonderful thing; we had not long been talking round a fire of spruce, which spat sparks upon the carpet, before we felt ourselves carried away to Australia. We yarned before dinner, during and after until late into the night, till we seemed to sense the scent of gum leaves in the room. If our chairs had not been so comfortable, I believe we would have squatted on one heel, and looked around upon the floor for a bit of barley grass to chew.

We started by 'did you know?' and for some hours on that day and the next two, we went on with 'have you ever met?' Thus we discovered that we knew half the population of New South Wales, anyhow, quite four dozen of them.

Men We Know

After the porridge next morning, we began to talk about 'Gossip'. Yes, he knew old Mac, knew him well. Then, while I was stroking the Persian cat with which the children entrusted me, I mentioned Souter, he of the cat and the cattish women. The *Bulletin* staff got their turn, and Brennan the walking encyclopedia and a lot of others. I remembered with pleasure some hours I spent one night in Sydney with a group of artists and writers, all good fellows, and full of interesting stories. We had dinner at the Trocadero, then drinks at .... well several places; and never did I hear a word about football, a word about "urdle races'; it was grand; it was fine! But then, I am a rotten sportsman!

Gummies as Good as Lambs

Later, we flew into the bush, landed in Forbes and reviewed the natives of the district. We knew the stock and station agents, the fellows who sell you old gummies 'as good' as lambs; second hand pianos guaranteed for three winter months, or a tip top property drought and rabbit proof. They do sell you some good stuff, too, and they are hard workers, many of them. We mentioned squatters, cockies, policemen; we both knew a few of the force, and even some of the pubs. We talked of the Forbes Show, where I once carried off the first prize for the best pen of Brussels Sprouts, my gardener really grew them, so I have no doubt he was perfectly just in getting gloriously drunk over his success.

Yes, I knew Eugowra well, one of the historical spots of New South Wales. I knew Canowindra, Cookamidgera. I had heard of Nelungaloo. I listened to Ogilvie talking about Ben Hall, and Morant the Breaker, and many others.

Then — And Now

That morning Ogilvie took me up the hill overlooking the house. We saw in the adjoining paddock some sheep eating turnips in a greedy, hoggish way; nothing of the dainty manners of our merinos out there, feeding on clover burrs or on bits of grass forgotten by the rabbits. The hills all round were gently undulating, covered with coarse grass. There were streamlets everywhere rushing to a little river down below called the Ale.

Ogilvie has not forgotten Australia; he can talk about droving four thousand wethers, although his flock at Kirklea is only starting, and counts but four goats. He still loves the 'Warrigals', the Outlaws, and the Rebels, though his stable holds a Shetland pony thirty inches high, which looks a trifle heavier than a prize ram.

We both had been new chums to the hour of parting. We carried on, spinning yarns like swaggies round their billies.

And from snowy Kirklea on the Scottish border, both sent our love to the land where, under the dazzling sun Fair Girls coo-ee, and Gray Horses still shake their manes.

The next caller at Kirklea who was to write about his visit was Clem Christesen, founding editor of *Meanjin*. The item appeared as an obituary for Ogilvie in *Meanjin Quarterly* for March 1963. The only logical explanation for Ogilvie's odd behaviour subsequent to this visit is that perhaps Christesen was too enthusiastic a radical and that Ogilvie wanted retribution! The obituary read:

Will H. Ogilvie, who wrote some of our finest ballads during his twelve years in Australia, died on January 30 at the age of 93 years. I stayed with him at his home at Ashkirk, near Selkirk, during 1939, and found him to be a charming host. He inscribed for me a book which he said contained 'the only poetry I have written'. It was stolen from me at Montreal, and I can't recall its title. My pleasant memories of the visit were dampened when I subsequently learned he had enrolled me as a member of 'The Link', a Nazi-front organisation in London. The president, Admiral Domville, and other members were interned at the outbreak of war.

One of Will Ogilvie's most enthusiastic admirers was Thelma Williams, wife of the well-known R. M. Williams. During the 1940s Thelma, assisted by Reg, set about assembling a collection of all their favourite pieces. With the poet's approval this was published by Williams in 1952 under the title of *A Saddle for a Throne*. The edition did much to build up Ogilvie's following in outback Australia, in spite of Douglas Stewart's somewhat critical remarks upon its editing:

A collection of his best verses (with also much that is inferior and repetitive) lately compiled by Thelma E. Williams . . . It is a pity, since all the balladists are due for re-assessment, that *Saddle for a Throne* is such an unsatisfactory collection; being neither a Complete Works which would be valuable to criticism and scholarship nor a Selected Poems which would present Will Ogilvie at his best in the ballads that really matter in Australian literature. However, it is pleasant to see him in print once more; and all his best Australian poems are at any rate included in the volume.[1]

In his autobiography, *Beneath Whose Hand*, Williams describes his meeting with Ogilvie on a trip to the U.K. in the late 1940s. Having heard that England was a small place, he took a taxi from London to Selkirk! Ogilvie greeted him with enthusiasm and the two men discussed which poems should be included in the book Williams had a planned. *A Saddle for a Throne* was published with an optimistically large print run of 10 000 copies that took more than twenty years to sell, but was reissued in 1982.

Ogilvie's first poem to be published by *The Bulletin* was 'Beyond the Barrier', in April 1894, written while he was at Broken Hill and posted in from the Silver City. Naturally he is remembered in that place so it followed that when Dorothy Tapp, a member of the Broken Hill Historical Society was visiting England, she should call on the Ogilvies. Subsequently her visit was recorded in the proceedings of the society, and she presented a paper describing her visit. In introducing Miss Tapp, the Journal states:

In 1959, during an overseas visit, Miss Dorothy Tapp of Broken Hill, was guest in the home of Mr and Mrs W. H. Ogilvie at Kirklea, near the village of Ashkirk, Scotland. Will Ogilvie was then 90 years of age. Miss Tapp's father, Mr E. P. Tapp, was a former manager of Yanncannia Station, previously owned by Thomas Shaw, whose daughter Joan married Thomas Scott Anderson. Their daughter Madge married Will Ogilvie in 1908.

At a meeting of the Society held on 11 November 1968, Miss Tapp gave an address on the life and works of Will Ogilvie, with particular reference to the period of eleven years which he spent in Australia.

MISS TAPP'S PAPER
'Will Ogilvie was born at Holefield, Scotland, in 1869. At the age of 20 he left for Australia and, during the next eleven years, worked on sheep stations in Central and Western New South Wales, as well as Western Victoria and the

southeast of South Australia. He developed a love of the bush, of horses and the ways of the Australian outback, which he soon put to verse. As a writer of bush ballads, he is placed slightly below Henry Lawson and A. B. (Banjo) Paterson. Will Ogilvie first published *Fair Girls and Gray Horses* in 1899, and Hearts of Gold in 1901. [Actually 1898 and 1903.]

J. Corrie, writing in *The Scots Magazine*, December 1958, says:

'In the Australian stockyards, Will had broken in over 60 head of bush horses, the wild brumbies of the outback. An Australian cattleman, a contemporary has left a graphic description of him: a handsome, quiet-spoken Scot of medium height and comprehending glance, with a fair moustache and brick-red complexion, deeply sun-tanned; a dusty, modest figure who had little to say when other bushmen were boasting of man-killers they had ridden, but who showed as soon as he approached a horse, however untameable, that he had little to learn about handling them.'

According to the late James Buchan, of Parkes, Will Ogilvie wrote 'Beyond the Barrier' during a visit to Broken Hill in 1894. Mr. Buchan also stated that Ogilvie worked at colt-breaking on Nelungaloo, Gunningbland, Botfield, Coradgery and Genanegie properties in the Parkes district. The poem, 'The Rose Just Out of Reach' was written about a Miss Rose West, whose father owned Botfield Station and what was then the Bogan Gate Hotel. A 'monument' to Will's sporting spirit lies just north of the old Bogan Gate Hotel and Botfield Station, consisting of a cleared piece of ground in a flat among heavy timber which he and others made into a polo field.

Ogilvie was a friend of Harry ('Breaker') Morant, the vice-admiral's son, who later was to face a firing squad during the Boer War. Will Ogilvie brought a touch of chivalry into his verses which was in contrast to the outback tradition of slovenliness, 'soiled moleskins', sloppy elastic-sides, and battered felt hats.

Will Ogilvie returned to Scotland in 1901 and devoted the rest of his life to authorship and writing for literary magazines. He had published sixteen volumes of verse at the time of his death in 1963. From the library of Will Ogilvie, an extract was obtained, showing the names of the places where Ogilvie wrote a number of the poems featured *in Fair Girls and Gray Horses*, which is printed below.

(There followed a list of forty-eight poems and localities, along with a list of titles and publishers of sixteen volumes of verse and prose.)

In an undated article submitted to *The Bulletin*, George Mather, writing as 'Milky Way', wrote fondly of his old friend Will H. Ogilvie and expressed sentiments that must have been shared by many:

Of Ogilvie I have many memories, memories that can never fade from gold to grey. More than that he is with me with his music everywhere; on the plains out back, in the bush township, in the city. I can always feel his presence not at my side, but in my heart. Throb! Throb! Throb! Oh the lyric life of him!

Ah! That dinner at the Savoy and the artist friend, the two girls — my girl particularly — and the wine — the sparkle of it is in my blood still, and the dinner! Oh, I do remember now. Fair Girls (dear, womanly, lovable girls) and Gray Horses! Oh I love him for both! And for that little spider-web rainbowed with morning dew and for that truest and bravest of bush verse, to me, for Rainbow in the Yard. But, alas, he is no longer here. Will he ever return? Surely his place is vacant still.[2]

In the Introduction to this book, Ogilvie writes of the reception *Fair Girls and Gray Horses* received from the critics. When the book was reissued in 1905, it was reviewed enthusiastically by fellow poet Roderic Quinn:

Stouter than in his first edition and more gaily costumed in green and gold, Ogilvie makes his second appearance — a graceful scrolling of liquid lines and large stars enwreathes his title and when the book opens to the gaze the pages tell a story of like advancement. Well assured of the pleasant path before me, I turned the leaves and did not put the songs away till some of their charm had tinted my mood, making my mind a place enchanted.

I thought how happy Ogilvie must have felt when he put his pen aside and saw his volume finished and wondered at the strange power which had caught him up in enchanted arms and carried him through his work. The singer knows no sweeter hour than that attending him when his task is at end. Critics may say exalted things of him afterwards, lifting their voices high almost to the note hyperbole but no matter how his praises be trumpeted they must always fail to bring that sense of genuine satisfaction which greets him in the hour of good accomplishment.

Ogilvie is sentiment and recollection. He sings from the heart, gladdening us like clear water and fresh air. He is never gloomy. Sunlight and starlight forever enrich his singing and charm his sight, though like Gordon in his Australian love of the horses, he never attempts that ecstasy of the damned soul which at times lifts Gordon so sublimely.

Now that the second edition of *Fair Girls and Gray Horses* is available no one should be satisfied with the first. It is well to have the best of anything always, particularly Ogilvie's best . . .

And now having read Ogilvie once You must read him twice, but when you have read him twice, you will not need reminding to read him again, but you will be so altogether charmed with him that this book will lie very constantly at your elbow, like a good friend who tells you pleasant news.[3]

PART II

STRAYS, CLEANSKINS AND SCRUBBERS

Introduction

Thirty poems of Will Ogilvie's have been included in the biography in places where they relate to the incidents that inspired their composition.

The criteria I have used in selecting a further twenty-three poems are twofold: some were fugitively published in obscure journals and have never been included in collections of his work; the others are pieces for which I had an empathy and a few items that have entered the oral tradition and have been recited for me by old bushmen from western New South Wales.

Ogilvie developed a habit of writing up his poems from inspirational lines that came into his mind during his working hours, and then immediately sending them off to *The Bulletin*. When they were later being assessed for publication in book form, he made many alterations.

An example of how just changing one word can alter the effect of an entire poem exists in 'How the "Fire King" Crossed the Swamp', published under that title in *The Bulletin* of 16 July 1896. 'Fire King' conjures up an image of ruthless destruction by fire, or of a rampaging bush fire consuming everything in its path. For inclusion in *Fair Girls and Gray Horses*, the waggon name was altered to 'Fire Queen', thereby creating a softer image: that of a mysterious lambent blue flame carrying with it a suggestion of that Gaelic mystique that is present in much of his work.

Although written at Maaoupe in South Australia, 'How the Fire Queen Crossed the Swamp' was suggested by the swamp below Belalie Station, and perhaps the title needs an explanation. In the nineteenth century all of the big waggons used in the outback had a name painted on the side, as is done with boats, and, like boats, most of the names were feminine. As one old bush reciter, Ernie Sibley of Mudgee put it — 'The waggons all had girl names; I never did see a boy waggon!'

But, as shown by this list of waggon names, Ernie was wrong. In the Riverina and Central West of New South Wales the following waggons might have been met with: Nil Desperandum, Killarney, Esperance, Indomitable, Rock of Cashell, Pull Me Through, I'm Coming, Here I Come, Mountain Maid, Morning Star, Fire King/Fire Queen, Wanderer, Hawkesbury, Wombat, My Jessie, Good Boy, Flying Dutchman, Try Again, Get There, Star of the West and Fear Not.

In his work as a horse-breaker, drover and station overseer, Will Ogilvie must have come into contact with the Koori people of the central west, yet they appear but rarely in his poems. They are featured in just two pieces — 'The Black Tracker' and 'Bucking Horse Bend' — and in each of them with a sympathetic treatment. Then once, an Aboriginal horse-boy rates a mention when a frustrated overseer calls him a 'black imp!'

In his biography of his father, George Ogilvie recounts a story of Will, galloping madly off to fight a bush fire and being thrown heavily and knocked unconscious. He awoke to find an Aboriginal woman massaging his bruised and gravel-rashed body with a soothing oil — probably emu or echidna oil, both of which are used for their emollient properties.

Many of his characters were taken from real life, and 'The Stockyard Liar' was one of them. The poem was written at the Lackeys' Nelungaloo Station, and 'The Liar' was none other than Percy Weston, a respectable stock and station agent in Parkes. Ogilvie has named Weston as the original, and further writes of him in a letter written to Alexander Irvine in 1907: 'since the days when I and Regie [his mate Reg Lackey] used to sit on the table swinging our spurred feet and listening to Percy Weston telling us how he used to "ride 'em to a finish" when he was our age!'[1]

'Beyond the Barrier' marked the beginning of Ogilvie's Australia-wide fame as a bush balladist. Acceptance of this piece by *The Bulletin* opened the way for a stream of contributions over the next fifteen years — elevating Will H. Ogilvie to equal rank with Banjo Paterson and Henry Lawson.

The scene of several Ogilvie ballads is a station called Tringadee, the location of which nobody has ever traced. Ogilvie gives a clue in 'The Station Brand', when he notes: 'Written at Nelungaloo. Suggested by an old horse carrying the old Belalie brand'. Yet, in the poem, the brand mentioned is 'Tringadee'. So, was Tringadee the original name for Belalie, and did Robert Scott inherit the old brand with the property and use it until he had registered his own 'RS-' brand? It seems more likely that Ogilvie simply used Tringadee as a fictional name for Belalie. This device would allow him to write about the station and its people without their knowledge.

Tringadee is the setting for 'A Draft from Tringadee', 'Off the Grass', 'The Station Brand' and, in both prose and ballad versions, 'The Lifting of Myall King'. In 'After the Horses', which is set on Belalie, Ogilvie is mounted 'On a reefing R S bar', obviously Robert Scott's brand.

In both versions of 'The Lifting of Myall King', the setting is nominally Tringadee, yet, going by the descriptions of the locality, it could easily be on Belalie. The ballad version of the incident is highly emotive and few people can read it without pausing to dash away a tear. On the other hand, the prose account (see Part III) is dramatic, and one person, when reading it, began to cheer and thump the table as he came to the description of the fight for possession of the stolen stockhorse!

SELECTED VERSE

AN 'ORSETRALIAN ALPHABET

A is Australia — 'Orsetralia, you know;
There was wit in the wisdom that christened her so.

B is the Buckjumper, I may suppose you
Have heard of the creature that jumps up and throws you.

C is the Crowd that comes down to look on,
And makes scornful remarks when the buckjumper's gone.

D is the Devil that seems to get free
As soon as the saddle is under your knee.

E is the Energy shown by the beast
When he changes his tail from the west to the east.

F is the Fence where the spectators sit
And fling at you fragments of wearisome wit.

G is the Ground you are likely to hit
If you have not been practising riding a bit.

H is the Hump that he puts on his back,
And also your Horror to find your girth slack.

I is the Idiot, perched on the race
For the purpose of waving a hat in his face.

J is the Jester whose Joke is displayed
In the shouted enquiry: 'Your will — is it made?'

K is the Kick that is rather un-nerving,
When it happens to come between bucking and swerving.

L is the Lurch when you almost come over,
And also the Laugh when by Luck you recover.

M is the Merriment caused by your danger,
And shared by five stockmen, the cook, and a stranger.

N is the Notion he takes in his head,
If he can't get you off that he'll eat you instead.

O is the Offer the Overseer makes
To ride him all day for a hatful of snakes.

P is the Pebble Prepared for his ear
In case he should show inclination to rear.

Q is the Question you rightly ignore:
'Shall I bring you some stick-phast along from the store?'

R is the Rail that a fellow lets fall
While your mount buckets through like the devil and all.

S is the Snaffle that's d—d little use
To stop him. As well might the beggar be loose.

T is the Terrible Tug that he takes,
And the Thrill that you get when the surcingle breaks.

U is Yourself when the saddle is shed,
And he flashes above you and kicks at your head.

V is the Venom he puts in that kick,
And the Vice of the breeding that taught him the trick.

W's the way that he goes down the plain
When he finds himself free of the saddle again.

X is the paltry Xcuse that you make,
Of a flaw in the leather, for decency's sake.

Y is the Youth who comes up to declare
He can ride any horse ever coated with hair.

Z is the Zenith of all your ambition;
It looks pretty far from your present position!

AT THE BACK O' BOURKE

Where the mulga paddocks are wild and wide,
That's where the pick of the stockmen ride —
   At the Back o' Bourke!
Under the dust-clouds dense and brown,
Moving Southward by tank and town,
That's where the Queensland mobs come down —
   Out at the Back o' Bourke!

Over the Border to and fro,
That's where the footsore swagmen go —
    At the Back o' Bourke!
Sick and tired of the endless strife,
Nursing the bones of a wasted life
Where all the sorrows of Earth are rife —
    Out at the Back o' Bourke!

Whether the plains are deep or dry,
That's where the struggling teams go by —
    At the Back o' Bourke!
North and Southward, in twos and threes,
Bullocks and horses down to the knees,
Waggons dipped to the axle-trees —
    Out at the Back o' Bourke!

That's the land of the lying light
And the cruel mirage dancing bright —
    At the Back o' Bourke!
That's where the shambling camel train
Crosses the Western ridge and plain,
Loading the Paroo clips again —
    Out at the Back o' Bourke!

That's the land of the wildest nights,
The longest sprees and the fiercest fights —
    At the Back o' Bourke'
That's where the skies are brightest blue,
That's where the heaviest work's to do,
That's where the fires of Hell burn through —
    Out at the Back o' Bourke!

That's where the wildest floods have birth
Out of the nakedest ends of Earth —
    At the Back o' Bourke!
Where the poor men lend and the rich ones borrow
It's the bitterest land of sweat and sorrow —
    But if I were free I'd be off to-morrow
    Out at the Back o' Bourke!

BEYOND THE BARRIER

Are you tired of the South Land, comrade
    The smoke and the city's din,
And the roar of the chiding ocean
    When the sobbing tide comes in?
Would you ride to the northward, rather,
    To the skirmish-posts of earth,
Where the darkest dust-storms gather
    And the wildest floods have birth?
Are you tired of the revel, comrade,
    The life of folly and wine
With its one half lived in the shadow
    And one half lived in shine?
Are you tired of the poison glasses,
    The lawless love and the kiss,
Out East where the brown range passes
    Do you hope for dearer than this —
Where the sweetest maid that ever knew
    Love's bliss and parting's pain
Is waiting open-armed for you
    Beyond the Barrier Chain?
Let us steer to the northward, comrade,
    To the Bush, with her witching spells,
The sun-bright days and the camp-fire blaze
    And the chime of the bullock-bells —
Down the long, long leagues behind us
    The rain shall cover our track,
And the dust of the North shall blind us
    Or ever we follow it back,
Away from the old friends, comrade,
    The grasp of the strong, brown hand,
The love and the life and the laughter
    That brighten the brave North land —
So long as the sunlight fills it,
    So long as the red stars shine,
So long as the Master wills it
    The North is your home and mine.

BLACK TRACKERS

Swart bloodhounds of the fenceless West,
    Black gallopers that lead the Law,
To whom your victims stand confessed
    By every lightest line they draw;
The hawks that high above you sail
    Have eyes less keen to pierce the blue,
The dingo on his hunting trail
    Runs slacker in the chase than you!

Your naked fathers, seeking food
    By signs upon the sand grew wise,
And tracked their quarry till it stood,
    And bore it home, a hard-won prize.
Now, clothed and horsed and paid in gold,
    Ye ride across the selfsame sands
To track the outlaw to his hold
    And leave him in his foeman's hands!

With head upon your horse's mane,
    With eyes intent on every clue,
By swamp and river, ridge and plain,
    Ye follow as the Fates pursue.
Behind you, blood on spur and heel
    And foam on chain and rein and ring,
With hands that tighten on their steel,
    Ride fast the troopers of the King!

The killer's threat is in your eyes,
    The falconer's and the hunter's pride;
Athwart your brow a vengeance lies,
    Unborrowed from the band ye guide.
The hate that shaped your fathers' spears,
    The wrath that armed some ancient sire,
The blood-lust of a thousand years
    Comes back to fan your hearts to fire!

Yet I have seen your passion sleep,
    Your hate and lust and anger die,
When, stirred by human love as deep
    As ever moved a mother's sigh,
Ye rode upon a gentler trail
    And followed, through the scrubland wild,
In sorrow that ye scorned to veil,
    The footprints of a lost bush child.

THE BRUMBIES

There are steeds upon many a Western plain
That have never bowed to a bit or rein,
That have never tightened a trace or chain.

They feed in the blue grass, fearless, free
As the curbless wind on the bit-less sea,
And the life they lead is a song to me.

For I know there are those in the world to-day
Who are just such rebels at heart as they,
Running uncurbed in the brumby way.

Men that have never been bridle-bound,
Bitted or girthed to the servile round,
Men of the wide world's stamping ground.

Who have wheeled to the Dawn: have kept lone guard
When the soft Bush nights crept golden-starred;
Rebels that never the world shall yard.

There is room on this earth for the toilers too,
And some must draw where their grandsires drew,
And some must lope on the trails anew.

But as long as the girth and the harness scar,
As long as there's land unfenced and far,
The wild mob feeds under moon and star.

BUCKING HORSE BEND

I sing of the babies of Bucking Horse Bend
    As I've oft seen them sitting, each babe on its end,
'Mid the sand and the flies of that town on the rise
    When hot winds are hov'ring and dust storms descend.

They raise to the welkin disconsolate notes,
    In so far as they can for the dust in their throats,
Or they doggedly play through the heat of the day
    On the patch of dry desert they share with the goats.

Their playthings are simple: a broken ox-bow,
    A dead cat they found in the river below,
A bent mallee root and a swagman's old boot
    And a jam-tin or two — all set up in a row.

I wonder what Fate in the future will send
    To those little brown babies of Bucking Horse Bend.
Will they grow like their sires with no other desires
    Than to fatten the purse of their publican friend?

Will they grow like their mothers, lean, flat of the breast,
    Yet brave in the war of that wonderful west?
As I watch them at play for those babies I pray
    That Dame Fortune may yield to each one her best.

COMRADES

Do the shearers still go riding up the Warrego to work,
Where the Thurulgoona woolshed flashes silver in the sun?
Are the bullock-teams still bending through the coolibahs to Bourke?
Is there racing at Enngonia? Is Belalie still a run?
Do the Diamantina cattle still come down by Barringun?

Is the black soil just as sticky? Is the mulga just as dense?
Are the boys still rounding cattle on the red Mulkitty plains?
Are there still some brumbies running on the Maranoa fence?
Still some horsemen always ready with more gallantry than brains
To race them through the thickest scrub with loose and flapping reins?

Does the flood-wrack still go rocking round the barren boxtree bends?
Do the scorching winds still steal the grass that means dear life to you?
Do you still receive the message that a ravished Border sends
Of 'Water done all down the road, and starved stock coming through'?
Does Drought still ride by Hungerford and Death by the Paroo?

Heigh-ho! But those were battle days and hungry days, and hard;
With carcases and bones picked bare at every turning met,
Lean steers upon the cattle-camps, lean horses in the yard,
And weariness and bitterness, and toil and dust and sweat!
Good luck to you, brave comrades, who are battling with them yet!

DUST CLOUDS

We were droving down the Lachlan
    With five thousand woolly wethers;
The sun was like a furnace
    And the sky a misty glow;
The dust was in our nostrils
    And the dust was on our leathers,
And blotted out the landscape
    As we zig-zagged to and fro.

We were drowsing in our saddles
    And our snaffle-reins lay idle,
And, turning and re-turning
    Without a hint assigned,
Our horses did the droving
    While we scarcely touched a bridle;
And the dust clouds hung above us
    And the tired dogs crept behind.

It was dust — dust — dust
    In the myalls and the gidyeas;
Dust — dust — dust
    Till we coughed and spat and swore;
Dust that hid the Lachlan
    And the frontage and the ridges —
Dust for all eternity
    And dust for evermore.

One horseman drowsing dreamily
    Had crossed the leagues of ocean
Beyond the drifting dust clouds
    To the windy English leas,
And there had gone a-worshipping
    The gods of his devotion,
A pack of hounds before him
    And a horse between his knees

Across the wintry meadows
    With his fancy he went roving
Where hounds were running Reynard
    With a heart-bestirring song,
Where twenty thousand miles away

From plains where men went droving
They were dust — dust — dust — dust —
　　Dusting him along!

His favourite flicked the fences
　　Like a housemaid with a duster,
And all was going well with him
　　And all was right as pie
Till his old crock fouled a tree-stump
　　And he came a pretty buster,
And woke again a drover
　　With the Lachlan lapping by!

THE BRIDLE TRACK

This worship of Horse
　　Is a sin and a curse,
So we hear in our parson's talk;
　　But we're steering straight
　　For the Golden Gate,
And we may as well ride as walk.
　　Shall our friendship break
　　O'er the way we take
Since neither will follow it back?
　　Let him hump his load
　　Down the two-chain road —
I'm going the Bridle Track!

THE WHALER'S TEXT

'Ashes to ashes and dust to dust!'
Said a prophet in one of his brilliant flashes,
But the text that the Lachlan travellers trust
Is 'Dust to damper, and damper to ashes!

FAIR GIRLS AND GRAY HORSES

Fair Girls and Gray Horses! A toast for you
   Who never went wide of a fence or a kiss,
While horses are horses and eyes are blue
   There is never a toast in the world like this!

To all Fair Girls! For the sake of one
   Whose bright blue eyes were awhile my star,
Whose hair had the rich red gold of the Sun
   When his kisses fall where the leaf lips are!
To all Fair Girls! How the red wine gleams
   To the glass's rim as it gleamed that night
In the jewelled hand of my Dame of Dreams —
   O, jewelled fingers so soft and white!
To all Fair Girls! Turn your glasses down.
   Here's 'Blissful bridals and long to live!'
And if I am slighting your eyes of brown,
   O, Gypsies Born of the Night, forgive!

To all Gray Horses! Fill up again
   For the sake of a gray horse dear to me;
For a foam-fed bit and a snatching rein
   And a reaching galloper fast and free!
To all Gray Horses! For one steed's sake
   Who has carried me many a journey tall
In the dawn-mists dim when the magpies wake,
   In the starry haze when the night-dews fall!

To all Gray Horses! Now drink you deep,
   For red wine ruins no rider's nerves,
'Light work and a long, long after-sleep!'
   As each gray horse in the world deserves.

Fair Girls and Gray Horses! To each his way,
   But golden and gray are the loves to hold!
And if gold tresses must turn to gray
   Gray horses need never be turned into gold!

FROM THE GULF

Store cattle from Nelanjie! The mob goes feeding past,
With half a mile of sandhill 'twixt the leaders and the last;
The nags that move behind them are the good old Queensland stamp —
Short backs and perfect shoulders that are priceless on a camp;
And these are *Men* that ride them, broad-chested, tanned and tall,
The bravest hearts amongst us and the lightest hands of all.
Oh, let them wade in Wonga grass and taste the Wonga dew,
And let them spread, those thousand head — for we've been droving too!

Store cattle from Nelanjie! By half-a-hundred towns,
By Northern ranges rough and red, by rolling open downs,
By stock-routes brown and burnt and bare, by flood-wrapped river bends,
They've hunted them from gate to gate — the drover has no friends!
But idly they may ride today beneath the scorching sun
And let the hungry bullocks try the grass on Wonga run;
No overseer will dog them here to 'see the cattle through',
But they may spread their thousand head — for we've been droving too!

Store cattle from Nelanjie! They've a naked track to steer;
The stockyards at Wodonga are a long way down from here;
The creeks won't run till God knows when, and half the holes are dry;
The tanks are few and far between and water's dear to buy;
There's plenty at the Brolga bore for all his stock and mine —
We'll pass him with a brave God-speed across the Border line;
And if he goes a five-mile stage and loiters slowly through,
We'll only think the more of him — for we've been droving too!

Store cattle from Nelanjie! They're mute as milkers now;
But yonder grizzled drover, with the care-lines on his brow,
Could tell of merry musters on the big Nelanjie plains,
With blood upon the chestnut's flanks and foam upon the reins;
Could tell of nights upon the road when those same mild-eyed steers
Went ringing round the river bend and through the scrub like spears;
And if his words are rude and rough, we know his words are true;
We know what wild Nelanjies are — and we've been droving too!

Store cattle from Nelanjie! Around the fire at night
They've watched the pine-tree shadows lift before the dancing light;
They've lain awake to listen when the weird bush-voices speak,
And heard the lilting bells go by along the empty creek;
They've spun the yarns of hut and camp, the tales of play and work,
The wondrous tales that gild that road from Normanton to Bourke.

They've told of fortune foul and fair, of women false and true,
And well we know the songs they've sung — for we've been droving too.

Store cattle from Nelanjie! Their breath is on the breeze;
You hear them tread a thousand head in bluegrass to the knees;
The lead is on the netting-fence, the wings are spreading wide,
The lame and laggard scarcely move — so slow the drovers ride!
But let them stay and feed to-day for sake of Auld Lang Syne;
They'll never get a chance like this below the Border line;
And if they tread our frontage down, what's that to me or you?
What's ours to fare, by God they'll share! For we've been droving too!

————————

HIS GIPPSLAND GIRL

Now, money was scarce and work was slack
    And Love to his heart crept in,
And he rode away on the Northern track
    To war with the World and win;
And he vowed by the locket upon his breast
    And its treasure, one red-gold curl,
To work with a will in the farthest West
    For the sake of his Gippsland girl.

The hot wind blows on the dusty plain
    And the red sun burns above,
But he sees her face at his side again,
    And he strikes each blow for Love;
He toils by the light of one far-off star
    For the winning of one white pearl,
And the swinging pick and the driving bar
    Strike home for the Gippsland girl.

With aching wrist and a back that's bent,
    With salt sweat blinding his eyes,
'Tis little he'd reek if his life were spent
    In winning so grand a prize;
His shear-blades flash and over his hand
    The folds of the white fleece curl,
And all day long he sticks to his stand
    For the love of his Gippsland girl.

When the shearing's done and the sheds cut out
   On Barwon and Narran and Bree;
When the shearer mates with the rouseabout
   And the Union man with the free;
When the doors of the shanty, open wide,
   An uproarious welcome hurl,
He passes by on the other side
   For the sake of his Gippsland girl.

When Summer lay brown on the Western Land
   He rode once more to the South,
Athirst for the touch of a lily hand
   And the kiss of a rosebud mouth;
And he sang the songs that shorten the way,
   And he envied not king or earl,
And he spared not the spur in his dappled grey
   For the sake of his Gippsland girl.

At the garden gate when the shadows fell
   His hopes in the dusk lay dead;
'Nellie? Oh! Surely you heard that Nell
   Is married a month!' they said.
He spoke no word; with a dull, dumb pain
   At his heart, and his brain awhirl
He turned his grey to the North again
   For the sake of his Gippsland girl.

And he rung the board in a Paroo shed
   By the sweat of his aching brow,
But he blued his cheque, for he grimly said,
   'There is nothing to live for now.'
And out and away where the big floods start
   And the Darling dust-showers swirl,
There's a drunken shearer who broke his heart
   Over a Gippsland girl!

HOW THE 'FIRE QUEEN' CROSSED THE SWAMP

The flood was down in the Wilga swamps, three feet over the mud,
And the teamsters camped on the Wilga Range and swore at the rising flood;
For one by one they had tried the trip, double and treble teams,
And one after one each desert ship had dropped to her axle-beams;
So they thonged their leaders and pulled them round to the camp on the sandhill's crown,
And swore by the bond of a blood-red oath to wait till the floods went down.

There were side-rail tubs and table-tops, coaches and bullock-drays,
Brown with the Barcoo Wonders, and Speed with the dapple greys
Who pulled the front of his waggon out and left the rest in the mud
At the Cuttaburra Crossing in the grip of the Ninety flood.

There was Burt with his sixteen bullocks, and never a bullock to shirk,
Who twice came over the Border Line with twelve-ton-ten to Bourke;
There was Long Dick damning an agent's eyes for his ton of extra weight,
And Whistling Jim, for Cobb and Co., cursing that mails were late;
And one blasphemed at a broken chain and howled for a blacksmith's blood,
And most of them cursed their crimson luck, and all of them cursed the flood.
The last of the baffled had struggled back and the sun was low in the sky,
And the first of the stars was creeping out when Dareaway Dan came by.
There's never a teamster draws to Bourke but has taken the help of Dan;
There's never a team on the Great North Road can lift as the big roans can,
Broad-hipped beauties that nothing can stop, leaders that swing to a cough;
Eight blue roans on the near-side yoked and eight red roans on the off.
And Long Dick called from his pine-rail bunk, 'Where are you bound so quick?'
And Dareaway Dan spoke low to the roans and aloud, 'To the Swagman's, Dick!'
'There's five good miles', said the giant, 'lie to the front of you, holding mud;
If you never were stopped before, old man, you are stopped by the Wilga flood.
The dark will be down in an hour or so, there isn't the ghost of a moon,
So leave your nags in the station grass instead of the long lagoon!'

But Dan stood up to his leader's head and fondled the big brown nose,
'There's many a mile in the roan team yet before they are feed for the crows;
Now listen, Dick-with-the-woman's-heart, a word to you and the rest,
I've sixteen horses collared and chained, the pick of the whole wide West,
And I'll cut their throats and leave them here to rot if they haven't the power
To carry me through the gates of Hell — with seventy bags of flour!
The light of the stars is light enough; they have nothing to do but *plough*!
There's never a swamp has held them yet, and a swamp won't stop them now.
They're waiting for flour at the Swagman's Bend; I'll steer for the lifting light;
There's nothing to fear with a team like mine, and — I camp in the bend to-night!'

So they stood aside and they watched them pass in the glow of the sinking sun,
With straining muscles and tightened chains — sixteen pulling like one;
With jingling harness and droning wheels and bare hoofs' rhythmic tramp,
With creaking timbers and lurching load the 'Fire Queen' faced the swamp!
She dipped her red shafts low in the slush as a spoonbill dips her beak,
The black mud clung to the wheels and fell in the wash of the Wilga Creek;
And the big roans fought for footing, and the spreaders threshed like flails,
And the great wheels lifted the muddy spume to the bend of the red float-rails;
And they cheered him out to the westward with the last of the failing light,
And the splashing hoofs and the driver's voice died softly away in the night;
But some of them prate of a shadowy form that guided the leader's reins,
And some of them speak of a shod black horse that pulled in the off-side chains —
How every time that he lifted his feet the waggon would groan and swing,
And every time that he dropped his head you could hear the tug-chains ring!

    *   *   *   *

And Dan to the Swagman's Bend came through mud-spattered from foot to head,
And they couldn't tell which of the roans were blue and which of the roans were red.
Now this is the tale as I heard it told, and many believe it true
When the teamsters say in their off-hand way — ' 'Twas the Devil that pulled him through!'

THE JACKEROO

Here he comes — a bit of a freak,
    With a glass in his eye and a rosy cheek!
Useless, of course; no good on a horse;
    And taking a buster twice a week.

Slewed at the muster and lost in the yards,
    A figure of fun to our old diehards;
A hopeless mutt, a bit of a butt,
    And àpt to be rooked when playing cards.

Donning the gloves with an air of gloom
    When somebody belts him round the room,
For any who asks doing menial tasks
    As humble as those of an English groom.

But under the eyes of a kind adviser
    He soon gets bolder and soon gets wiser,
Turning out rough and calling their bluff;
    And, as for the station — he'll surprise her!

For stock-work now he displays some wit;
    He can ride a horse that can root a bit;
He can sink a post as well as most,
    And a broken wire — he can deal with it.

He can brand a calf, he can milk a cow;
    He never gets lost in the paddocks now;
When scrubbers race he can keep his place
    And gauge the height of a bloodwood bough.

In fact, he's a bushman — more or less,
    With suitable oaths and proper dress,
And faced with a fight has a handy right
    That can make his opponent's face a mess

*   *   *   *

So here's good luck to the jackeroo!
    Let him come along as he used to do,
For, though raw and green, as they've always been,
    He'll just grow up as the old ones grew!

KELPIES

Out where the scrubs stand dark and dense
    And the great plains blaze in the sun,
Where the wide sheep-paddocks, unmapped, immense,
Reach out to the Queensland border fence —
    It is there where the kelpies run.

Where the dustclouds spin on the dry claypans,
    Where the dancing brolgas play,
Where the dingo fashions his furtive plans —
It is there that the little black-and-tans
    Toil on in the heat all day.

There is the kingdom of Nip and Nell,
    Of Tweed and Swallow and Sweep,
Of the racing beauties I loved so well;
And many a tale I yet could tell
    Of what they could do with sheep.

Hustling their mob through the barley-grass
    Or turning a wing inside;
Often in fancy I see them pass
Leaping to answer the call, 'Here, lass!'
    And the caution, 'Wide, go wide!'

Many a time I can see them lie
    In the shade of a kurrajong,
Chester, or Connie, or Flip, or Fly,
Searching a foot for a bindi-eye
    That has lain in a pad too long.

When the sun goes down in a crimson glow
    And a wave of golden foam
I can see them snatched to a saddle-bow
With a 'Come along, pup, you're tired, I know',
    And given a free ride home.

We have dogs in the North of world-wide fame,
    And champions not a few
Of grander coat and of stouter frame,
But none more gallant and none more game
    Than the kelpie friends I knew.

THE LIFTING OF MYALL KING

His brand's a brand of Cooper's Creek, his breed's a breed of fame,
And far as falling whipthongs speak the bushmen know his name;
At musters on the Red Barcoo, where all the best are known,
He threads the rounded cattle through to single out his own,
And where our lazy fats are spread, or lean, wild scrubbers ring,
There's not a Queensland stockman bred but's heard of Myall King!

We've raced him with the colours up at bush-hotel and town,
And none could take the Gumleaf Cup against the grass-fed brown!
And fairer still the fame he bought, if need of further sign,
The night that Death and Donald fought beside the Border Line,
When, with the wind of dawn that stirred the sleepy leaves a-swirling,
At Bourke upon the bridge, men heard the hoofs of Myall King!

One morning on the blue-grass plain, and down the lignum side
The blackboy cracked his whip in vain to start the station's pride;
The mob swept down across the road, light-heeled and breathing hard —
For once no streak-faced camp-horse showed the short way to the yard;
We heard the racing hoofs go by, we heard the stockwhip ring,
And watched them pass, and wondered why he brought no Myall King!

We rode the paddock east and west and searched from fence to fence
The wilgas where the horses rest, the buddahs branching dense,
We searched by waterhole and creek, we rode the six-wire round —
We might have ridden week to week and searched and never found!
We knew the brown horse had not strayed; we swore the man should swing
That broke our bound'ries, unafraid, and lifted Myall King!

He might have stolen eight or nine longtails from our long list,
And still have reached the railway line before the colts were missed;
He might have sneaked a mare and foal that ran in Number Two,
And reached Rockhampton as a goal before we found a clue,
But though he took a d—d good horse, he did a risky thing
The night he dropped the sandhill rails and lifted Myall King!

That night, before the sun went down, we found the mark of hoof
Close hid among the grasses brown, but proof — and bitter proof;
Shod tracks and bare, that told us true, beyond the reach of doubt,
How one shod horse was ridden through, and one, bare-hoofed, led out.
We looked, one hasty, careless look — it was a simple thing
To read, as in an open book, the tracks of Myall King!

And side by side the hoof-tracks showed on flats made bare by Drought,
Until they joined the river-road — the wide road to the South,
And here the keenest sight was vain, the soundest art at fault,
And night came down across the plain, and so we called a halt,
And slowly to the homestead turned, the evil news to bring,
And in our hearts the vengeance burned, for love of Myall King!

For there was not a Tringa man from boss to blackboy down,
But loved, as only horsemen can, a good horse like the brown;
Yet, though we loved him, worst and best, and worshipped him, 'tis true
A grief more deep than all the rest Jack Fitch, who rode him knew!
For five years back, without a break, at racecourse, camp and wing
To guard the station pride at stake Jack Fitch rode Myall King!

That night, when stars were bright o'er head, Jack had a tale to tell,
'I'm going southward, boss', he said, 'I'm sick and want a spell!
Make up my cheque! I'll get the nags and sling the rugs across!'
But Jack's excuse was thin as rags and did not 'ceive the boss;
He looked the stockman through and through, and smiled, the slightest thing,
'All right! Jack Fitch! Good luck to you! And bring back *Myall King!*'

He packed the race mare Maori Belle, and rode his hack, Gray Cloud,
We wished to pay his way but — well, Jack Fitch was always proud!
We lent a hand to strap his load and then fare-well we bade
And wished him luck upon the road — Jack's white as they are made!
And at the rails he shouted back, it seemed a manly thing —
'I'll come no more the Border Track unless with Myall King!'

It was an hour before the dawn while gold stars glittered still,
We saw him on the sky-line drawn, a dim wraith on the hill;
He turned and waved his cabbage-tree, then cantered down the rise,
We turned away! and as for me, the mist was in my eyes!
I knew the man; his word's his thrall, and not a light-flung thing;
I knew if he came back at all he'd come with Myall King!

The border roofs shone dimly white; 'neath one a lone lamp showed,
And Gray Cloud snorted at the light that barred across the road;
Then gate and gate were won and passed, and mile and mile flung by,
And when the stockman camped at last the sun was hot and high,
He gave the nags a southward start, short-hobbled on one ring,
And boiled his billy, but his heart was South with Myall King!

He thought of fights they both had fought, of toils they both had shared,
And wondered what old Myall thought, and wondered if he cared.
He dreamed of how they won the Cup a year ago that day —
How game the old horse finished up and beat the little bay!
He thought of how some slower steed would race to block the wing,
And wondered how they'd hold the lead without old Myall King!

Then flung the saddles on their backs, and mounted and away,
And never stayed to look for tracks, but rode by night and day;
One question on his lips in Bourke, one question down the line,
Yet none could speak to aid his work or give a favouring sign,
If all was truth the bushmen told, they had no light to bring,
No horse had passed, was seen, or sold, the least like Myall King!

While day by day, from night to noon, the scorching summer went,
By naked road and dry lagoon Jack Fitch rode ill-content;
He crossed the hungry Nyngan plains, south-east, and down the Bland;
He drew his weary horse's reins in Riverina land;
With sheep he toiled among the rest all winter till the spring,
But never once forgot his quest — the quest of Myall King!

And now and then, when work was slack, he raced the Maori Belle,
Till, winning on the Wagga track, he sold her more than well,
And riding northward on the gray for station work to seek,
He camped at noon one sunny day upon the Yanco Creek.
Some yards away a tent was spread, a camp-fire in full swing,
And tied below a gum-bough-shed the stock-horse Myall King!

His brand was not of Cooper's Creek, for brands a thief can mould;
His face had lost the long white streak it used to wear of old;
His white hind foot jet-black had grown, and they had docked his tail —
And yet that style was all his own of standing at a rail,
Though doctored brands work wonders rare, and paint's a curious thing,
Jack Fitch could swear to every hair that grows on Myall King!

He tossed his rough bush-blanket down and hobbled out the gray,
And hailed the owner of the brown and passed the time of day;
And lunched with him to try and learn some facts across the fire,
But, spite of all, his eyes would turn towards his heart's desire,
And when the beef and tea were done and pipes were well a-swing,
He said, 'Good stamp of horse, my son!' with nod to Myall King.

'The sort of horse you see round Bourke; I'll swear, a dainty hack!
The stamp of horse for cattle work — deep-ribbed and short of back;
And if I'm any judge of pace, I'd say that nag could go,
He's got no white upon his face? Ah! no! I thought not! No!'
The stripling's cheek had blanched with fright — a hopeless, cornered thing —
He seemed to borrow half the white he took from Myall King!

Then Jack stood up, stockwhip in hand, and looked him in the eyes
'I'd know that horse in Zululand for all his faked disguise!
I've looked for him eight months or so — I don't care who you be
Take up your thieving traps and go! I'll take the horse with me!'
The stranger looked him up and down, Jack gave his whip a swing
And, on his bearded face a frown, stepped up to Myall King!

The grass was girth-high on the plain and summer winds a-roam
When, pulling on the halter-rein, old Myall King came home.
We saw the dust far down the bend, two horses on the track,
The rider somehow seemed a friend, and then we knew 'twas Jack!
We knew he would not pass the place, unless — he chanced to bring —
And then we saw the old streak-face, and cheered for Myall King!

And now along the Western side in cattle mustering time
They watch two champions undenied, the heroes of my rhyme
The finest stockman, mouth to source, along the Big Barcoo;
The grandest type of cattle-horse the Border ever knew,
And when foam-splashed they head the van, or thunder down the wing,
The bushmen tell you — 'That's the man who lifted Myall King!'

THE MAN WHO STEADIES THE LEAD

He was born in the light of red oaths
 And nursed by the drought and the flood,
And swaddled in sweat-lined saddle-cloths
 And christened in spur-drawn blood;
He never was burdened with learning,
 And many would think him a fool,
But he's mastered a method of 'turning'
 That never was taught in a school.
His manners are rugged and vulgar,
 But he's nuggets of gold in our need,
And a lightning flash in the mulga
 Is the Man who Steadies the Lead!

When the stockwhips are ringing behind him
 And the brumbies are racing abreast,
It's fifty-to-one you will find him
 A furlong or two from the rest
With the coils of his whip hanging idle,
 His eyes on the mob at his side,
And the daintiest touch on the bridle —
 For this is the man who can ride!
And the stallions that break for the mallee
 Will find he has courage and speed,
For he rides the best horse in the valley —
 This stockman who steadies the lead.

When they're fetching in 'stores' to the station
 Through tangles of broken belar,
And the road is a rough calculation
 That's based on the blaze of a star;
When they're quickening through sand-ridge and hollow
 And rowels are spattered with red,
And sometimes you've only to follow
 The sound of the hoof-beat ahead;
Then we know that he's holding them nor'ward —
 We trust in the man and his steed,
As we hear the old brown crashing forward
 And his rider's 'Wo-up!' to the lead.

And again in a journey that's longer,
    In a different phase of the game,
Dropping down the long trail to Wodonga
    With a thousand or so of the same;
When the blue grass is over our rollers,
    And each one contentedly rides,
And even the worst of the crawlers
    Are stuffing green grass in their hides;
He is ready to spread them or ring them
    Or steady them back on the feed,
And he knows when to stop them or string them,
    The stockman who rides in the lead.

But when from the bend of the river
    The cattle break camp in the night —
O, then is the season, if ever,
    We value his service aright!
For we know that if some should be tardy,
    And some should be left in the race,
Yet the spurs will be red on 'Coolgardie'
    As Someone swings out to his place.
The mulga boughs — hark to them breaking
    In front of the maddened stampede!
A horse and a rider are taking
    Their time-honoured place in the lead!

As an honest, impartial recorder
    I'd fain have you all recollect
There are other brave men on the Border
    Entitled to every respect;
There's the man who thinks bucking a tame thing,
    And rides 'em with lighted cigars;
And the man who will drive any blamed thing
    That ever was hooked to the bars . . .
Their pluck and their prowess are granted,
    But, all said and done, we're agreed
That the king of 'em all when he's wanted
    Is the Man who Steadies the Lead!

MULGA MAXIMS

If the cattle-pup's careless at heeling, get him kicked if you possibly can —
An occasional heels-over-header is good for a dog and a man.

If there's doubt in the breed of the yearling, put the circle-and-bar on his rump,
For the man that 'has' others is clever, but the man that is 'had' is a chump.

If he bucks with the tackling, get on him and ride him — there's nothing to fear;
But beware of the colt who will watch you and stand when you've buckled the gear.

A leader's a good thing to follow in scrub or in life, I allow,
But don't come too closely behind him — you might get the swing of a bough.

When long-tails get going in timber, when wives set their tongues out of slip,
Don't harass yourself or a good horse, but fill up your pipe — let 'em rip!

If the sheep-pup cuts in on the wethers and splits them, be kind to him, please;
We, too, have run riot as youngsters, and scattered our charge to the breeze.

Hurry home when the revel is over; when it's cold and the moon's going down,
One light in the horse-paddock timber is better than ten in the town.

To steer by the stars up above you on bush tracks is all very well,
But his course is erratic who follows the twinkling three-star of Martell.

If a fellow talks fight after whisky, let him talk, there is nothing to blame;
But keep wide of the beggar at polo, he's too hot of head for the game.

If you want to get rid of a rival, don't shoot him or poison his grub,
But shout for him twice in succession at any known Warrego pub.

Don't trust to a light-coloured chestnut, keep wide of a redheaded dame,
If you don't want to carry your saddle and don't want to fall in the flame.

If the boss's girl gives you a rosebud, fling it out — you are fooling with Fate;
If the stockman's young wife is the donor, doff your hat to the devil, and wait.

If it rains on the eve of a journey, that journey had best be delayed,
For the man that drives out on the black soil is hired for a day with a spade.

Don't be foolish in yards full of cattle — 't will win you no medals or stars,
And bad-tempered heifers, like barmaids, are safest at back of the bars.

Run the team off its legs if it need be, flog the fall off the whip if you must,
But keep to the front on the roadway and never take any man's dust.

OFF THE GRASS
(MYALL KING)

They were boasting on the Greenhide of their nags of fancy breed,
    And stuffing them with bran and oats to run in Gumleaf Town,
But we hadn't got a racehorse that was worth a dish of feed,
    So didn't have a Buckley's show to take the boasters down.

For old Midnight was in Sydney and we couldn't get him up
    In time for Gumleaf Races if it *had* been worth our while;
The Chorus colt was far too light to win the Gumleaf Cup,
    And we didn't own a hackney that could finish out the mile.

But we couldn't watch them win it while we never had a say,
    So we mustered up the horses, and we caught old Myall King;
He's as brave as ever galloped, but he's twelve if he's a day,
    And we couldn't help but chuckle at the humour of the thing.

But, though shaky in the shoulders, he's the daddy of them all;
    He's the gamest bit of horseflesh from the Snowy to the Bree;
One of those that's never beaten, coming every time you call;
    One of those you sometimes read about but very seldom see.

He's the don at every muster and the king of every camp;
    He's the lad to stop the pikers when they take you on the rush;
And he loves the merry rattle of the stockwhip and the tramp
    Of the cockhorned mulga scrubbers when they're breaking in the brush.

He can foot the Greenhide brumbies if they take a mile of start,
    And if they get him winded in a gallop on the plain,
He's as game as any lion, and he carries such a heart
    You can never say he's beaten, for he'll always come again!

So we put up Jack the Stockman with his ten pounds overweight,
    And he lengthened out the leathers half-a-foot and gave a smile;
'I don't suppose you'll see us when they're fairly in the straight,
    But we'll make the beggars travel, take my oath, for half-a-mile!'

And they started and the old horse jumped away a length in front,
    And every post they came to gave the brown a longer lead,
Till it seemed that there was nothing else but Myall in the hunt,
    With his load of station honour and his weight of mulga feed!

Then the bay mare, Bogan Lily, started out to cut him down;
  She had travelled out five hundred miles to win the Gumleaf Cup,
And she couldn't well get beaten by a hack in Gumleaf Town
  When she had to pay expenses for her owner's journey up.

So she started out to catch the old brown camp-horse from the Bush,
  And a furlong from the finish she could nose his rider's knee,
Then you should have heard the shouting of the Bogan Lily push,
  And the flinging of their hats up was a sight for you to see!

But old Myall King had often been as nearly beat before,
  And he steadied off a little, while the mare shot out ahead,
Then he shook his ears and gripped the bit — you should have heard us roar
  As he came at Bogan Lily with his flanks a streak of red!

And the little bay mare, beaten, gave him best and threw it up,
  And we heard her rider murmur as he saw the brown horse pass,
And Jack the Stockman drop his hands and win the Gumleaf Cup —
  'Beat by a hungry cripple of a camp-horse off the grass!'

Then we led him in the winner, and they cheered him from the stand,
  With the black sweat running channels from his forearm to his foot,
And the white foam on his shoulder till you couldn't see the brand,
  And the crimson bloodstains scattered over spur and flank and boot.

So we carried off the honours of the meeting — and the notes,
  And the men on Green-hide River when they see our fellows pass,
Will tell you this in whispers, 'You can train your nags on oats,
  But be careful when you're racing those d—n scrubbers off the grass!'

A NEW YEAR SONG

This is the time of the year when folk
   Make resolutions good,
But since they're only made and broke,
   I don't see why I should!
And so let all who know me hear
   My purpose told in verse —
If I've been wicked all this year,
   Next year I hope I'm worse!

For every drink in nineteen-two
   Next year I'll toss two more,
For every girl I've kissed — mark you!
   I'm going to fondle *four!*
I don't care whether this is right
   Or whether it is wrong,
I only think, each New Year Night,
   'Play up! You've not got long!'

HISTORY REPEATED

My lady keeps upon her shelf
A comb, a tortoise shell affair,
Thus history repeats itself —
The tortoise following the hair!

THE RABBITER'S CURE

Robby the Rabbiter loved his glass —
Loved it a little too much, alas!
His camp was close to the Mulga Inn,
Which served as a shrine to his favourite sin.

Most of the nights in a week you'd see
Robby involved in a moderate spree,
Leaving the pub at a blameful hour
Full as a well-filled bag of flour.

Robby a rum-looking gee-gee owned
Light of the flesh but amply boned,
Ugly and lazy and underbred,
With a bumble-foot and a coffin-head.

Night after night this steed was tied
To the rail at the pub; and the horses shied
Time and again at the ancient wreck,
With its hat-rack hips and its hose-pipe neck.

Over a bottle of Ted's 'Three Star'
Bill and a mate at the Mulga bar
Fashioned a plot of the deepest guile
And left the pub with a four-inch smile.

Down the paddock the schemers sped
And found a horse that had long been dead,
One of those frames of bone and hide
That the crows have picked and the wind has dried.

When the sun went down old Rob appeared
With blood of rabbits and horse-sweat smeared,
Riding the crock he was wont to ride,
And he tied him up and he went inside.

Out of the big scrub crept the dark,
And the stars rose over the stringy-bark.
They took his crock to the stable yard
While Rob at the bar was drinking hard.

Then they saddled the horse that was dried and dead,
And slipped Rob's bridle over his head,
And stood him up by the dim horse-rail,
With a waggon propstick beneath his tail.

Then they greeted their man at the Mulga bar,
And they filled him up with good 'Three Star',
Till the hour grew late and the sleepy Ted
Gave a yawn or two and suggested bed.

Rob was enjoying himself just then,
But the clock in the bar said half-past ten,
So he called all hands for a final shout,
And emptied his glass and stumbled out.

He took his reins with a heavy sigh
From the rail, and murmured a thick 'Goo-bye!'
Then he lifted his toe to the stirrup-bar
With a 'Woh, my beauty!' and 'Stand there, Star!'

Now, as soon as the framework felt his foot,
It fell to the ground like rotten fruit,
And Rob with a shriek and sundry groans
Clasped to his bosom the bunch of bones.

They picked him up and they led him in
To the beer-stained shrine of his ancient sin,
Where, gibbering under the darkened bar,
He sought relief from the ghosts that are.

To the Mulga Inn on the lonely rise
The teamsters flock like thirsty flies,
And the drovers gather like gulls offshore,
But Robby the Rabbiter comes no more.

THE RIDING OF THE REBEL

He was the Red Creek overseer, a trusted man and true,
Whose shoulder never left the wheel when there was work to do;
Through all the day he rode the run, and when the lights grew dim
The sweetest wife that ever loved would wait and watch for him.
She brought him dower of golden hair and eyes of laughing blue,
Stout heart and cunning bridle-hand to guide the mulga through;
And when the mob was mustered from the box flats far and wide
She loved to mount the wildest colts that no one else would ride.
And once it chanced a wayward steed, half-mouthed and roughly broke,
Denied the touch of gentle hand and gentler words she spoke,
And, plunging forward like the ship that feels the autumn gales,
He reared and lost his footing and fell backwards on the rails.
Her husband bent above her with cold terror at his heart —
The form was still he loved so well, the wan lips would not part;
And all the day in trance she lay, but when the stars smiled down
He heard his name low-whispered and he claimed her still his own.
And afterwards he spoke his fear, 'Heart's Love, if you should die!
Unless you take your orders from some other man than I,
You shall never finger bridle, never mount on horse's back,
Till the outlaw on Glenidol is a broken lady's hack!'

There's an outlaw on Glenidol that is known through all the West,
And three men's lives are on his head, bold riders of the best;
The station lads have heard the sneer that travelled far and wide,
And flung the answering challenge, 'Come and teach us how to ride!'
Roll up, ye merry riders all, whose honour is to guard!
We've mustered up the ranges and The Rebel's in the yard,
His open mouth and stamping foot and keen eye flashing fire
Repeat the temper of his dam, the mettle of his sire.
Roll up, ye merry riders all, from hut and camp and town!
You'll have to stick like plaster when the stockyard rails go down.
But the boss will come down handsome, as the boss is wont to come,
To the first who brings The Rebel under spurs and greenhide home.
And the stockmen heard the challenge from the Cooper to the Bree,
And rode from hut and cattle-camp by one and two and three
To keep the horseman's honour clean and play a hero's part,
To best the bold Glenidol boys and break The Rebel's heart.
And Ruddy Neil, the breaker, from the Riverine came through
With all the latest breaking gear and all the wiles he knew,
But ere the saddle was secured, before a girth was drawn,
The Rebel's forefoot split his skull — they buried him at dawn!

Marora Mick, the half-caste, from the Flinders River came
To give the South-the-Border boys a lesson at the game;
But he got a roguish welcome when he entered New South Wales,
For The Rebel used his blood and brains to paint the stockyard rails!
And Mulga Jack came over from the Yuinburra side —
The horse was never foaled, they say, that Mulga could not ride;
With a mouth as hard as a miser's heart, a will like the Devil's own,
The Rebel made for the Stony Range with the man who wouldn't be thrown;
The Rebel made for the Stony Range, where the plain and the scrub-land meet,
And the dead boughs cracked at his shoulder-blade, the stones leapt under his feet,
And the ragged stems of the gidyeas cut and tore as they blundered past . . .
And Jack lay cold in the sunset gold — he had met with his match at last.
And once again the challenge rang, the bitterer for scorn,
And spoke the bold Glenidol boys, their jackets mulga-torn,
'A week have we been hunting him and riding fast and hard
To give you all another chance — The Rebel's in the yard!'
And the stockmen heard the challenge from the Cooper to the Bree;
But 'I'm getting old!' 'I'm getting stiff!' or 'I've a wife, you see!'
Came whispered to the border; and the horse they could not tame
Had saved Glenidol from disgrace and cleansed a sullied name.

But ere the reddening sun went down and night on the ranges broke
A stranger youth to the sliprails rode, and fastened his horse and spoke
Softly and low, yet none so low but that every man there heard,
'I've come to tackle your outlaw colt,' — and he looked as good as his word.
He bridled The Rebel in failing light, and saddled the colt and drew
The straps of his gearing doubly tight, and looked that his 'length' was true.
He mounted The Rebel and gave the word, and the clattering rails went down,
And the outlaw leapt at the open gate and into the shadows brown;
But he settled himself to the soothing voice and the touch of the fondling hand,
As it followed the curve of his arching neck from wither to forehead band;
His flanks were wet with the fresh-sprung sweat, his shoulders lathered with foam,
And he bent to the bridle and played with the bit as he came at a canter home.
And the boys were dumb with wonder, and sat, and the Red Creek overseer
Was first to drop from the stockyard fence and give him a hearty cheer.
He raised his hat in answer and — the gold hair floated free!
And the blue eyes lit with laughter as she shouted merrily,
'You can reach me down my bridle, give my girths and saddle back,
For the outlaw of Glenidol is a broken lady's hack!'

THE STOCKYARD LIAR

If ever you're handling a rough one
    There's bound to be perched on the rails
Of the Stockyard some grizzled old tough one
    Whose flow of advice never fails;
There are plenty, of course, who aspire
    To make plain that you're only a dunce,
But the most insupportable liar
    Is the man who has ridden 'em once.

He will tell you a tale and a rum one,
    With never a smile on his face,
How he broke for old Somebody Some-one
    At some unapproachable place;
How they bucked and they snorted and squealed,
    How he spurred 'em and flogged 'em, and how
He would gallop 'em round till they reeled —
    But he's 'getting too old for it now'.

How you're standing too far from her shoulder,
    Or too jolly close to the same,
How *he* could have taught you to hold her
    In the days when he 'followed the game';
He will bustle, annoy and un-nerve us
    Till even our confidence fails —
O Shade of old Nimrod! preserve us
    From the beggar that sits on the rails!

How your reins you are holding too tightly,
    Your girths might as well be unloosed;
How 'young chaps' don't handle them rightly,
    And horses don't buck 'like they used'.
Till at last, in a bit of a passion,
    You ask him in choicest 'Barcoo'
To go and be hanged in a fashion
    That turns the whole atmosphere blue!

And the chances are strong the old buffer
   Has been talking for something to say,
And never rode anything rougher
   Than the shaft of old Somebody's dray;
And the horses he thinks he has broken
   Are clothes-horses sawn out of pine,
And his yarns to us simply betoken
   The start of a senile decline.

There are laws for our proper protection
   From murder and theft and the rest,
But the criminal wanting inspection
   Is riding a rail in the West;
And the law that the country requires
   At the hands of her statesmen of sense
Is the law that makes meat of the liars
   That can sit a rough buck — on the fence!

PART III

THE HONOUR OF THE STATION

Introduction

IN DECEMBER 1903, almost three years after his return to Scotland, Ogilvie wrote to A. G. Stephens that he had twenty to twenty-five prose sketches on bush subjects which had been printed in various first-class British journals and that he was going to try and get them published in book form.

The anthology was rejected by London publishers on the grounds that the stories were too slight for a book. When he went to Iowa in October 1904, Ogilvie took the manuscript with him and tried to place it with an American publisher. It was rejected by Macmillan of New York as not being of commercial value in the States on account of the small interest in Australia.

From America, in 1905 he tried *The Bulletin*, which had already had great success with several editions of his poetry collection, *Fair Girls and Gray Horses*. Again, he was unsuccessful. The London and New York publishers thought the book was good, but could only succeed in Australia. *The Bulletin* said 'Good — but suited to a foreign audience'. Ogilvie wrote to Stephens: 'I'm stumped!'

Back in Scotland from the U.S.A. Ogilvie did not give up hope of getting his prose pieces published, but put the 'sketches', as he called them, away for the time being and submitted another book to Fisher Unwin — *My Life in the Open*. This is not, as the title suggests, an autobiography, but rather a collection of essays descriptive of life and conditions in several countries where he had visited or worked, covering South Africa, Australia, America and his native Scotland. This work was accepted and published in 1908.

Working from his home in Selkirk, Ogilvie supported a wife and two children by freelance writing. He became almost as well known in the United Kingdom of the early twentieth century as he had been in Australia during the 1890s. It was this rise to fame that eventually enabled him to place *The Honour of the Station* with Holden & Hardingham of London, who in 1914 issued the book as one of their series of paperback 'Sixpenny Novels'. The little book is a collector's item today.

During 1995, four book search services in London and Edinburgh, plus an appeal in the Stockman's Hall of Fame newspaper, failed to locate a copy. Then a librarian at the Mitchell Library of New South Wales called up the National Bibliographic Display in the computer catalogue and located what are probably the only four copies of the work in Australia. There is a copy in Hobart, there are two in Melbourne, and the fourth one is in the library of the Australian Defence Forces Academy in Canberra. A photocopy supplied by the Academy has enabled this 'lost' work to be made available again to Australian readers.

The Honour of the Station is important in that it provides an intimate insight into life on the sheep and cattle stations of the outback a hundred years ago. An insight with more depth than that given in verse by *The Bulletin* bush balladists of the 1890s: Lawson, Ogilvie, Paterson and Morant, for example. The sketches are now published in Australia for the first time.

When describing the book to Stephens, Ogilvie wrote:

These sketches don't deal with the red-shirted bowie-knifed bushman of the English novel. They are *life* and *true*. No man not a bushman born has had better chances to get at the inner life of all sections of Bush Society than I have. I hope and think that I have kept my eyes open and I have tried to write down what I have seen. It is not literature but it's Australian *life*.[1]

While the stories have doubtless been based upon actual events, the identities of people and places are generally disguised — albeit sometimes thinly. Thus Skuthorpe's Buckjump Show becomes 'Grimthorpe's'; the township of Condobolin is 'Condobarin', and a horse called Boona gets its name from a property near Condobolin managed by Ogilvie's friends the McLean brothers. Internal evidence in several poems and prose pieces suggests that 'Tringadee' is a pseudonym for Robert Scott's 'Belalie' station where Ogilvie lived and worked during his first two years in Australia. 'The Last Straw' obviously describes Ogilvie's arrival at that station.

The Honour of the Station

FIVE OF US stood with bridles on our arms on the store verandah at Mulga Plains, and peered into the gathering darkness. A rush of hoofs came down the paddock, and the clang of a slip-rail dropped in place told us that the black boy had yarded the horses.

'Is it worth it?' asked Hammond, the book-keeper, jingling his snaffle against the verandah post, 'the wind's rising — it's going to rain — it'll be a rotten show anyway — is it worth riding ten miles in the dark for?'

'Oh, come on, Hammond; no slacking, you promised to come!' So we rallied him through the dark.

In the end we all went to catch our horses, David Wilson the overseer, Hammond, myself and Hughie and Albert — two of the boundary riders.

So dark it was that the piebald mare struck the gate with her shoulder before Hughie realised that he was near it; we rode through and followed Davie in single file as he picked up the track on old Mosquito. The clouds parted a little, and a thin wisp of moon showed above the river-timber. Davie shook Mosquito into a canter.

We could hear Hammond grumbling behind us as his old mare stumbled in the wheel-tracks, but our leader cantered on, humming a bush song; he had an eye like a hawk, and the perfect confidence in his horse that exists only between the superb horseman and his mount; behind him we struggled along, trusting to luck. At last far ahead a light twinkled, another and another, and the township loomed before us. The lighted verandahs of the hotels were black with people.

'Quite a crowd', said Davie cheerily, tapping his pipe-bowl on the pommel of his saddle.

We drew rein in front of Donaldson's, and someone shouted from the verandah, 'Here come the Mulga boys!'

We stabled our horses under a brush shed behind the hotel, and clanked along the boards in our trailing spurs to mingle in the crowd and drink success to Grimthorpe's Buckjump Show.

The walls of Donaldson's bar were plastered with posters of a magnificent black horse, bucking furiously beneath a wiry horseman, who smiled down upon the bar-room loafers, hat in hand. Under this picture was written: —

STEAM ENGINE.
£10 TO THE MAN WHO CAN SIT HIM FOR 2 MINUTES IN A HUNTING SADDLE.

In little knots of two and three the bushmen stood and drained their glasses, and everywhere the talk was of Grimthorpe and his horses.

'I saw the show up in Rockhampton last year', said Dally Stevens, the drover, 'and, take it from me, the black horse can buck; he threw four of our best men one after the other; there isn't a chap in this sheep country that could follow him for two bucks, and my money's ready to back what I say!'

'Now then, you Mulga boys', said someone, 'take him up; he's only talking: those show horses are only tricky; a man who can ride can do what he likes with 'em.'

'Some of 'em can buck, some of 'em can't', said Hughie, with a wise shake of his head. 'I want to see this horse first.'

'Well, let's get down to the show', said Dave, linking his arm in mine; 'Come along, Billy!'

In the township a steady stream of people was pouring into the large tent erected on a vacant piece of ground below Loughran's Hotel. As we paid our money at the door a gust of wind shook the canvas, and a few heavy drops began to fall.

Our party took seats together, and presently the show began. The first part of the programme consisted of some clever high-jumping by two grey horses, and some trick-riding by Grimthorpe's men; one of these, dressed as a clown, did some clever tumbling off a bucking pony, falling off in every conceivable attitude, and always in perfect safety, at once gaining the good opinion of the crowd. This was followed by a clever exhibition of stock-whip cracking and lasso-throwing; then there was an interval of ten minutes before the important work of the evening began — the challenge riding of Grimthorpe's buckjumpers.

A sturdy little roan horse was led into the ring, and Grimthorpe came forward and announced that one of his men would ride the horse, a notorious buckjumper from the Flinders River and that afterwards £5 would be given to any man in the audience who would remain on his back for two minutes. A murmur of approval greeted this sporting offer, and the crowd settled down to watch while the half-caste rider saddled the roan.

There was a dead silence as the man crept slowly into the saddle, then a shout of applause as the roan sprang into the air and went bucking round the enclosure in a cloud of dust. In a very few moments the horse stopped, and his rider vaulted down and waved his hat to the occupants of the two-shilling seats.

The general opinion of the crowd was that the horse 'couldn't buck for sour apples', and had no pluck, and no one was surprised when the butcher's son stepped forward 'to have a cut at that there fiver', only stipulating that he should use his own saddle. But the little roan seemed to know what was expected of him, and with a flying forward buck and a quick side-lurch, he had the boy in difficulties at once, and following up his advantage he flung his rider heavily against the canvas at the end of the tent, which fortunately broke his fall.

Grimthorpe dusted the boy's coat with his riding whip and turned with a smile to the crowd. 'My five pounds is still waitin', gentlemen!' he said. Hughie stirred in his seat. 'Shall I have a cut at him, Dave?' he asked, but even as he spoke a little wiry horsebreaker from Merrigal Springs stepped into the arena with his huge saddle on his arm.

He rode prettily; beneath his iron thighs the little roan was powerless, and though he bucked his hardest he was conquered from first to last, and a great ovation greeted the breaker as he received Grimthorpe's five pounds and returned modestly to his place.

'Gentlemen', said Grimthorpe, 'I have often heard of the Border riders, and there's not the least doubt that you've got some good men in the district, but I have a horse in my show that has tested the best, and to show my confidence in him I will double my usual wager and give £20 to the man who can sit him for two minutes in a hunting saddle, but any man who tries and fails to ride him must pay me a forfeit of £5 and take all risk of accident. Bring in Steam Engine!'

A murmur of applause rippled round the ring as the beautiful black horse was led in; he stood fully sixteen and a half hands, of immense bone and muscle, and carried a proud head so high that he seemed even taller than he really was. His eye flashed fire upon the tiers of rapt brown faces, and as the groom faced him up in the centre of the tent he squealed and lashed out in very wantonness.

Then the crowd began to talk, calling on the noted horsemen present to take up the challenge.

'Now then, Hughie! Now then, Dall! Come on, Dave Wilson! Where's Jack Grieve?' and so on.

Hughie shuffled his feet impatiently, and I noticed the hand that rested on his knee shook as though with some nervous resolve.

Dally Stevens, the drover, shook his head good-naturedly. 'I've seen him buck', he said, and there was a wealth of meaning in his words.

'Have another try, Jack Grieve, he's no worse than the roan!' called somebody; but Jack sat still, looking thoughtfully at his saddle.

'Dave, Dave Wilson! Come on, Dave!' yelled the crowd. 'What's become of the Mulga boys!' But Davie's handsome brown face betrayed no interest in the proceedings; he stooped to strike a match, and held it to his pipe.

A gust of wind shook the great canvas into bellying waves, and a clatter of rain swept down upon the roof: The black horse started and pawed the ground impatiently.

'Will I have a cut?' Hughie's face was a little white, I thought, as he bent across me to ask Dave the question.

'Please yourself, Hughie!' said the overseer, 'but mind you, he's a bad one. Dally Stevens wouldn't be off him unless he was something out of the common.'

But Hughie had already made up his mind. 'Let me use my own saddle, and I'll ride him', he called out. Grimthorpe demurred, but finally gave way on the point, and Hughie, with the honour of our station in his hands, stepped out into the arena.

The black horse was blindfolded and saddled, and Hughie made a little speech to the crowd.

'I don't want you fellows to think', he said, addressing the crowd generally, 'that I'm riding this horse to try and make a big man of myself before you; and I know there's two or three fellows in this tent that can ride both sides of me; but I don't believe in these Queensland fellows coming down here and poking fun at us chaps because we happen to work among sheep and not cattle; more than that, I'm a Mulga Plains man, and I'm going to have a try at this black horse for the honour of the old station.'

Great applause followed this impromptu oration, for Hughie was a sterling fellow and a favourite with all, and a first-rate horseman into the bargain. Then he waved his hand to us and took hold of the reins, and quick as a cat was down in the saddle. The bandage was snatched from the black's eyes, and he reared straight on end, gave a sudden twist and nearly fell, then, coming down, he dropped his head, and, squealing viciously, bucked hard and high across the ring. At the second buck Hughie slipped forward, at the third he left the saddle as though slung by a catapult, and fell a dozen feet away with a crash that resounded through the tent. For a moment we thought he was seriously injured, but he rose and staggered unsteadily across the ring.

Grimthorpe stood tapping his riding-boot with his whip. 'I have twenty notes here', he said, 'for the man who can ride him'.

Jack Grieve got up from his place in the front row and walked forward, carrying his heavy saddle, with the stirrup irons jingling to his stride.

They took off Hughie's saddle and put Jack's in its place. The big horse, now thoroughly roused, struck and plunged, and it took twelve minutes to saddle him, while the crowd hummed with excitement: 'By heaven, that horse can buck!' 'Jack can never ride one side of him!' 'Nor any other man South of the Border!'

In a dead silence the famous horsebreaker stole into the saddle, the cloth was pulled from the horse's eyes, and up he went in a savage buck. Jack Grieve loosened his reins and drove home the spurs; with a roar of pain the great horse gave one bound into the air, and surely never before or since did a horse buck so big and high; like an arrow from a bow the trim little figure of the breaker shot through the air, and he landed twenty feet away at Grimthorpe's feet, while a shout of wonder and dismay rose from the benches;

The horse was caught and unsaddled and Jack Grieve went back to his place, and under the tan his face was very white.

Grimthorpe smiled up at the audience.

'It takes the cattle-men to ride a horse like that', he said, with quiet scorn. 'I should have brought something easier down here.'

There was some hissing and booing from the back of the tent at this speech, and somebody called out, 'Let's see you ride him yourself!'

But Grimthorpe only tapped his boot with his riding whip and smiled.

I looked across at David Wilson. Dave had a reputation second to no man as a buck-jump rider, and if any man in that tent could ride the horse I knew it was the tall, lithe overseer of Mulga Plains. A far finer rider than Hughie Warren, but less addicted to displaying his prowess, we knew at once that if Dave consented to try we should see such a battle between man and beast as had seldom been seen before.

'Try him, Dave,' I said. But he shook his head. Somebody heard me, and caught at the name, 'Dave Wilson, Dave Wilson! Now then, Davie!'

In a moment the cry was taken up by a hundred throats.

'Dave', I said, 'remember the honour of the station'.

A sudden gleam awoke in his keen, honest blue eyes. If there was one thing above all others that was a cherished fetish with David Wilson, it was the honour of Mulga Plains. His ambition was that our station should be first in stock, first in honourable dealing, and, before everything, first in sport, and that it should be beaten in horsemanship was a thought intolerable to him. He turned to me quickly.

'Run and fetch your little hunting saddle, Billy!'

I hesitated. 'But, Dave', I said, 'the little saddle — he'll let you — '

'Hurry up', he broke in authoritatively, 'your hunting saddle!'

I was out of the tent in a flash. When I returned with the dainty English saddle on my arm the bushmen stood up all round the ring and cheered lustily. Dave was talking to Grimthorpe. He turned to me, took the saddle and unstrapped its silk web girths and surcingle, and attached the leather gear from Hughie's.

In a few more minutes the big black horse was ready for the fray, and Dave stepped forward, cool, watchful, and determined. Before we had realised that he had gathered the reins he was safe in the saddle, and up went the black with a snort of anger. Coming down with a nasty turn in the air he lost his footing and fell, but Wilson sprang clear, and, still holding the bridle, gave the black a kick in the ribs.

The horse rose, and as he did so Dave threw his leg over him, and as man and beast leapt six feet in the air a great cheer burst from the crowd.

Then began a royal battle for supremacy; the outlaw bucked straight forward big and high, side-lurched, bucked backwards, reared and turned in the air, or spun like a top in one place; but through it all the tall, lithe figure of the rider swayed easily to every motion, and seemed to be a part of the whirling catherine-wheel below.

Suddenly there burst from the audience a wild yell of triumph. 'Time's up! Time's up! Good old Dave!' The bushmen, mad with delight, stood up on the benches and waved hats and handkerchiefs and whips. The black horse made one more terrific attempt to unseat his rider, and then, bolting for the opening in the tent that led to his rough bush stable, he suddenly disappeared from view. We leapt from our seats and rushed to the doorway in an excited stream. Outside a crash of thunder met us, and a great flash of lightning showed for a moment the big black horse and his gallant rider forging through the night.

There came a sudden jingle of wire and then silence. Someone called, 'Into the fence, by Jove!' and we ran over to the spot.

As we reached it another flash revealed the black horse lying on his side, and Dave standing over him unhurt. Then his cheery voice rang out, 'Sit on his head, somebody; I don't want to get that saddle smashed!'

The saddle was none the worse except for a scar on the flap, where a ragged edge of wire had touched it; but I'm proud of that mark, for it calls to mind the night when Dave Wilson saved the honour of the station.

The Fence Builders

THE FIERCE SUN, somewhat tempered in decline, still beat down with an arrogance of power upon the shadeless plain, where a long straight line of posts broke the interminable level of the burnt brown grass. At the end of the line of newly erected posts two men were working. One with shovel and bar was digging post-holes in the hard, unyielding black soil; the other was setting up the yellow posts of split pine, one by one, with a mathematical accuracy and a conscientious thoroughness, beating down the earth round each with a wooden rammer, shovelling in the clods from time to time, or stepping back to glance along the yellow tops with a practiced eye, to make sure that no post leaned so much as an inch from the level line. He was a tall, well-built young fellow, this setter of the posts, but he looked a mere boy beside the swarthy giant who, with determined thrusts of the bar and rapid dips of the long-handled shovel, was swiftly adding brown heap to brown heap as he prepared the three-foot apertures for the posts. Broad-shouldered, heavy-armed, bull-necked, he showed a massiveness of build unusual among the bushmen, and his height was far above the ordinary.

Ned Jackson, in addition to his enormous physical strength, was the possessor of a restless energy not usually connected with men of great bulk. No matter what work it was upon which he happened to be engaged at the moment, he gave his whole soul to the doing of it. He was proud of his strength, and proud of his quickness, and in all his work he was conscientious and thorough. Two more able and reliable bush workmen than he and Jim Arrol, his mate, it would have been difficult to find in the length and breadth of the Western District.

They were the best of friends, too, with a mutual admiration for each other's good qualities. They had done a great deal of heavy contract work together, sharing the burden of the burning western days with a brotherly unselfishness; each working his hardest for the common good of 'The Firm', as they called themselves.

*   *   *

Arrol had a little cottage and a wife and child in Wonbilla township, ten miles from the scene of their work. Ned Jackson was independent and unattached, one of the floating population of the Bush, his home a shifting quantity that followed his work, and consisting of a small canvas tent which was at present pitched upon the red sandhill which rose out of the level plain a mile away to the northward. Arrol, whose grey horse was now tinkling his bell upon the same sandhill and tugging mouthfuls of dry grass, rode home each night at sundown.

The two men toiled on at their heavy labour: they were clad only in shirt and trousers, yet the sweat poured off them as they worked. They were too far from each other for conversation; each was intent upon his own work, and cast scarcely a glance in the direction of the other.

So busily engaged was big Ned Jackson that he did not hear the pad-pad of a horse's hoofs in the dry earth, and he looked up suddenly with a start as a shadow came between him and the sun. It was the manager of Wonbilla Station, who had ridden out to inspect the new line of fence. The manager was a square-shouldered, active-looking young man, with a well-trimmed beard and moustache which failed to hide the hard and cynical droop of a rather cruel mouth. His blue eyes had a steely glitter in them, and a certain haughty insolence about the man did not prepossess one in his favour. He smiled rather contemptuously at the startled look of the big bushman. 'Good day, Ned!' he said, civilly enough. 'G'day!' said the big man, very shortly; he had no love for his employer, who had lashed him more than once with a bitter satirical tongue, for no reason but to make a fool of him.

'You're gettin' 'em up pretty quick', said the manager; the words were complimentary, but the tone was unpleasant. Ned Jackson made no reply, but bent again to his work, prodding the hard ground furiously, as though some enemy lay there beneath his hand.

'Queer thing it is', went on the manager, in his haughty and aggressive tones, 'that you fellows can work like galley slaves when you're on contract labour, and when you're on wages you're just cursed loafers; queer thing, eh?'

'I've never worked for you on wages, Mr Hamilton', said the bushman, 'so I don't see as you've any right to say that about me'.

'Oh, you're all the same', said the manager contemptuously, 'every blasted one of you. There's no honour about you. That hole's not three feet, eh?'

For answer Jackson quietly picked up a lath which was lying near him, with measured feet notched upon it, slipped it into the hole in front of him and looked up at his employer; the measure showed the hole to be a couple of inches deeper than the contract demanded. The manager bit his lip.

'Mind, if I find you cheating me, and a single one of those holes shallower than three feet, I'll not pay you a shilling! Do you hear me, eh?'

'We'll do what we contracted to do, Mr Hamilton', said Jackson, quietly.

The manager wheeled his horse and cantered off to where Jim Arrol was working, cursing at his horse as it shied at a post upon the ground. Jackson looked after him with a dark shadow on his sunburnt face. 'Bullyin' hound!' he said.

*   *   *

If Ned Jackson thought little of his employer, Jim Arrol thought less. As he saw Hamilton approaching, he dropped his rammer and strolled back along the line of posts to where he had left his coat. Taking his pipe and tobacco from his pocket he began leisurely to cut up a pipeful of the black weed and to roll it deliberately between his palms. He seldom smoked when working, but something always prompted him to idle when the manager was present, some sense of shame at letting this man whom he heartily despised see him sweating in his interests.

Hamilton eyed the last few erected posts with a scowl on his face. Then he walked his horse up to the fencer. 'Those last three are clean off the line. None of your careless work for me, Jim Arrol; I want a straight fence. Pull 'em up and put 'em in again! You fellows are going a deal too fast here. Nothing but greed for money!'

Jim Arrol was a good workman and he knew it. It hurt him to have his work faulted, but he remained outwardly calm and, striking a match with slow deliberation, he lit his pipe, and having got it fairly started lifted it from his mouth and said:— 'The posts is dead straight, Boss. You can't see 'em right from a horse's back. If you get down and look along 'em you'll see they're not an inch out anywhere.'

'Don't talk to me, Arrol', said the manager, haughtily, 'do you think I don't know what I'm speaking about? Take up those last three, and plant them straight. I want this job done according to contract, and, by Jingo, I'll have it done right. Do you hear me, eh? — Eh?'

Jim Arrol smoked furiously and said nothing. Driving his spurs into his horse, the manager cantered off across the plain, and the bushman with a sigh of relief went back to his work. 'An' if he wants them straight posts lifted he can do it himself', Jim muttered as he plied the rammer with renewed energy. The sun slanted down towards the horizon, and the men worked the harder as the fierce heat waned. Not until the red ball of fire had actually dipped beyond the far-off fringe of myall trees did they lay down their tools and walk side by side back to their camp on the sandhill.

Both men were annoyed at the manager's visit, as good men must always be when their honest work is found fault with without reason. Jim Arrol spoke bitterly of the interference, which he resented, and even talked of throwing up the contract. Big Ned Jackson swore in sympathy, and then became moodily silent. It was evident there was something on his mind, over and above the harshness of his employer.

*   *   *

At last he seemed determined to speak. 'Jim', he said, laying his big hand kindly on the shoulder of the younger man, 'there's something about that big sneerin', bullyin' boss of ours that hurts me more than anything he can say about your work'. And then roughly but kindly he unburdened himself of a secret which he had found ill to keep.

He had found out that the whole of the township, as well as all the station men, had begun to talk about the attention which Hamilton, the manager, had lately been paying to Jim's wife. Mrs Arrol was a light-hearted, frivolous little woman, who had been a servant at Wonbilla Station before she married the young bushman; and even then there had been talk about herself and the manager. This old intimacy, it appeared, had lately been renewed, and it was an open secret in the district that Hamilton frequently visited the little cottage on the outskirts of the township when Jim Arrol was absent at his work. The neighbours had begun to talk; but no one had thought to tell Jim of the intrigue, being fearful of hurting by any word the loyal heart of this honest man, without positive proof of his wife's infidelity. But in the last few days there had been ugly rumours abroad, and Ned Jackson, in his present mood of resentment, thought this a fitting moment to tell his mate something at least of what he had heard.

Jim Arrol, though not blind to his wife's frivolous and shallow nature, was still very much in love with her; and Ned Jackson's words were a severe blow to him. He turned white under his healthy tan, and staggered as though the weight of that kindly hand on his shoulder was too much for him.

'Out here', he said, at last, 'Bob Hamilton is my boss; but if ever I catch him sneakin' about my house I'll break his neck for him. An' more than that', he went on, with vicious emphasis, 'I'll break the neck of any man I hear making light of my wife's character. You let 'em say those things before you, Ned?' he asked, suspiciously.

The big hand gripped his shoulder like iron. 'Don't doubt me, Jim, my boy', said his mate, 'I'll stand up for you before all the world, but woman's a thing no man can understand, and no man can answer for!'

'You believe these tales, then, Ned?'

'I don't believe, nor disbelieve', said Ned, guardedly, 'but I believe in you, Jim Arrol, and any way I can help you to bowl out that rotten bully, or to choke off any flamin' liars that may be traducin' your wife — I will, s'help me God!'

And, then, somehow Jim knew that there was something of truth in this scandal that had touched him.

The two men spoke no more on the subject, but sat down to their simple supper. Then Jim saddled his grey and lit up his pipe preparatory to his departure.

'Well, I'll be away for three days, Ned!' He was summoned to Bourke on certain land business. 'I'll be out to work on Thursday mornin' again. Don't sweat too hard at them holes. I don't want you to be breakin' your back here while I'm loafin' in town.'

'That's all right, Jimmy, my boy', said the big man cheerily, 'I'll be always sloggin' along. I'll be very near across to the timber by the time you're back. So long! An' look here', he put his hand on the horse's mane as Jim mounted, 'don't you be frettin' about them tales I was tellin' ye. Lies, likely enough!'

Jim wrung his hand and then, touching the willing grey with his heel, cantered off round the edge of the sandhill to pick up the road to the township. That night he said nothing to his wife, but sat and watched her with a certain sadness in his eyes that was infinitely pathetic. He had always trusted her implicitly. His married life had been happy. He had a pretty little girl two years old, who brought sunshine to his modest home. He had worked hard and saved some money and had put in an application for a homestead lease upon Wonbilla; it was on business connected with this that his presence was now required in Bourke. Only a day previously life had seemed a very good and desirable thing, and now by reason of those well-meant hints given him by his mate the poison had entered his blood, and life to him had become a worthless thing. As he sat and watched the pretty face of this woman that he loved, his heart grew bitter against Robert Hamilton, and he swore to himself that he would be revenged upon him for his many sneers, and for his real or attempted intrigue with his wife.

*   *   *

At the first streak of dawn he was in the saddle, ambling down the Bourke road upon his free-stepping grey; while very little later Ned Jackson, the giant, was back at work upon the myall plain, singing contentedly as he plied shovel and bar, determined to have a brave show of accomplished work to set before his mate when he returned.

And at the head station Hamilton, the manager, wove his plans.

On the second day of Jim Arrol's absence, Ned caught one of his horses and rode to the township to see about rations for the camp. It was the custom for Mrs Arrol to supply the fencers with scones and cakes, and to see about these Ned rode up to the little cottage that stood by itself a little apart from the other houses. Biddy, the baby, saw him coming and toddled out to meet him, and Ned, stooping from his big brown horse, caught her up in front of him on the saddle and rode up to the door. Mrs Arrol made him welcome, and the bushman tied his horse in the shade of a neighbouring tree and entered the house. 'I have all your things ready, Ned', said the woman, 'all but a few eggs they're keeping me at the hotel. I'll run down and get them now if you'll watch Biddy till I come back.'

'All right', said the bushman, cheerily, 'come on, Biddy Malone, an' I'll give ye a ride on my back!' He hoisted her on to his broad shoulders; and the little room rang with childish laughter, as he galloped up and down with clumsy step. The mother had only been gone a moment or two, but was out of sight among the houses, when the station blackboy rode up on a sweating horse with a letter in his hand. 'Hulloh, Fred! What's that you've got?' called Jackson.

'Letter from Boss — fur Missus Arrol.'

'Well, give it to me; she's gone to the township!'

The boy hesitated. 'Boss said baal me gibbit any feller only Mistress Arrol!'

'O, get out, ye yellow nigger, ye know me, don't yer? I'm Jim Arrol's mate. Give it here!'

The boy hesitated, but was afraid to refuse. He rode close up to the verandah and handed the note, carefully sealed and addressed in Hamilton's well-known bold hand, to the big bushman.

'Now, cut home as quick as you like, or I'll take a whip to you.' The boy needed no further hint; leaning over his mare's neck he disappeared in a cloud of dust.

Ned Jackson set the child down and turned the note over in his hand. Quickly he made up his mind. 'It's not meant for me', he said to himself, 'taint honourable to read other people's letters, but Jim's honour's worth more than mine — so here goes!' He broke the seal and read: 'Will be up to-night at eleven o'clock. — R. H.' That was all, but it was enough. He thrust the piece of paper into his pocket just as Jim's wife approached the verandah. He put the things she had prepared for him into a billy-can and a small bag, swung himself into the saddle, and with a cheery good-bye to the little girl, ambled off towards the township.

But he did not collect the rest of the rations and go back to camp as he had intended to do. Instead of that he stabled his horse at the hotel and lingered about the township talking to his friends until long after dark. Then by a roundabout path he approached the Arrols' house. With the exception of a couple of small trees which stood by a small railed stockyard there was very little cover, but in the house all was silent, and there were no lights burning. Ned stooped down, and creeping round the end of the house slipped into the back verandah and so into the narrow passage that ran through the cottage from front to back. There were only three rooms in the house proper: the kitchen being a separate building at the back. On Ned's right as he stood in the passage was the one large room which was used as a sitting room; on his left were the two bedrooms, in the front of which he knew that Jim's wife and child slept. The sitting-room door was open and Jim stepped cautiously inside; he had left his boots some distance from the house, and he sat down noiselessly in a large chair. Very cautiously he laid upon the table a heavy willow stick he had spent an hour of the evening in choosing from the willow clump at the creek. In the dim light he settled himself to his lonely vigil, burning with an honest man's wholehearted eagerness to get a grip upon the neck of this thief of honour.

*   *   *

Meanwhile Jim Arrol was cantering home as fast as his gallant grey could carry him. He had traversed more than half the long distance to the western capital when the mailman met him with the news that the land meeting was postponed, and that his services would not be required, and now he was making the best of his way home that after an hour or two's sleep he might be ready to join his mate on the fence in the morning and recover at least one day of the three that he thought he must lose. There was a light in the men's hut at Wonbilla head station as he passed, and he reined up for a moment to tell the men of the postponed Land Court and of his long and futile ride. As he was turning to ride away the head stockman drew him aside. 'Jim', he said, 'take this that I'm tellin' you for what it's worth. I'm maybe thinkin' you're home before you're expected. I seen the boss givin' the nigger a letter for your missus this afternoon; an' the boss went up the road on his chestnut not ten minutes ago. Maybe you're not expected to-night, Jim.'

With an oath the fencer wheeled the tired grey horse and galloped up the horse paddock. Once out upon the open road he stood up in his stirrups and raced over the four miles that separated him from his home, but he saw no signs of the manager of Wonbilla, who was either ahead of him or had left the road.

Nearing his house, Jim Arrol reined the grey into a walk and then, dismounting, tied his horse in the little stockyard and crept stealthily towards the front verandah of the cottage. The house was very still, but Jim, with hatred and a raging jealousy in his heart, refused to be soothed by its apparent peacefulness. As he crept onward in the shadow of the nearest tree, he drew from his belt a loaded revolver, which he always carried, and his fingers closed lovingly on the trigger guard.

In the dim starlight that filtered through the shutterless window of the sitting-room, big Ned Jackson sat still as a statue, brooding on the wrongs of his mate, and determined, however long the wait and however desperate the chance when it came, to avenge those wrongs for the man who was absent and could not strike for himself. The sound of a horse's hoofs woke him from his reverie: and at the same time a slight sound reached him from the bedroom opposite. Ned rose cautiously from his chair, picked up the heavy stick, and peered out into the dim passage. The light footfall of a man stepping stealthily on the verandah set his nerves tingling. A great joy came over him. At last his chance had come, his chance to avenge the honour of his mate, and at the same time to take revenge for the insults he himself had suffered from this arrogant bully, this cowardly destroyer of homes. The muscles of his great right hand swelled in anticipation. How he thanked God for this almost superhuman strength of his, this strength that had made him disdain any other weapon than the simple willow bludgeon. He knew that with his splendid naked hands he could throttle the life out of this paltry coward, but he had thought the stick the more suitable weapon to use upon so mean a foe. He moved a little further into the passage. A shadow darkened the outlet and Ned involuntarily raised his arm, but before it could descend the crouching figure before him leapt up. A shot rang out, then another, and Ned Jackson fell forward on his face, shot through the heart, filling the narrow passage with his great bulk.

The shriek of a woman woke the sleeping township, and when the first of the men arrived they found Jim Arrol, white and trembling, bending over the dead giant, the guardian of his honour and the keeper of his home.

The Crossing

MORE THAN forty years ago, when bridges were not so numerous on Australian rivers as they are to-day, most of the stock-routes which led from the north crossed the Murray River independently, wherever the banks were sound and not too steep and the river bed was clear of snags and quicksands. At a crossing place such as this lived Barney Allen, well known to all the drovers who brought cattle to Melbourne by that particular route. Barney's modest hut stood on the Victorian side of the river, half-hidden in the tall gum timber, and Barney made a living by assisting the drovers to cross their stock by swimming. He was practically amphibian. A strong and resolute swimmer, he had grown to accept the rushing waters of the Murray as his home. With a couple of clever horses which swam as well as he did himself, he made himself simply indispensable to the drovers, many of whom were but poor hands in the water, and were apt to lose their heads when the river ran strongly and the frightened cattle began to bellow and circle, and refused to make a straight course from bank to bank. Then it was that Barney, swimming out on his famous grey horse, or scarcely less famous brown mare, straightened up the swerving irresolute leaders and drove them to the landing place in spite of themselves.

Reckless, gallant, cheery, and a master in his own particular class of work, Barney was one of the most popular figures between Melbourne and the Gulf Country, and was the friend of every drover on the road. He had a wife and one child, and one night when the wind was roaring down the Murray flats and the river was thundering past the hut in tawny tossing flood his wife died and left him with a little five-year-old girl to cherish and work for. Allen reverently buried his help-meet on the low sandhill, fenced her grave with a square of white railing, and went back to his work; and Lassie, the baby girl, planted bush flowers on the grave, and cried bitterly — and forgot.

*   *   *

As the slow bush seasons came and passed, these two became wholly sufficient to each other. Lassie kept the little hut clean and tidy for her father, cooked his meals for him, and rode bare-backed to the nearest township for provisions when her father was busily employed with the cattle at the river.

With plenty of time and opportunity for practice, the girl became an expert swimmer, and thoroughly at home in the water with or without a horse. Even before her mother died she had crossed the river on a swimming horse in the crook of her father's arm, and at seven years of age she could cross alone on either of the horses and guide the cattle in the water.

Before she was twelve she had become indispensable to her father as assistant and understudy as well as in the capacity of housekeeper and cook. Intrepid, clear-headed, and alert, and sitting astride upon her bare-backed horse, she swam the river with the crossing mobs and guided one wing of the cattle while her father looked after the other. She was the apple of his eye, his pride and admiration, and eagerly he drank in every word of praise which the drovers bestowed upon her. She was a merry, lighthearted little witch, beloved of all who knew her, content with her humble employment, and unstirred by any desire for the great unknown life that lay behind the purple fringe of the mallee.

It was Leonard Murray, the Rockhampton drover, who broke up at last the idyllic, careless, boyish existence which had been thrust upon her by circumstance and environment. Murray was a married man with a wife and two grown-up daughters in Rockhampton. He earned good money in his profession, lived in a large house in the suburbs, and had had his girls educated at one of the best schools in the city. He talked to Barney one day at the riverside, as the last steer of two thousand crept dripping up the paddled bank and trailed away across the sandhill. 'You should send that girl to school, Barney — she's getting too big for this game now. You can well afford it. It's only fair to the woman she will be. A handsome girl and a good one. Send her to school.'

'Oh! I can afford it right enough', said Allen, 'and I know she oughten be wastin' her time like this, up here; but, bless yer heart, Len, I couldn't *never* live without her. Yer see ever since her mother died she and me's never been parted. If she went to school for a year or two she'd maybe forget her old daddy, and then it would never be the same again for me. It would break her heart, too, leaving the horses and the swimmin' and the river an' all. Come here, Lassie, my girl!'

The strangely-garbed little figure, seated on a dead log, rose and came towards them. The wide blue dungaree trousers, wet and clinging, outlined the delicate roundness of the limbs. The face was piquant, pretty, and mischievous. The long hair was coiled tightly and pinned to a blue handkerchief tied round the brows turban fashion. The loose white shirt clung closely to wrist and arm and bosom. Already, seen thus at infinite disadvantage, there loomed in this childish figure the possibilities of a rich and glorious womanhood. She stood in front of the men without a trace of shyness, legs apart, hands clasped behind her on the bridle rein of the old grey horse. 'Would you like to go to school in Sydney, Lass?' asked her father.

She pouted prettily. 'And leave you, Dad? And old Flying Fish, and Wild Duck? And the clashing horns when the cattle crowd, and the rush of the water when the river's big, and the sunsets, and the white cranes and — no, no, Daddy, I'd rather stay here with you!'

'You're a young woman, now, Lassie', said Murray kindly, 'you can't run about like a boy all your life. You must learn to dance and play the piano and do fancy needlework and be a lady like the rest of them. Then you'll meet some nice young Sydney fellow and get married.'

The girl laughed merrily, 'I'm happy here with Dad', she said simply, 'I can read and write and cook and bake and darn, and swim and ride. I'm all the lady I want to be.' A faint note of yearning crept into her voice, belying her last words, and Murray, quick in his knowledge of human nature, detected it, and was glad.

Barney, less sensitive, heard only the sentiment expressed. 'She don't care for them things', he said.

But Murray's interest was awakened, and it was mainly through his efforts, and on account of his having won the girl's confidence and given her some good advice, that she allowed herself to be sent away shortly afterwards to a boarding school in the capital, and Barney piloted the mobs alone.

Those were dreary days in the little hut on the sandhill. At first he could hardly bear the separation. But, as the days went by, and the autumn brought its usual busy period, Allen found peace in hard work and in the satisfaction of a voluntary martyrdom in the interests of his daughter. Letters came to him from Sydney, long letters at first full of homesickness and weariness, detailing hatred of the city and the people and the school and the dull and deadly routine of it all. Then came letters that showed a waking interest in the new life, letters describing dances and picnics and moonlit trips across the harbour; then letters reticent, distant, distrait; letters strangely out of touch with the old life; letters that forgot to ask about the floods and the horses, and the river steamers and the drovers.

Three years went by, and the time of her exile was fulfilled, and still Lassie lingered in Sydney. She could get work, she said, in the city. She told of many situations that had been offered to her; and expressed a fear that she could never settle in the Bush again. And always there were requests for money, money, money. Allen was fairly well off for a man in his position. For many years he had been able to save something from the money he made at the river, but this constant strain was telling on his bank account. At last he was obliged to shorten the supplies, and at last the daughter whom he had not seen for three and a half years agreed to return to the hut by the Murray. Allen was delighted. He went whistling about the place like a boy, set the hut in apple-pie order — he was always a tidy man — and made ready with loving care the little bedroom with its humble fittings and lined log walls. He gave the pots

and pans a special cleaning, and spent hours in polishing the snaffle bit on the
bridle which had always been Lassie's particular property. His was a secret that
his favourites, the horses, must share.

*   *   *

'Lassie's coming home on Monday', he whispered into the grey ear of
Flying Fish as he swam him over to meet Jim Murtrie with his two thousand
steers from the Warrego; 'Lassie's coming back', and the old horse as he heard
the words seemed to put fresh power into his shoulders as he buffeted the
brown water and blew through his great red nostrils, forging onward to the
northern bank.

On the appointed day Allen borrowed a waggonette from his nearest
neighbour, Hamilton the selector, and drove in to Albury to meet his daughter.
When the Sydney train drew up alongside the platform he searched the windows
in vain for a glimpse of Lassie. The people began to alight, and he scanned
wistfully each female figure with a great sorrow of disappointment gripping at
his heart. In the horde of well-dressed travellers he failed to find the girl whom
he sought. While he paused irresolute, and the hurrying, chattering throng
swept past him, a tall, good-looking, but rather flashily dressed young woman
tapped him on the shoulder with a sudden 'Hulloa, Da!' He turned and saw his
daughter. Those three and a half years had changed her out of all knowledge.
Certainly it was Lassie, and yet — and yet! —

'My girl!' was all he could say, as he threw his strong arm round her.

'Don't, Dad; don't crush my frock like that!' she said petulantly; 'your hands
are so dirty, too!'

A couple of girls, passing, sniggered, and looked back over their shoulders,
and, suddenly ashamed, the bushman looked down at his rough red hands,
innocent of cuffs, engrained with the dark contact of the river mud, and freshly
smudged now with the black grease of the harness. For many months he had
dreamed of this meeting, his loyal heart beating in anticipation of the thrill of
its coming rapture, and now the hour had come and had brought some strange
sense of disappointment. It was his Lassie, grown to splendid womanhood, but
somehow different from the witching happy girl he had loved and lost.

'My word, you're a swell now, Lass, in your fine clothes', he said, rather
shamefacedly; 'yer wouldn't have minded a streak o' black on yer blue dungarees
once on a time. Well, well, never mind! Where's yer bag?'

'Bag!' she said scornfully. 'I've two boxes and a hat-box and a dressing-case
in the van. Oh, do let go my hand. It looks so silly!' She swung away from him,
and challenged boldly with her eyes a broad-shouldered young fellow who
was standing near, watching her with unconcealed admiration.

Allen walked unsteadily towards the van, where people were claiming their
luggage. Realising it as yet but dimly, he was, nevertheless, stricken to the heart.
Busying himself with the luggage and strapping it securely on the back of the

waggonette he soon grew more cheery, and helping his daughter up to the high front seat — she would have made light of the effort in the olden days — he sprang up beside her, and soon the sturdy Bush horses had drawn them through the town and were tossing up the grey dust in clouds upon the river road.

'Now, tell me all about what yer bin doin', Lass! I've been longin' and longin' to see yer, till I thought I could bear it no longer and I'd have to come down and fetch yer home. Old Flying Fish'll just go off his head wi' joy when he gets you aboard again. Burnett's gived notice fer to-morrow — fifteen hunder' fats — and the river's big. I've got the old togs out an' aired 'em fer yer.' He glanced with a smile at her dainty city clothes. 'Yer'll be spoilin' fer a swim agen, eh Lass?'

*   *   *

She looked across to where a glimpse of brown betrayed the old river surging down bank high beyond the gum-trees on their right.

'Ugh, how I hate it all', she said, 'the dust and the dead gum leaves and the rotten dying sheep and the blistering sun and all. I wish I'd never come. *Do* put the whip on those crawling brutes and let's get on into the timber!'

'Crawling brutes? Why, Lassie woman, that's the best horse on the Murray River', he said, laying his whip gently on the quarter of the near horse, a long, low bay with a swinging, earnest step and a bold high-carried head. 'Jim Hamilton wouldn't take a hunder' pound for that feller — only lent him to me to-day because it was a sort of special occasion — your coming home, Lassie!'

The girl winced at the word home. 'You've never put up a decent house yet, I suppose', she said, pouting, 'the same old tumble-down shack, is it?'

'Well, Lassie, it ain't much of a place, certainly', he said slowly, 'but I've never wanted no other, nor your mother didn't neither, nor you when we was so happy there together. It'll surely do us two for all we want.' He spoke cheerily, but his heart was heavy. How was this dainty, over-dressed girl to live in the poor place that he knew as home. He wished he had mended the broken shutter before he left and nailed a bit of calico over that torn patch near the window — yes, he wished he had thought about that bit of calico.

For miles they drove in silence. The girl would not talk about Sydney, nor would she let herself be interested in the river and the horses and the mobs that had lately crossed. She cared nothing about what the neighbours were doing, nor that the Wandarra woolshed had been burnt down, nor that Murray's fine old roan camp horse had been drowned the last time he crossed with cattle. All these things were outside the world in which she now lived, and very sadly her father at last recognised the fact. Hurt and disappointed he relapsed into a meditative silence. 'It's not Lassie — not *my* Lassie, at all', he kept saying over and over to himself with pathetic insistence. He looked down at his rough red grimy hands, and wondered if it was he who had changed; grown careless perhaps as he had grown older. And so in the shadows of a bitter disillusionment on both sides Barney Allen brought his daughter home.

He watched her anxiously next morning as, in a long blue wrapper, she toyed with the uninviting chops and damper of the Bush breakfast. 'You'll be coming to help me cross the cattle', he suggested, rather doubtfully.

'What *do* you take me for?' she asked, with withering scorn. 'Don't you see I *hate* your cattle and your drovers and your wretched monotonous life. Dad, I'm going back to Sydney; I can't stay here.'

Her father paused with half a chop on his fork, and his jaw fell.

'You're — going — back — to — Sydney!'

'Yes! I couldn't stop here. Dad, can't you see it's impossible? You don't understand — this life — it's impossible to me — this hut — the desperate loneliness — ' She stopped suddenly, for the man's face had grown ashen pale, and he reeled as he stood up. 'Do yer mean it?' he asked in a low earnest voice, 'ye're going back?'

'Yes! I must go back', she said.

He rose from the table without another word, and, taking his bridle from the verandah, went to catch his horse, and over the river came the ringing coo-ee of the drover waiting to have his cattle crossed.

The river was running deep and brown as Allen led old Flying Fish down to the edge of it. Without hesitation he leapt on to the horse, bare-backed, and urged him into the tawny, angry tide. On the opposite bank the drover's men, in a group, watched his progress with anxious eyes. The grey horse was caught by the strong running tide and carried swiftly down stream, but, swimming determinedly with his head lying low on the water, he gradually forged across, and, with his master floating lightly above him with one hand on his mane, he eventually landed safely, and scrambled up the sloping bank, snorting, and tossing his gallant head.

Burnett rode forward from the group. 'By Heaven, Barney, that's a ripping horse in the water — I never saw anything to beat him yet. She's running big to-day. Can we cross 'em?'

'Sure thing', said Allen. 'I've crossed when it was four foot higher, but we'll have to put 'em in above the island to allow for the swing of her, and, of course, we'll have to watch for trees coming down.'

'Right', said the drover, 'I don't want to stop on this side if I can help it. We'll put a hundred in first and see how they get on. He sent a couple of his men back to bring up the leading bullocks.

* * *

Allen stood by his horse. His shirt and trousers clung to him, and the drip of the water darkened the sand where he stood. He was strangely silent and forbore to laugh and jest as was his wont on these occasions. Now and again he patted the grey horse on the neck or stroked his wet ears. Presently the bullocks came up, big-horned, wild-eyed, ringing and frightened.

'Gently there!' said Burnett, steadying the great nervy creatures down to the water. There they checked and tried to turn, but the little band of men pressed them down the bank, and presently, lowing with a low moaning note, they took the water in a bunch.

Burnett and one of his men swam their horses on the top side of them; Allen, as was his usual custom, took the dangerous position on the lower side, and with it the main responsibility and burden of the crossing. With a confidence born of years of practice, he set the grey into the water, and the old horse, well broken to the work, started swimming quietly without fuss or fret. For twenty yards or so the bullocks swam steadily, then the full force of the current caught them; they began to waver and ring round, and try to turn back to land. Allen urged his horse forward, and swung the stock whip which he always carried. It would have been a dangerous moment for any man less practiced in his work than Barney Allen, but he knew every move in the game, and so did the horse, and veering upward in the strong current, they straightened the leaders and compelled the bunch to swim forward. Presently they seemed to catch sight of the further shore, and ploughing steadily on, with horns clashing and heads low in the water, they made straight for the landing-place. Behind them the three men floated above their strongly-swimming horses, and though carried swiftly down stream, seemed in no imminent danger. Allen, looking forward over the grey ears of his favourite horse, saw, far off in the gum-trees, the glitter of a white dress. A low groan escaped him, and was lost in the thunder of the angry waters. Then a strange thing happened. This man, who had crossed many hundreds of thousands of cattle, and had swum his horse over the flooded Murray waters times out of number, who knew every move of his dangerous trade, suddenly seemed to lose his head, dropped his weight upon his horse and pulled like a tyro at the bridle.

The grey plunged and snorted as the current pressed him and he found himself helpless to resist it. Vainly he fought for his head, his master seemed to be suddenly bereft of his senses, he tugged and hauled at the reins, and turned the grey completely round. For a moment there was a whirling struggle with the tide, and then both went under, to re-appear — apart — forty yards further down the river.

Burnett's man was the first to land. 'Good God!' he cried, as he slipped from his dripping mare, 'Barney's gone — what made his horse turn over like that — I never knew that grey horse fail him before.'

Burnett splashed past him through the trodden slush of the landing place. 'There was nothing wrong with the grey', he said, 'it was Allen himself — he pulled him over — I don't know why — but he pulled him over!'

A couple of hundred yards further down the cruel river flung up on a bank of sand — dead — those two strong swimmers, horse and man; and only the girl in the white dress guessed why Barney Allen had chosen that crossing for his last.

Mulberry

MULBERRY was an old ragged-lipped, splint-covered red roan mare which we used on the station for running up the horses, lending to the Chinese gardener when he wanted to ride to town, and putting at the disposal of any visitor who was timid and required a quiet and reliable hack. Her paces were rough — 'She'd shake a man's teeth down his neck!' was the head-stockman's verdict — but she was honest and trustworthy; and Billy, the horse-boy, who rode her oftener than anyone else, said she could gallop like a racehorse. However, as Billy always had a tale about his horses being able to gallop, no one paid any attention to him.

Mulberry was not bred on the station, but had been sold to the Boss for a mere song by a passing drover, when she was too thin and weak to travel further with his mob of horses going south to grass from the drought-bound Queensland Border. She carried a Queensland brand, a dainty, well-bred head, and a heart as big as a bullock. We simply knew her as a good, honest old slave, by no means a beauty, but not the worst horse on the station by any means.

One night we were all racing in from the drafting-yards, a practice winked at by the authorities, though it was generally admitted to be the very deuce on horses' legs to come hammering down the woolshed road when the ground was like iron. Billy, the boy, happened to be with us that day, as we were short-handed, and he was riding old Mulberry. The last man was scarcely on his horse before Dave, the overseer, shouted 'Off!' and stole a couple of lengths start on Brown Duchess. I jammed the spurs into Skylark and followed; Ted, Hughie, Mulkitty Fred, and Harry flashed up in a cloud and joined us. Nobody thought it worth while to wait for the boy, and he was only tumbling into his saddle when the rest of us were a dozen lengths away. It is just short of a mile from the yards to the horse-paddock gate, and we cut it down at racing pace.

Now, Harry was riding Rosebud, and Rosebud is pretty fast. You need to steal a good few lengths from her in a mile if you expect to beat her on the average station horse, so Dave sent the Duchess along for all she was worth, and soon had a clear lead. Skylark can go no faster than you can kick your hat, and I very soon dropped behind and swallowed buckets of dust for the rest of the journey. Even old Mulberry passed me, as I noted with a cynical smile. Hughie was the next to drop back; he was riding that half-broken St. Clair colt,

green as grass, and it soon had enough. Mulkitty Fred was riding First Toss, and
she began to buck, and he had to pull up. Dave, Ted, and Harry had the race to
themselves with Billy the boy slogging along somewhere behind them. So, at
least, we thought; but when we reached the gate we found the true state of
affairs disclosed. Dave had led on Brown Duchess for three-quarters of a mile,
looking back for Rosebud to make her inevitable dash to the front. Three
hundred yards from the winning tree something flashed past him. It wasn't
Rosebud; it was old Mulberry, and she won by ten lengths; Rosebud beat Dave
a neck for second place, Ted on Blue Bonnet was half a dozen lengths behind
them.

'What the devil' Dave was saying as I came up. 'How the devil did you get
here, kid, on that old crock?'

'I told you she could gallop', said the boy.

'How far behind were you when we started?' asked Dave, ignoring the
triumph in the tone of the winner.

'Bout a quarter o' a mile', said the boy, lying bravely.

Harry snorted, but Hughie, who came up at that moment, said 'Well, he
was nearly a hundred yards behind you, anyway. That old mare's as fast as the
wind!'

Billy looked pleased.

'I told yer she could gallop', he said.

We all rode thoughtfully home together, and many a glance was thrown at
the ragged-looking old mare as she paddled along the track, throwing her lean
head up and down, the black sweat dripping from her red-brown flanks.

'If that mare was fed and trained', said Hughie, 'she'd win a good race in
Sydney. Rosebud can beat Mark Twain over a mile at level weights, and Mark
Twain won the Opening Handicap at Rosehill with eight-stone-seven.'

We said nothing, but eyed the mare with renewed interest.

Billy leaned forward and patted her neck. He was a proud boy that evening.

That night at supper in the homestead I made up my mind to try and buy
old Mulberry. I was fond of racing, in fact, all we fellows on Gidyea Plains had
a leaning towards it, and I thought of the fame I might win and the money I
might make if I owned a horse which could beat Rosebud over a mile,
remembering that Rosebud could beat Mark Twain, and that Mark Twain had
beaten some very good horses on a suburban course.

After supper it was the custom for Harry and me, as young jackeroos, to
retire to the verandah for our smoke, while Dave interviewed the Boss about
the next day's work and reported the happenings of the day just over.

This evening I thought, as I lay at ease in the big cane chair and puffed
rings of smoke and dreamed of winning the Sydney Cup with a red roan mare
that started at the nice price of 25 to 1, that I overheard Dave say something
about 'Mulberry'. This annoyed me, for I didn't want the Boss to hear about

the race and put a prohibitive price on the mare. But I need not have worried
about that. As I found out afterwards, Dave had merely remarked casually: 'I'm
buying up a few old screws to send to that brother of mine at Winbadgery. Do
you want to sell old Mulberry? I'm afraid I can't go higher than a couple of
quid for the sort my brother wants.'

The Boss looked up quickly.

'No, I think not', he said, and the interview ended.

Knowing nothing of this question of Dave's, I entered the dining room as
he came out, and after reporting to the Boss on some business he had given me
to do that day, I asked carelessly:

'What would you take for old Mulberry, Boss?'

The old man looked at me quizzically, then he said quietly:

'I don't wish to sell the mare at present, thank you!'

There was no more to be said, and I retired. As I reached the verandah,
Mulkitty Fred, the stockman, swaggering as usual, with a loosely-knotted red
handkerchief round his neck came across the little garden.

'Boss in?' he asked, in his free and easy manner, hand on hip, hat on the
back of his head.

'Yes', I said. 'Shall I tell him you want to see him?'

The man nodded, and I delivered the message. The Boss heaved himself
out of his easy-chair and came to the edge of the verandah.

'Well?' he asked, rather sharply — he was annoyed at being disturbed at this
unorthodox moment. *'Well?'*

'Can I speak to ye alone, Boss?' asked the bushman.

The Boss courteously stepped out into the garden. Fred spoke low, but I
heard the word 'Mulberry' — and then, 'if she's cheap.'

Presently the Boss was back with a smile on his face, and Fred clicked the
latch of the garden gate and went away towards the men's hut with a dejected
look about his shoulders.

Harry got up and followed the Boss into the dining-room. He told me
afterwards about it. He began proceedings by saying it looked like rain; and to
his great surprise the Boss burst out laughing.

'Get to business!' said the Boss.

'Well, I was only going to ask you, sir, if you felt like selling old Mulberry —
the old roan mare, you know!'

'Yes, I know', said the Boss, facetiously. 'No, my boy, I'm afraid I can't let
you have her!'

Harry was very much disappointed, and came out to me on the verandah.

Later on, when Dave and Harry and myself went into the house, the Boss
asked the overseer what it all meant.

'What's the game, Davie? Has old Mulberry grown gold hoofs, or what is
it?'

Dave looked a little shamefaced at being caught by the rest of us, and as he had had first chance, the biggest laugh was against him. He told about our race and the newly discovered speed of the old roan mare.

The Boss leaned back in his chair and laughed uproariously; we thought he would hurt himself.

'Well, you see', he said at last, 'I couldn't have sold her to any of you, anyway, for I got rid of her just before supper.'

'Who to?' asked Dave, eagerly and ungrammatically.

'Billy, the horse-boy!' said the Boss.

The Mountain Hut

SEVERAL YEARS ago the Lachlan River district of New South Wales was thrown into a state of unusual excitement by the desperate deeds of an aboriginal named Barwon Jacky. This native, who was employed on one of the large sheep stations in the neighbourhood, had fallen foul of another black fellow, had split his skull with a waddy and flung him into the river. The local police attempted to arrest the murderer, who had escaped to the rough country in the ranges of the upper Lachlan, and was known to be armed with a stolen Winchester rifle and a considerable supply of ammunition. The fugitive, hard pressed by a mounted trooper and his black trackers, shot the policeman and again escaped for the time being to the Bush. Branded with the blood mark of double murder, with a price upon his head living or dead, the outlaw had, at the time I speak of, evaded pursuit for a fortnight or more. A large force of police had been drafted into the district and the mountains and gullies were full of troopers and trackers searching for the cunning black fellow whose bushcraft and knowledge of the lie of the land made his capture a difficult, and some thought an impossible, undertaking.

When, after many days' search, nothing had been seen of the fugitive, the local bushmen gave it as their opinion that the murderer had succeeded in getting safely away from the district and was probably by that time across the Queensland Border and hidden in the huge camps of the Warrego or the Barcoo, where the identification of any one black fellow among hundreds of his fellow natives would be impossible except to the private individual or policeman who knew him intimately.

At a moment when even the most sanguine of the pursuing officers of the law had begun to accept this theory, a settler in the ranges, who knew Barwon Jacky, rode into the town of Forbes and reported that the outlaw had appeared at his lonely house the previous night, had covered the inmates with his rifle, and demanded food and a horse. He was given some meat and flour but, becoming alarmed, had left before a horse could be procured from the horse paddock. The black trackers were at once put upon the trail and the outlaw was followed in the direction of Parkes, where again all trace of him was lost.

One day, one of our boundary riders coming in from the back of the run brought a tale of having seen a ragged and footsore black fellow with a rifle in his hand threading through the thick scrub in the mountain paddock just ahead of him. As the sound of the boundary rider's horse hoofs reached him the native swung quickly round and tossed his rifle to his shoulder and the bushman, knowing the desperate character of Barwon Jacky, and assuming that it was he, wheeled his horse and rode rapidly away through the covering trees. Buoyed with fresh hopes from this information the eager police drew their cordon closer, and the sergeants who called almost hourly at the head station had ever some fresh tale of a still more recent clue, until the capture of the murderer seemed to be only a matter of hours. Things were in this state when one morning we stood about the-stockyard holding our saddled horses and awaiting the Manager's arrival for our day's orders as to the working of the sheep. Presently he opened the wicket-gate of his garden and came striding towards us with a clink of dragging spurs. After giving the boundary riders and stockmen their orders he came over and said to me: 'I hear some of our sheep have been getting out of the Mountain Paddock into Henderson's selection, I wish you would ride the East side fence to-day, Billy, and see that it is all right; camp at the Hut and come in early in the morning. To-morrow's Christmas Day you know, and you'll want to go up to the races at Allan's!'

I nodded, to show him that I heard; but the order was not a pleasant one, for I remembered that the outlaw black fellow was somewhere in the ranges of the Mountain Paddock, and it had even been suggested that he made the Mountain Hut his headquarters. This hut was an old tumble down place that had once been a boundary rider's dwelling. It was in the loneliest part of the great heath-covered ranges, was seven miles from the nearest house and thirty miles from the head station. The Mountain Paddock was a huge enclosure of thirty thousand acres, and so far away that to ride the whole way round the fence in one day was too serious a journey, so we were in the habit of riding one half of the fence and carrying a blanket and some food and camping for the night at the old hut. It was an eerie picnic at any time; now, with an armed black fellow, hunted and desperate, liable at any moment to arrive upon the scene, the outlook was less inviting than ever. I hesitated, then mounted my mare and rode after the Boss.

'I don't much care about camping alone at the Mountain Hut to-night', I said, 'what if Barwon Jacky should pay me a call. I think I'd rather ride home here, even if it takes me till ten o'clock to do it.'

'Oh! Rot, Billy!' said our Manager, who feared neither man nor woman, horse nor God nor devil, 'Barwon Jacky is much too busy dodging the troopers to come near a hut where, for all he knows, the police may be camped waiting for him. Don't be such a suckling, man!' He gathered up his reins as though argument were at an end but, being as kindhearted as he was brusque, he turned in his saddle and called out: 'Well, it is a lonely hole, Billy; take young

Steve with you; let him ride the West fence, meet at the hut at dark; come in as early as you like in the morning!'

I sought out Steve, the horse-boy, and he was delighted to vary his usual routine of water-carting and wood-chopping with a long ride through the paddocks. 'I hope we'll get a look at Barwon Jacky', he said, and off he went to catch his horse.

We strapped blankets in front of us on our saddles, got some bread and cold mutton from the cook, some tea and sugar from the store, and with our quart-pots jingling from the saddle-dees rode slowly away into the shimmering sand ridges. It was fiercely hot and we nodded drowsily over our reins, though the sun was not yet at its full height. At the slip-rails leading into the Mountain Paddock we parted, Steve jogging away down the right hand fence across a cane-grass swamp, I to the left over a rocky ridge and into the shade of a deep scrub.

There is nothing in the world in dull monotony to be compared with riding fences on a sheep-station. Mile after mile the little horse track follows the post and wire, now leaving it for a moment to avoid a fallen tree, now coming so close to it that one's knee almost brushes the posts; and all the time one's eyes must be keen to detect a loose wire or a broken one.

It was hot and close in the shadow of the scrub. It was hotter still on the open plain, where the wires shimmered and danced in the heat haze. After following the fence for five or six miles I halted at a little pool in a creek that crossed the boundary, and getting off the mare pulled the saddle off and put on the hobbles. Then I lit a fire, boiled my quart-pot and made tea and ate my humble lunch of cold mutton and damper. After a half-hour's smoke I saddled up and rode slowly on, stopping here and there to tighten a wire or straighten a post. As we topped a rocky rise the bay mare pricked her ears, and presently I heard the drum of hoofs approaching. Then a trooper on a splendid brown horse appeared suddenly in front of me on the narrow path. After exchanging the usual bush greetings I asked him whether they had run Barwon Jacky to ground yet. 'Not actually', said the sun-browned trooper, 'but we know to within a few miles where he is, and it's only a matter of hours. Sergeant Peters saw him not three miles from where we are standing, yesterday morning. He is done up, short of food and, I believe, thoroughly desperate; and riding through these ranges is nervous work, for he may be lurking behind any bush, and if he gets first drop on anything in uniform he won't mind pulling the trigger!'

'And I daresay he won't be very particular to ascertain that it is a uniform before he shoots', I suggested, feeling a little uneasy, 'even boundary riders are his enemies now!'

'Quite true', said the trooper. 'Have you got a fill of tobacco on you? — Thanks! — Good afternoon!' And he gathered up his reins, touched the brown with the spur, and clattered away down the ridge.

I rode on, thinking deeply, and not feeling very comfortable. It was a queer sensation, this jogging along in the undergrowth of the ranges, miles and miles from any human habitation, with the understanding that at any moment a hunted and desperate man, hearing the hoofs of a horse and imagining the presence of one of his pursuers, might crouch behind one of the low bunches of heath which edged the track and with well-aimed rifle end one's hopes and fears for ever.

The sun dipped behind the gum-saplings, and the shadows began to settle on the Bush. I found my eyes often straying from the fence as I glanced from time to time into the darkening undergrowth. Once the mare stopped suddenly and snorted as something crashed out of a bush beside her. My heart leapt into my mouth; but it was only a frightened wallaby that went scurrying away into the rocks above us. Gradually the gloaming thickened and I was still half a mile from the old hut, so I set spurs to the bay and trotted briskly along till I came to the wicket-gate that led through the fence towards the hut There was no sign of Steve yet but, as he had a few miles further to go than I had, I hardly expected him to be at our rendezvous before me. I rode through the gate and along the little path that led to the hut. There it stood, weird and ghostly in the gathering shadows, not by any means the sort of place which a man would choose to spend the night in by himself, and least of all when the surrounding bush was the resort of a notorious criminal.

The weather had been very hot and dry, but there was a splendid pool of water in the small creek below the hut and plenty of grass on the little patch of open plain which surrounded the building. I took off my saddle and bridle, hobbled out the mare, and gathered sticks to make a fire. With my thoughts still running on Barwon Jacky I peered into the hut, half expecting to see him rise, rifle in hand, from its shadows. But the old one-roomed house wore its usual aspect of uninhabited decay The old bagging fluttered in rags from the walls. The fireplace was full of the usual grey ashes where we had burned many myall logs to the Goddess of Loneliness in unappreciated vigils. There was no furniture in the place except a couple of upturned soap boxes. In one corner lay a half-bag of potatoes, the only provisions we thought it necessary to leave in this lonely camp. Instinctively I assumed that as the potatoes had not been taken Barwon Jacky was not in the habit of making this place his headquarters, and I felt relieved. A loud rattling noise made me spring to my feet as I was putting a match to some dry twigs in the fireplace, and my heart began to thump. I soon realised that it was only the mare, nosing about on the bank of the creek, who had set a tin bucket rolling among the stones. I lit the fire, found an old bucket and took it and my quart-pot to the creek for water. It was now quite dark and every sound in the gum-saplings suggested a possible enemy, dark-skinned, treacherous, sneaking into position for a rifle shot.

I filled the tins and went back to the hut. Here I busied myself with boiling a few potatoes, and water for tea. Then I stepped out into the darkness to listen for Steve's coming. The Bush was absolutely, ghostily, still. Not a cicada chirped, not a frog croaked. I thought perhaps Steve had gone home after all. I could not even hear the hobbles of my own mare. The loneliness was overpowering. I returned to the desolate ingle and made up the fire, but half the hut remained in shadow and I found myself looking round from time to time as vague shapes seemed to gather out of the gloom. The water boiled in the quart-pot, the potatoes were cooked and strained and heaped on the rather rusty tin plate which comprised our dinner service, and once again I went to the door and looked out. The silence was more accentuated than ever, the Bush seemed to be preparing with bated breath for some fearful tragedy. I could stand it no longer, the deathly stillness was getting on my nerves. I raised my voice in a loud 'Coo-ee!' The sound died away in a kind of sob among the ridges. There was no answer, and I began to get anxious about Steve, who, unless he had lost his way, ought to have been with me an hour before. Again I coo-ee-d, and again. The silence crept closer than ever, and I closed the door and went back into the house, piling every available bit of timber on the fire and so chasing the shadows out of the corners. There was nothing to read; there was no work to do; nothing to take my mind from the one thought that now completely obsessed me.

I began to curse Steve who had left me in this uncomfortable position Was he lost, or had some accident happened to him? Perhaps he had run across Barwon Jacky and that rifle — ! Hark! What was that? The snapping of a dead branch just outside the hut, then the long whistling snort of the bay mare, then the scramble and clatter of her hoofs as she rushed through the darkness. Then there came a sound like the soft fall of naked feet tap-tapping round the hut. I shivered, then roused myself sharply. A wallaby of course. The gully was full of them. It was a wonder the old mare did not get used to them. Then something fumbled at the string of the doorlatch. Hulloh! Steve, of course. The door was opened quickly and I felt every hair on my head slowly rising, for there, barefooted, bare-headed, with a scratch across his forehead where some branch had torn him, pathetic with his fluttering rags and pleading hunted eyes, stood Barwon Jacky, the outlaw. He was apparently unarmed, and he held up one hand with a gesture of truce. He caught sight of the steaming plateful of potatoes, and with a wolfish eagerness he fell upon them, gobbling and grunting like a wild beast as he thrust handful after handful into his mouth while the other hand was held towards me as though to stay any possible interference. Instinctively I knew I had nothing to fear from the poor hunted creature, and I forgot the loneliness of the spot. I knew that he was unarmed and weak from hunger and that, man to man, I was more than a match for him if we had to wrestle for our lives; still I watched him narrowly, for I meant to throw no chance away, and to give no opportunity for treachery.

He finished the potatoes, then crammed my portion of bread and beef into his mouth, and still I never stirred. The poor wretch was famishing, and though I saw my last hopes of supper disappearing I raised no hand to stay him. He lifted the bucket in which I had boiled the potatoes and searched greedily in it, still unsatisfied. I shook my head. Then for the first time he looked at me steadily. His eyes expressed anger, then fear, then childish pleading, and, in a hoarse tone, holding out both hands in supplication he said in accents that might have melted the hardest heart 'Baal you givem me up to the troopers, Boss!'

'No, Jacky', I said standing up and facing him, touched by his pathetic appeal, 'I won't give you up, never you fear! Sit down here and rest and have a drink of tea!' He approached cautiously, evidently suspecting treachery. I held out my hands to show I had no weapon concealed, then said quickly to gain his confidence. 'Didn't you hear my horse, Jacky — weren't you afraid there might be a trooper waiting in the old hut?'

'Too dam hungry! Better bin shootem 'n die all same a jumbuck longa drought!' said the black fellow, heaving a great sigh which might have been the protest of a too suddenly loaded stomach or the relief of a soul that has suspected an enemy and found a friend.

'Where's your rifle?' I asked.

'Cartridge all done. Sling him away. Too dam heavy', said the outcast.

He finished the tea and set the quart-pot down in the ashes, then his head drooped forward, and huddled up on the empty soapbox, worn and exhausted, poor Jacky fell asleep. I stood at the opposite side of the big open fireplace and watched him. There was something pitiful beyond all expression in the emaciated frame on which the tattered rags hung loosely, in the drawn and haggard face shining like ebony in the firelight, and in the thin claw-like hands that rested on his knees. Were we right, we the white sons of civilisation, the slaves of law and order and a stringent moral code, to hunt down this poor creature whose primitive instincts had impelled him to use the club and the rifle in a moment of mad passion? I had seen much of the blacks at station work, had flung them their scraps of meat at the dinner hour as one flings a bone to a dog, and had counted them but little better than the brutes; but now I faced a human being in dire distress, a man, of primitive passions, but still a man.

And then I remembered my position, the loneliness of the hut in which I stood unarmed and alone, face to face with a half-wild creature who had taken life on two occasions and who might in a frenzy of sudden hate or fear be tempted to take it again. As I watched the sinister sleeping face of my companion and harboured such thoughts as these he suddenly started to his feet, gazing wildly around him like a hunted beast at bay. Then he recognised me. 'Baal you givem up, Boss!' he pleaded, and again I reassured him. 'Lie down and camp, Jacky, I'll not let anyone touch you.'

I might have explained to him that we were many miles from any human being, except perhaps poor Steve who might be wandering somewhere in the barren ridges having lost the fence line in the dark, but I did not wish to call his attention to the defencelessness of my own position. I showed him a heap of old bags in the furthest corner of the hut and there he lay down, utterly exhausted, and fell again into a deep slumber, while I made up my mind to a long hungry vigil. At first I thought of stealing out of the house, catching my horse, and taking my chance in the pitch-black Bush, but it occurred to me that the black fellow might wake, suspect treachery, and creeping on me in the cover of the darkness make his own escape by a well-directed blow. So I determined to stay beside him, to rouse him at the first streak of dawn, and then bidding him a friendly good-bye to leave him to cope with his fate as best he might. I had no power, had I wished it, to protect him from the inevitable consequences of his actions, yet I felt that I could not give him up to the police or bring him nearer to his punishment by a single word of mine. And so the outlaw slept and I nodded, sleepy, by the low fire, rousing myself every now and then with a start as I fancied that an ebony hand was raised above me.

The slow night dragged its interminable length along. There was no sound in the absolute stillness save the heavy breathing of the black fellow and the occasional rustle as a burnt stick fell into the ashes.

At last a faint grey light in the wide chimney betokened the dawn. I rose from my cramped position and moved towards the door. The black was on his feet in an instant with the quick apprehension of the hunted. 'Time to be on the road, Jacky!' I said, pleasantly. The light of understanding crept into his tired eyes. Suddenly he drew himself up, listening intently. I, too, listened and heard the tramp of hoofs on stone, shod horses, and it needed no click of dangling carbines and whisper of bridle chains to tell me the police were upon us. I turned to Jacky, doubly anxious to secure his escape and to make him understand that it was by no treachery of mine that the troopers were there. 'Police! Look alive, man! Tear a hole in that bagging at the back, run for the clump of saplings, then into the bed of the creek and go for your life! So long, Jacky! Good luck to you!' For a moment he hesitated, then tore at the ragged hanging and broken laths; a scramble and he was gone. The trampling hoofs came nearer and out of the morning grey rode a sergeant and three troopers with blankets strapped on their saddles and hobbles tied round their horses' necks. The troopers turned off to water their horses in the creek and the sergeant heeled his tall chestnut right up to the doorway where I stood. 'Good morning, young fellow!' he said, 'You've a lonely camp here; you're from the station I suppose?'

'Yes! My mate failed to turn up last night. Got bushed I suppose. It is a lonely place, I assure you!'

'Well!' said the officer, 'you've a good nerve to camp alone here with that nigger loose in the ranges. By Gad, you have!'

I received the undeserved compliment as though it were mine by right. 'Sorry I can't offer you breakfast, Sergeant, but I only carried enough tucker for myself. Where's your tracker?'

'Sent him back to town for bread and meat. He's to meet me at the Black Waterholes, three miles from here at sunrise; so I must be pushing on.'

'When are you going to nail the black fellow?' I asked, bidding for time, and wondering how far down the creek the poor fugitive had travelled.

'In two days at latest', said the big man, as his comrades rejoined him, crashing through the dead timber on the creek bank. Waving his hand to me he set spurs to the chestnut and the little party of four cantered away over the ridge at right angles to the creek.

I hurriedly caught my mare and threw the saddle on her and sped home to the station, breathing no word of my adventure to anyone until three weeks later I heard of Barwon Jacky having safely crossed the Queensland Border, three hundred miles away.

Steve, who had left the fence to chase a kangaroo, had been lost, and after riding all night in the Mountain Paddock arrived at the Station only half an hour earlier than myself. From all accounts his night had been nearly as weird and lonely as my own.

Barwon Jacky was eventually run to earth by the Queensland police, and paid the penalty of his misdeeds, but somehow I never regretted — murderer though he was — that I acted squarely to him that Christmas Eve in the Mountain Hut.

Click O' The Latch

DAVE WAS riding the frontage plain in the Woolshed Paddock, driving weaners back from the stock route, when a man on a legweary chestnut rode up to him and asked: 'Have you seen anything of a piebald horse with a bell on him?'

'A white-eyed brute, as lean as a rake, with hook bones like a cow?' asked the overseer.

'That's him!' said the stranger.

'You'll find him standing in that clump of mulga over there. If you don't rescue him soon and give him a feed the crows'll have him!'

'It'll take a fast crow to catch him', said the man.

'How's that?' asked Dave, interested at once.

'Because that old piebald's one of the speediest half-milers that ever came out of Queensland.'

'Rot!' said our overseer.

'It's gospel truth I'm telling you', said the drover, for such he turned out to be.

Now Dave happened that day to be riding My Lady, the little brown mare that won the Autumn Handicap in Bourke, and she was 'pretty slippy', as the bushmen say, over half a mile, or indeed over any distance up to a mile.

'I'll run this mare against him from here to that dead pine tree on the sandhill for a pound a side, owners up!' said he, always ready for a match on the slightest provocation.

'Done!' said the drover quietly, 'I'll catch him now.' They rode down together to the mulga trees and the drover caught the piebald without trouble, and changed the saddle from his chestnut, tying the latter to a tree.

'Better leave that bell on him', suggested Dave, as he watched the man fumbling with the strap, 'it'll help to frighten the crows off him. Besides, if he drops dead in the race, as he looks likely to do, I'll know to stop riding when the bell stops ringing, and that'll save me riding with my head over my shoulder.'

The stranger laughed good-naturedly, but he removed the bell. Dave's chaff did not disconcert him, and the overseer guessed that he had a fast horse and knew it; so, as they jogged quietly towards the point from which they had agreed to start the race, he took a careful look at the piebald. He was very, very thin, and you could have hung your hat on his hip bones; but he had a superb shoulder, deep galloping quarters, a long rein, a lean, determined head, and flat-boned legs of steel. A wicked eye showing a deal of white, and his unfortunate circus colour, detracted from his appearance, otherwise, in spite of his poor condition, you would have called him a good-looking, racing-like horse.

For a moment the overseer repented of his wager. He knew well that many of the cattlemen get hold of extraordinarily smart horses from the northern stations, with which they make money out of boundary riders and jackeroos who fancy their pet horses can gallop. Dave was no new chum, and no pigeon to be plucked by these hawks of the road, but a man of experience, and only the fact that he knew he was riding a specially fast mare had induced him to make this match with a man of whom he knew nothing. However, it was too late to withdraw, and, in any case, Dave was a good sportsman who loved a race for its own sake — win or lose — and he knew he would have a good gallop for his money.

The ground chosen for deciding the wager was a stretch of rather more than half a mile, the first part of it over loose and rather rough ground, the second part over the firm, red surface of the sandhill, finishing up a slight incline at the dead pine-tree that formed the winning-post.

The start was by mutual consent. Like most speedy short-distance horses the piebald was off the mark like a dash; but the mare was a quick starter too, and both were into their stride simultaneously. For a hundred yards they ran neck and neck, then the mare drew out a length ahead, the piebald rolling in the crumbling ground.

Once out upon the firm going of the sandhill, however, the big horse lay down to his work like a racer, and, drawing away at every stride, won with ridiculous ease by half a dozen lengths.

Dave got off his sweating mare and loosed the girths. 'Well', he said, 'that old bit of patchwork of yours is most undoubtedly a flier, for I know this mare of mine is none too slow.' He fumbled in his pocket and brought out a crumpled one-pound note, which he handed over to his opponent. 'Here you are', he said, 'you've won it fair enough. When I saw that chap standing under those trees this morning I wouldn't have given that note for him — bell and all. I daresay you wouldn't take fifty pounds for him?'

'Try me!' said the drover, pocketing the note, and rubbing some river-mud off the piebald's shoulder.

'I'll give you twenty pounds for him', said Dave.

'Done!' said the stranger, 'and you can have his bell. When it rings round your camp at night it will remind you what a fast horse you own'.

Then he went on in more serious tones, 'Mark my words, Boss, you've got a hack to be proud of, and a racehorse that can beat the best of them!'

'I don't think much of his colour, anyway!' said Dave.

'O, colour! You can paint him blue if you prefer it. It won't make him go any faster!'

'That's true enough', said the purchaser of the piebald. 'Come up to the station and I'll write you a cheque for him.'

'Thanks. I'll take him up to the camp first and knock some of that mud off him, and comb the burrs out of his tail, and pull his mane a bit. He'll look better then. I'll bring him up this evening. He just wants a week or two's rest on good grass, and he'll be as nice a horse as ever you looked at!'

'Right you are', said Dave, 'bring him up this evening.' And he rode home well pleased with his bargain, for a horse that could beat My Lady as easily as this piebald had done, even supposing there was ten or twelve pounds' difference in the weights, was a horse not to be despised. Dave chuckled to himself as he looked forward in fancy to the matches he would win against Queensland drovers and their half-mile sprinters.

At sundown the drover, who gave his name as Nick Pierce, and said he was travelling out to Eulo to pick up his droving plant there, came jogging up on the chestnut, leading Dave's piebald bargain, which looked all the better for the grooming it had received. The long tail had been pulled and combed, the mane thinned, the coat well brushed. Even the wicked eye seemed to show less white than before, and though nothing could hide the horse's poverty, he was really a very good-looking framework, and apparently only wanted good feed and a rest.

After learning that the horse's name was Click o' the Latch, and that he was a famous sprinter well known in Queensland, Dave handed over his cheque, took possession of the seller's receipt, and led his new purchase away to the paddock.

Except for an occasional glimpse of his spotted hide flashing in and out among the trees in the spelling paddock, we saw no more of Click o' the Latch for over a month. Then he came in, bucking fresh from the bluegrass, seemed annoyed at finding that Dave was a finished horseman who could not be thrown, and eventually settled down to quiet work as a station hack. No sooner was the fat worked off him than Dave pulled him out to run a half-mile with old St. Clair, the station trial-horse. The bay beat him easily by a dozen lengths, and Dave was disgusted. He trimmed the piebald's hoofs, put up a lighter rider, and tried him again with My Lady, who romped away from him with her head in the air.

Dave, who had been bragging to us a good deal about his new racehorse, was rather downcast, but said little, and went on hacking the piebald at station work.

It was a month or two after this that a travelling horse-breaker put up for a night at the station. Seeing Dave's piebald in the yard in the morning he said: 'By Jimminy, that old piebald horse is the dead spit of Nick Pierce's Click o' the Latch.'

'It *is* Nick Pierce's Click o' the Latch', said Dave, with a remnant of pride still left regarding his purchase, now that he had found at last some one who had evidently known the piebald in his days of fame.

'No, *that* he ain't', said the breaker, 'for I saw old Click win the Birthday Cup at Hughenden only last week. It's very like him, though!'

Dave stroked his fair moustache meditatively.

'*Very* like him', the breaker went on, 'same markings, same build; not as big a horse though, and not near as wild a looking customer.'

'Do you know Pierce at all?' Dave asked.

'Know him!' said the tamer of two-year-olds. 'I know him like a book, an' I don't think much of him. Him and me travelled down the Paroo together one summer, but he played me a dirty trick, he did, and we parted not exactly friends.'

'What sort of a fellow is he?'

'What sort of a chap? Well, he'd go through your pockets for your false teeth; he'd rob a child of its bread and jam; that's the sort of chap *he* is!'

Dave whistled softly. 'Pretty wise about horses?' he asked.

'What he don't know ain't worth tellin' to a priest', said the horseman.

Dave told of the match — of the deal — and of the delivery of the horse, spruced up and looking a different animal from what he appeared in the morning.

The horsebreaker leaned on the stockyard fence, and spat with deliberation into the sand of the yard. 'Piebalds ain't so *very* rare up here', he said significantly.

'You think he had two of them?' Dave asked.

'Knowin' the sneakin' hound as I know him', said the breaker 'I'm dead *sure* of it!'

Silverfoot

SILVERFOOT was the shapely brumby stallion which, with his little mob of four mares, three three-year-olds, a two-year-old, and two foals, constituted the remainder of the once considerable community of wild horses which ran on the Warrangoona boundary. He was a beautiful dark brown horse, with four white feet and fetlocks, from which he had gained his name among the bushmen. He was wild and shy, with all the cunning of his outlaw ancestors; and though many a horseman would have forfeited a year's wages to have had him safely in the station stockyard, with a green-hide, halter on that lean, beautiful head of his, Silverfoot ran free in the bluegrass, holding his mastery over the young stallions, and leading the wild mares to the water in the moonlit nights. The boundary rider at the Box Hut would often hear the wild horse whinny to his mob as he trotted down through the scrub to the river, and, turning over on his rough bunk, would sink into dreams of following brumbies through the mulga, and of a white-footed horse in the lead, that no stock-horse could keep pace with; for the dark brown stallion was in the minds of many men. They knew his breeding, these horse-loving bushmen; they knew the story of the brown thoroughbred which had escaped, some twelve years before, from Opal Downs station — breaking away from his groom at exercise, and which, in spite of the best efforts of the hardest riders in the West, was never recovered; they knew that this Silverfoot, as they called him, was the progeny of that same famous Silver King, and that, in spite of the brumby cross in him, he was likely to be one of the fastest fliers in the Border country. Marvellous tales were in circulation of his extraordinary bursts of speed when chased by the fastest stock-horses. Nothing could live with him for pace, and the further he went the further he distanced his pursuers — a token of his great stamina and endurance. Even George Lee on his famous cream horse, which the bushmen said could gallop all day without tiring, and which was fast as a deer to boot, was fain to confess that here at last was a brumby which he could neither head nor hold — a horse worth winning, by the gods!

In the earlier days of Western settlement a horse such as this, running wild in the Bush, might have escaped notice among the thousands of his brethren; but brumbies had become scarce upon the Border. They had been yarded in large numbers, and sold in the Southern markets; they had been decimated by drought — the increased amount of wire fencing having cut them off from their known watering-places; and in some cases they had been victims of the rifles of the station men, who considered them a menace to the grass-country, sacred now to sheep. The few that remained were wilder than ever. It was a case of the survival of the fittest, and only the fastest and most determined and most cunning could hope to elude the bush-riders who from time to time built yards in the pine scrub, and organised chases in the hope of their capture.

With every brumby in the district now known by sight, it was not to be wondered that the white-footed stallion attracted so much attention, and that wildly exaggerated tales of his speed and stamina were floating around every hotel-bar and station verandah. He became a fetish in the land, standing for everything that was desirable and unattainable — a sort of demi-god.

Of all the bushmen who coveted Silverfoot none was keener than Arthur Haverfield, the son of the owner of Warrangoona Station. Acting as overseer on his father's run, he was constantly brought into contact with the little mob of brumbies, and had long made up his mind that some day he would own the famous brown stallion. From time to time he organised hunts, in which he and the best riders of his staff did their best to yard the evasive wild horses, but time and again he failed to effect his purpose, and was obliged to return home empty-handed, with knocked-up horses and disgusted men. Yet he never made any secret of the fact that his great ambition was to yard Silverfoot. In this desire he was aided and abetted by George Lee, the selector, who never failed to lend his assistance when the station men were out after the wild horses.

One morning, when work at the head-station was slack, the usual little party of crack riders set forth for a gallop after the brumbies — Arthur, George Lee, Bob Galloway, and Teddy the horse-breaker. All were good men, and well-mounted. Galloway knew where the horses were running. The yard in the pine-scrub, with its long guiding wings, had been re-built. The chances seemed favourable.

Some hours after the men had gone out, Winnie Haverfield and her friend Lucy Drake had their horses saddled for a ride. Arthur had told them that if they took a canter out to the pine-yards in the Back Paddock during the morning they would have a chance of seeing the yarded brumbies. He spoke half in jest, for he well knew that they would have luck indeed if they managed to yard the white-footed stallion and his mob.

It was a beautiful morning, and the girls' horses played merrily with their bits as they cantered out from the river, along the dusty white track to the Box Hut. Winnie was riding the race mare Paleface, the only stable-fed horse on the station, in hard condition and fit to run for a man's life; her friend rode The Pearl, Winnie's favourite hack.

At the gate into the Back Paddock they met Ted the horsebreaker, with old Midnight dead lame, making the best of his way home.

'Have you yarded the brumbies?' asked Winnie, with her silvery laugh.

'No fear, Miss!' said the breaker with a grin. 'Last I seen of 'em they was goin' hell-for-leather for the Back Scrub, and nobody near 'em but Mr Lee, an' he was gettin' further behind every stride. My word! that Silverfoot can gallop all right!'

The girls rode slowly on in the direction of the clump of pines where, cunningly hidden among the thick saplings, stood the outlying wings of the brumby-yard. A horseman met them. It was Bob Galloway, his tired horse stumbling in the dried-up cattle tracks. 'No chance, Miss!' he said in answer to Winnie's question. 'They was too far ahead of us at the start. Mr Arthur's horse is knocked-up. He's gone on to the Hut. Mr Lee's still followin' on; but he hasn't a Buckley's chance now. They're well into the Back Scrub by this time!' He jerked up his leg-weary horse, and went slowly on.

'Well, I think we might as well go home, too, Lucy!'

'Hark! There's a whip!'

They reined up their horses and listened. There were sounds of galloping hoofs, and right in front of them Silverfoot, the beautiful wild stallion, broke from the scrub and passed close to them.

Winnie, who had several times seen him in the distance, had never before been so near him, and a little exclamation of admiration broke from her lips. The brown horse passed at a long loping canter; his deep slanting shoulder was white with foam, his flanks were wet with dark sweat, and his eye flashed with fire as he headed across the open plain, followed by his toiling mob.

Only two mares and two of the young horses were with him; evidently the foals and the others had found the pace too hot, and had broken away in the scrub, as hunted horses will.

Winnie's mind was made up in a moment. If only she could head Silverfoot — who had evidently been galloped for many miles and must be tiring a little — head him back between the wings of the yard, what a triumph it would be! Sitting down in her saddle, she caught the race mare by the head, and flew after the wild horses, her friend, a much less confident horsewoman, following more slowly.

At the same moment Lee, on his famous cream-coloured horse, appeared at the edge of the scrub. The gallant beast was black with sweat, yet galloping on with that extraordinary gameness that had made him a by-word in the West. When his rider saw how matters stood he pulled him up; knowing that there was just a chance that the flying race mare, fresh as she was, might overhaul the brumbies, and wheel them back, in which case his own good horse, given a minute or two's breathing space, might be able to assist in yarding them.

Silverfoot, who had been merely cantering, now became aware that a pursuer was close to him, and, stretching out with that beautiful easy stride which was the admiration of every horseman who had seen him, he gradually drew away from the others. But Paleface, disdaining the steadying pull of the slight arms of her rider, cut down the distance at racing pace, and in a quarter of a mile was on his flank.

For the first time in his life the speedy stallion was beaten for pace. His twelve-mile gallop forbade his making an extra effort and, as the swift mare shot up to his shoulder, he squealed in impotence and anger. Wheeling in upon him, the girl struck him sharply over the nose with her riding-switch. Slithering up on his haunches, the white-footed horse stopped short, turned, and raced back, picking up the others as he went, to the point where he had left the scrub.

And now or never, as Winnie Haverfield knew, was the chance to hammer him along at top pace, and break the gallant heart, already so severely tried. With a sound, hard-conditioned, clean-lunged mare beneath her, she knew that she could do it, and when that desperate half-mile to the scrub had been covered, the wild horse was reeling in his stride, and almost at the end of his tether. With a yell, and a roaring crack of his whip, that struck terror to the heart of the brumby, Lee dashed out on the cream horse, and together the three threaded the saplings in a reckless rivalry.

The great beautiful stallion had shot his bolt. The cream horse, that had given him so many rattling gallops, had at last won his triumph, and, wheeling him for the last time, turned him all unsuspecting between the hidden yard-wings. In another two minutes he was within the twelve-foot trap yard; the rails were up and the king of the Warrangoona boundary was a captive.

Outside, the man and the girl stood by their horses, and in both their hearts was the pride of great achievement. The cream horse stood with lowered head and pitifully heaving flanks; the black sweat ran down in channels from his fore-arm to his hoofs; it had been a hard gallop for a grass-fed beast. Paleface, with high head, and only a quicker breathing to betray the exertions of that full-speed mile, showed her magnificent condition. 'She may win the Squatter's Cup!' said Lee, looking at her with admiration, 'but this will always be remembered as her finest race!'

The Cook's Story

'Now, Ned', said the Boss to the cook, when the latter had finished washing up the tin plates after supper, and had flung a huge gumlog upon the fire, 'let's have some of your experiences'.

'Somethin' cheerful, for Old Nick's sake', said Flash Jack, with an accusing glance at Rawlinson. 'This ain't a bloomin' funeral.'

'Speak up, Cookie!' said Rawlinson, ignoring Jack.

The cook folded his arms across his chest, and surveyed us for a moment or two with a smile flickering round his large mouth. He was the accredited humorist of our little camp.

Then he remarked quietly, 'I killed a chap once with a bar of soap!'

'Ger out!' said Jack, surprised into sudden disbelief.

'You *what?*' asked the Boss.

'I killed a chap once with a bar of soap — common yellow soap!'

'Tell us about it!' I said.

Ned Dicken hitched up his trousers, lit his pipe with a fire-stick, and between puffs at it told in quaint fashion the following tale —

'I was born in the City of Goulburn, which I suppose even Jack Bryce knows is in New South Wales. They drowned the rest of the litter. I never cared for town life, as a small kid I used generally to be found on our ash heap playing with the thrown-out rhubarb leaves. Anything green attracted me, that's why my cousin John Dicken and I became such fast friends. We was always together as boys, and always in mischief, leastways I was always in the mischief, and John was hanging about in the neighbourhood of it, because he knew he'd get a kicking from me if he went away from it. I was eight years older than my cousin, but in wickedness and low cunning and smartness I was eighty years ahead of him. He was green as a youth, green as a boy, and green in petticoats, and I think he must have been a green baby. He'd believe anythink you told him. You could have put ink in his feeding bottle and he'd have believed it was milk. Green as grass he was.

'When I was about sixteen my people apprenticed me to a butcher, but my heart was never in the business. The only part of it I liked was ridin' round with the basket. We had an old bay horse with one eye and a bumble foot, and, bless yer! how I did rip him round them Goulburn corners, with one leg over the rails, so to speak!

'I might ha' been butcherin' yet, but the Boss and me had a difference of opinion about some sausages which had dropped out of the basket one muddy morning, and I slapped him in the face with a bullock's liver, which riled him, and I got the sack. Then I got a job yarding sheep at the sale-yards, but all the time the country was a-calling. The drovers used to tell me tales of the grand free life in the Bush, and at last I slung up my job, rolled up a blue blanket, and came out-back. There was nothing in my swag but a clean shirt and a dirty towel, and a copy of 'Gordon's Poems' that a cattle drover had given me, and a letter I had got from a housemaid at one of the houses I used to take meat to, saying she couldn't come for a walk that evening. That's how I began life in the Bush. There's not much change in my swag to-day, except that somebody sneaked my copy of Gordon at the last shed I was at, and I burned the biddy's letter a long time ago.

'At first I went pickin' up wool in the Lachlan sheds; from that I got on to shearin', and then drifted into cookin' — or poisonin', as Jack here would call it! Bein' strong and big, and useful with me hands, I could always hold me own, and after I had whipped one or two shearers for grumblin', they dropped makin' remarks about my cookin', and would take anythin' I put before 'em — meek as milk.'

Here Peter, the calf-caste, broke in with a snigger, and the Boss took the opportunity of reminding Ned that he (the Boss) was *not* as meek as milk, and that when he paid a cook to cook, he expected good cooking, and would see that he got it.

Smiling, but unabashed, Ned went on with his yarn.

'I had been several years at the game, following the sheds through the shearing season, and living for the rest of the year at Goulburn, when one winter, as I was preparin' to pack my shirt and towel for the track, my uncle said to me, 'Why not take your cousin John out with you?'

'My cousin John had grown into the most awful gawk you ever seen in your life. He was about nineteen then, an' a pretty specimen of greenness an' uselessness. They had put him in a shop to sell ribbons, but he was slower than a ham-strung sheep, and at last the Boss lost his temper because, while John was measuring two yards of tape, one of his best customers got sick of waitin' and walked out of the shop in a huff. The Boss vaulted over the counter and knocked my cousin down with an umbrella, an' told 'im to get out — which he did.

'Well, he didn't seem a likely piece of goods to take into the back country, but seein' we 'ad played together as kids I thought I could knock sense into 'im if anybody could; so at last I said he could come if he liked. He *didn't* like, but his father was sick o' keepin' him about the place, and Mr Johnny had to come.

'Right from that day my troubles began. I'm a good-natured sort of cove, 'ceptin' when anyone finds fault with my cookin', but my cousin roused me a dozen times a day; he was that slow and soft and sawney; no more brains than a maggot, and not as much gumption as a worm. If you kicked him he said, "I beg your pardon!" an' if you didn't he looked round expectin' it.

'Don't think that I bullied the feller! I'm not that kind of a man. I won't say I didn't boot him once or twice for worse silliness than usual; but he was that aggravatin' in his meekness that St. Peter himself would have knocked him down with the keys if he'd asked a question at the portals of Paradise.

'I'd send him up to a farm to ask for a bit of bread or meat, and perhaps the missus would give it to him and then ask him if he'd be good enough to cut a little bit of wood for her, introducin' him to the wood-heap and a blunt axe. Well, instead o' givin' a skelp or two at a log and knockin' off three splinters and then evaporatin' as soon as her back was turned, wot does the blighter do but put in an hour and a half's solid work while I'm kickin' my heels out on the road and frettin' to be on to the sheds!

'Or I'd send him up to a station store to try and get some tobacco, and to pitch a tale that he hadn't tasted a smoke for four days. And up he'd go and pitch his tale, with his pipe in his hand and the smoke rising to heaven as a silent protest to his idiocy. Long before we got to the Lachlan I was dead sick of him, as you'd ha' been, chaps, if you'd knowed him.

'I got so mad with 'im after some rotten thing he had done that I says to 'im, 'Look here, Johnny, if you think I'm goin' to own you as a cousin, or let such a stupid rhinoceros as you carry the good name of Dicken, you're much mistaken. So long as you travel with me your name is Albert Green, do you understand?'

'He begged my pardon very humbly, and said he understood, and consequently Albert Green he became.

'Well, when we got up to Boonathella on the Lachlan, where I had the cookin', my mate and his silly maggot-brained ways nearly drove me mad, and caused no end of fun to the shearers and rouseabouts. The Boss gave Albert a job at pickin' up fleeces, but, as you'd suppose, he made a poor show at that, being so desperate slow. One of the shearers gave him a kick on the trousers to liven 'im up, and was so dumbfounded to get "I beg your pardon, sir!" from him, instead of a bit of cheek, that he ran the point of his shears into his own leg. Then he wanted to kill Albert — that is, Johnny — and he'd have done it, too, if I hadn't promised to lick him into a jelly if he did. Not that I wanted to keep Albert alive, but as he had come to the shed as my mate, I felt it my duty to stick up for him.

He didn't last long at the pickin' up. One of the shearers — a bit of a wag — told him that one of his duties, as well as tarrin' the cuts on the sheep, was to tar the Boss's boots whenever he had a chance, as the Boss, bein' so busy, had no time to black 'em in the mornin's. So the first time the Boss came and stood beside 'im Mr Albert Green steps forward, pot in hand, an' makes a lick at the boots with his brush.

' "H—l yer doin?" said the Boss sharply. 'Blackin' yer boots, sir!' said Albert, innocent.

'Well, I never seen the Boss so mad in my life — or any Boss. He took my cousin up by the scruff of his neck and the seat of his trousers and pitched him down the shoot into the counting-out pen, brush, tar-pot an' all; an' then he swore like a regiment of dragoons. Albert would ha' been sacked off the place, but I begged to be allowed to have him to help me in the kitchen, and the Boss consented, so long as I promised to keep him out of his sight.

'Well, you may guess I had a lively time with him. What with the silly tricks he played me, and the rotten tricks the boys played him, my life was scarcely worth livin'. I had to lick a shearer every night and whip a rouseabout every morning to keep things in shape at all. I was precious glad I had made my cousin change his name, for I was ashamed to have any connection with him.

'Well, things went on like this for a week or two — and at last came the end. I found him one morning, when I was particular busy and had been lookin' for him everywhere to peel the potaters, sittin' on the edge of his bunk playin' with some live cockroaches.

'What yer doin'?' I asked. 'Here I been up to the shed and back lookin' fer you!'

Then he explained. One of the rouseabouts had told him the best way to keep the cockroaches off the sugar was to tie a little bit of thread round the neck of each, then when they began to feed they choked.

'It was more than I could stand. I'm a good-tempered man as a rule, except when my cookin's questioned, but he had got me at the end of my tether. I had one of those long square bars of soap in my hand, having just left a job of washing plates to look for him; I took it in both hands and brought it down with all my strength on his head, and Albert Green fell at my feet like a log.

I was that mad with him I didn't care if he never got up again. A swagman who came in at the door at that moment came over and looked at him. 'You've done for him, mate!' he said. Then I began to be a bit sorry, for he was such a harmless poor beggar, it seemed a shame to have killed him. I looked at the bar of soap in my hand; there was some of his brown hair sticking to it, and a little red stain at one end, and the bar was bent in the middle where it had struck him. That broke me up a bit, and I kneeled down and took his hand. Suddenly he came to himself, and there was a wicked look in his eye that I never seen there before. He staggered up on to his feet with an oath — a fearful oath it was, and him a feller who had never sworn in his life! He caught sight o' the unoffending swagman and made for 'im, and before I could block him he was into him with both hands like a prize-fighter. 'It was you that hit me, was it?'

says he, 'you son of a sweep!' and with that he rolled poor swaggie on the floor, and pummelled him till he yelled for mercy. I couldn't move for laughin', in spite of the fright I had got.

'Well, would you believe it, boys, from that moment he was a changed man. From being a poor-spirited worm of a chap he became one of the loudest-talking, most aggressive fellows in the shed. You couldn't say 'Boo!' to him but he'd want to hit you — and he *could* hit, like the kick of a mule.'

Ned Dicken ceased speaking, and turned to the fire to get fresh light for his pipe.

'But you said you killed him!' Jack Bryce remarked in an injured tone.

The cook puffed a leisurely cloud before he answered.

'So I did', he said. 'I killed Albert Green, and brought to life John Dicken, for he'd never let me call 'im anything else afterwards and indeed I've had no cause to be ashamed of 'im from that day to this.'

Rawlinson rose and began to arrange his blankets for the night. 'You're as good at a yarn as you are at a curry, Cookie!' he said.

'Far too much soap he puts in both of 'em', said Jack, who was annoyed at being cheated out of a corpse. But the cook only laughed.

The Shoeing Of Boona

BOONA WAS only a little thing, and he had come forty-seven miles since morning; but he flirted his head gaily and pranced under the snaffle as he topped the hill beyond which could be seen the white roofs of Condoboran township. We had crossed a number of flint-strewn ridges, and Boona's unshod feet, used to the softer surface of the plains, were troubling him; this I knew by the crampiness of his usual cat-like tread. I determined to take him to the first blacksmith I could find and have him shod at once. Then I laughed a little as I thought the blacksmith would assuredly earn his money, for Boona, game, gallant little roadster as he was, had a fiery temper, had an impetuous dislike for all strangers, and had never had his hind feet lifted by any man in the course of his four years of bush life. However, he must be shod; of that I was fully determined, for it was impossible that he could carry me further in this stony country without protection to his brittle little feet. Unconscious of my thoughts Boona neighed ringingly to a horse which cantered up to a log fence to inspect us, and he plunged sideways as I checked him with the bit. No gamer little beast ever stepped than this thirteen-hand black pony, and few wilder ever carried a saddle. He was hard to mount and hard to sit, self-willed and impudent and impetuous, brave as a lion, and stubborn as a pig when crossed in his wishes. He could kick like a mule or stand and spar like a man when his temper was roused.

Glances of undisguised admiration from a number of horsemen in the street followed him as he sidled proudly along the roadway till I drew him up at a large doorway over which was written 'T. Connolly, Blacksmith. — Horses Shod.'

I sprang from the saddle, and Boona struck playfully at me as landed, a proceeding embarrassing to the stranger, but one to which I had grown so accustomed that it had ceased to be disconcerting. A smoke-blackened tradesman appeared at the door with a hammer in his hand. 'I want this pony shod', I said, without circumlocution. 'Bring him in', said the blacksmith, with equal brevity. Boona hung back on the bridle, flashed fire from his wicked little eyes, and planted his sore feet firmly; his whole attitude said 'I'll be d — d if I will!'

I knew him in that mood and pitied the blacksmith. The latter approached and began to say soothing words, and I was obliged to warn him to keep beyond reach of the quick little hoofs, already beginning to lift ominously.

I managed to pull Boona slowly over the threshold of the doorway, protesting sullenly; then he bounded suddenly forward and upset some iron balanced on the anvil; this frightened him and he went up in the air in a cloud of dust, striking wildly and lashing out with his hind feet. The blacksmith and his assistant sprang back towards the door and prepared for a rapid exit should circumstances make it necessary. I spoke to the wild little black, and he stood trembling and snorting in the settling dust.

I picked up a tapping fore-foot and held it. The smith came over and took it from me. From his folded apron he produced a knife and began to use it tentatively, paring the ragged horn, and nervously watching the pony the while. Boona turned up the white of his eye and crouched, then he sprang forward and spun suddenly round, sending the blacksmith reeling into a corner. The man picked himself slowly out of the dust. 'Is that brute broken in?' he asked. 'Usual bush-breaking', I said carelessly; but I was rather ashamed of Boona's manners. A crowd of loafers and townspeople had meanwhile collected at the door and were taking keen interest in the proceedings. 'Too much for ye, Tom', said one of them. 'Better take him down to Peter Rogan', said another, 'he'll shoe him!'

This irritated Connolly, and, approaching cautiously, he lifted Boona's near fore-foot with the claw of his hammer, and, getting a good hold with both hands, he again took out his knife. Boona's eyes flashed fire, and he fought and bored and jumped, got his foot free at last, and sprang past the smith, lashing out savagely as he went by. 'You can take him out of here', said the man in a fury. 'I don't want my brains knocked out just yet.' 'Don't look as if you *had* many', called an enemy from the doorway, 'when you begin to fight that way with the pony!'

'Take him down to Peter Rogan', said someone again. I led Boona down the street, followed by an interested crowd of loafers and others, until the legend 'Peter Rogan — Horse-Shoer' loomed up in front, and a man in dusty leggings and long-necked spurs who had formed himself into the vanguard of the little procession announced ungrammatically 'That's 'im! Peter Rogan. There ain't a horse in the back-country 'e can't nail shoes on. Take 'im in there, young feller!'

Peter stood at his anvil — a big, good-natured-looking giant, with sleeves rolled up to the shoulders over huge muscular arms. He was not only a noted blacksmith and a horse-shoer famed for his success with wild bush horses, but was also a pugilist and wrestler of considerable fame, and incidentally the strongest man within a radius of a hundred miles or so. He looked at the little procession surrounding a led horse, guessed its meaning, and smiled in anticipation and conscious power. His smile broadened as we came nearer and he saw the diminutive size of the 'horse.' 'Hullo boys!' he grinned from his ample doorway, 'Been out catching rabbits? Where did you find the black one?'

'I've seen 'em catch quieter ones', said the man in leggings pleasantly; 'this is a rabbit wot kicks and bites!'

'Are you used to bush horses?' I asked as I hauled Boona unwillingly after me through the broad doorway. 'Want him shod?' asked Peter in return, disregarding the doubt implied in my question. 'Stand back there, you fellows, out of my light! Woa, my little beauty!'

Peter Rogan evidently understood horses, and had the 'way wid him' that won their hearts. But Boona was a Bush Bohemian, an Ishmael of the plains, and he had a hatred and a dread of strangers. He nuzzled his head into my waistcoat and shuffled his feet nervously. Peter approached and lifted a fore-foot, promptly, severely, and without hesitation, in the manner of a man who is accustomed to be obeyed. Boona, somewhat overawed for the moment, suffered the foot to be examined without protest; but when the knife was produced he began to edge about and plunge. Peter spoke to him softly and stuck manfully to the fore-foot, while I hung on to the pony's head. Boona became excited, and flung the big man backwards and forwards in his efforts to get clear. Peter laughed and hung on, but the sweat was rolling down his grimy forehead and the muscles stood out upon his great arms. Boona was stronger than he looked. Up and down the forge the battle reeled, the pony more and more determined to get free, the man more and more determined to keep his hold.

I was flung to and fro at the end of the bridle. Boona grew desperate; he had never been handled like this before. Fear gave him the strength of a sixteen-hand horse; he plunged and pulled and reared till the mighty Vulcan that held him was dragged off his feet. Then with a sudden wrench he tore his fore-foot from the hand that held it and sent the blacksmith spinning into a corner. Peter Rogan cursed volubly, but good-naturedly, and picked himself up from a pile of old horse-shoes. 'Bit of a daisy, that fellow!' he said carelessly to the crowd; but there was a quiet confidence in his eye that seemed to say 'I have still some cards to play!'

He strolled up to Boona and talked to him in serious vein, stroked his glossy neck and shining quarter, and whispered into his quivering, tense ears. Boona stood quietly enough, but there was fire in his eye, and his lip twitched nervously. Poor Boona, he recognised the strong individuality pitted against his own, and he knew swiftly and surely, as horses always do, that in the battle for mastery he must go down before this stronger will — and he was afraid. But he was also stubborn and determined; the spirit of battle was aroused in him, and he meant to fight as long as freedom was left to him. As for me, I think he had entirely forgotten my existence for the time being.

For several minutes Peter caressed and fondled the pony, and I noticed that he gradually moved him over towards the wall of the forge; but he made very little impression with his friendly overtures. Boona was angry and suspicious, and from time to time snorted apprehensively; he seemed to know that the blacksmith was merely 'sparring for wind', as the fighting-men say. Suddenly Peter stooped down and picked up the fore-foot next to him; Boona fidgeted and fretted, but with a quick movement the man had him jammed against the wall, and, pressing him there with all his strength, the pony was powerless. In vain he tried to plunge forwards; the blacksmith's weight was against his shoulder. He attempted to run back, but the cross-wall was immediately behind him. He pushed outwards, but the powerful man at his shoulder squeezed him against the unyielding bricks. 'Give me that knife!' called Peter to his assistant, and in five minutes the little foot was trimmed. A similar stratagem was employed with the other foot, by the use of the other wall. Then the shoes were shaped and hammered and cooled, and carefully fitted under similar methods. Finally, they were fastened on, and so skilful was the strategy of this master blacksmith that Boona was unable to make the slightest protest until the last nail was clinched, and he was strongly and securely 'shod in front.'

Then Peter Rogan wiped the sweat from his forehead, took down his coat from a nail on the wall, and crossed the road to the hotel to have his dinner. We left Boona tied up in the forge to contemplate his new slippers, and the crowd divided its attention between watching the fire in Boona's eye and the triumph in Peter's as he quaffed two deep glasses of beer at my expense.

'I've *got* to shoe him, you know, Mister', he explained to me; 'if I didn't the boys would never believe in me again. I've *got* to shoe him.'

But shoeing a horse 'in front' is comparatively easy, and Peter knew well that the hardest part of his task still lay before him. After dinner and a smoke we re-crossed the road to the smithy and shouldered our way through the little crowd, which received Peter with a cheer. Somebody asked him if he had had *rabbit* for dinner, but Peter had assumed a sudden dignity in the face of his responsibilities. His reputation was at stake, and he recognised the fact; only to me he whispered as he blew up the red coals in his fire; '*I'll* shoe him now, you'll see!'

Boona scooped up the dusty earthen floor with an impatient forefoot, wondering at its unaccustomed weight. Then he looked round at me reproachfully, and his wild eye was full of white. Somehow I felt that I had betrayed him into the hands of the Philistines. Rogan went over to him and patted his quarter, and spoke severely when Boona lifted a hind-foot threateningly. I unfastened his bridle and led him into the centre of the forge and held him. Peter stooped and lifted a hind-foot with his claw-hammer. The pony kicked savagely, and Peter let go. Boona stood resting his near hind-leg. In a moment his enemy had the foot in his hand and braced himself for a struggle. Squealing and fighting, the little rebel threw himself hither and thither in a struggle for freedom, but Peter stood like a rock with the knotted sinews thickening on his massive arms as he fought to keep his hold.

Minute after minute passed, while the blacksmith wrestled for his reputation and the pony for his freedom. The crowd in the doorway held their breath, and someone muttered 'Good boy, Peter!' Up to the present the big blacksmith had taken the struggle in good part, and his fine temper was a thing to wonder at, but at this juncture Boona tossed him roughly against the iron edge of the anvil, and a light, fiercer even than that which shone in the pony's, blazed suddenly in his kind brown eyes. Peter's patience was exhausted, and he was going to fight, terrible in his magnificent strength. Exerting every inch of his muscle and every ounce of his weight, he gave an upward twist to the hind-leg which he held, and flung the battling pony on its back.

Peter was breathing hard now, and a blasphemous word escaped him as he reeled out of reach of the upturned clattering hoofs. Boona rose and shook the dust from his glossy coat, staggered, and stood still, breathing no less heavily than his conqueror. The fire in his eyes dulled to the ashes of fear. Boona was cowed.

Peter, quick to understand, stepped in at once and seized the foot in his iron hand. The pony fidgeted and plunged; quick as lightning the powerful smith repeated the movement of the moment before, and the little horse again fell heavily. This time he lay for a few seconds, blowing the dust from his nostrils. I jerked the bridle and he rose, snorting in fear. 'Bring me the knife', said Peter. He had won.

In less than an hour the shoes were made, fitted, and fastened and Boona stepped cautiously over the threshold in unaccustomed bonds.

I paid Peter Rogan handsomely, and as he tossed down a deep draught of beer to the health of 'the toughest ever I tackled' he told me confidentially, 'You see, I *had* to shoe him, Mister. There never was a horse that beat me yet!' And, looking at his huge shoulders and massive fore-arm, at the weight and build and strength of him, I wondered if there ever would be one.

The Mulga Ridge

THE LONG, red road from Bourke to Hungerford stretched endlessly through the ridges, shimmering in the blazing sunlight of an Australian noon. Before it climbed the stony ridge the road crossed a level box flat, and on the left-hand side of it, about a quarter of a mile from the waggon tracks, rose the red earthwork of a tank. Near the tank stood a little bark-roofed hut, with a thatched and floorless verandah. At the back of the hut a small, square horseyard was built under the shade of two large box-trees. The sun blazed down relentlessly upon this lonely home, at which the only sign of life was supplied by a lean blue cattle-dog, which, with lolling tongue and drooping tail, crouched in the shadow of the hut wall in the cool dust of the earthen verandah. No sound came from the surrounding bush, no whisper of leaf or grass, no ripple or lap of moving water in the stagnant tank, no voice of any bird.

The sun moved slowly down the western sky, and at last the clink of dragging spurs on the boarded floor of the hut broke the almost uncanny silence. A tall, lean bushman came through the open door, and, going to the water-bag which hung from the verandah-roof, dipped in it a tin mug, and drank greedily. He was burnt brick-red by the rigour of the Western suns, stooping-shouldered and bow-legged from long hours spent in the saddle; a typical horseman of the Outer West.

Jack Devine, owner of the hut at the edge of the ridges, was in charge of one of the changing stations of Cobb and Co., the great coach proprietors of the West. To him fell the duty of looking after a dozen or so of coach-horses, of having four of them ready at stated hours to change when the coach arrived, and of rough-breaking the young horses which were brought in from time to time to strengthen the working plant.

Picking up his saddle and bridle in the verandah, Jack strode off to the stock-yard, and caught a brown mare which was standing in the shade of one of the box-trees. The coach would pass at five o'clock, and four fresh horses had to be waiting in the yard at that hour. This meant rounding up the little mob which ran in the mulga ridges, and, as there were two young horses in it which were wild and not easy to yard, Devine allowed himself a liberal margin of time. He mounted the old mare, and rode quietly towards the mulga. Knowing well the run of the horses, he went almost exactly to the spot where they were feeding, fifteen of them, of which thirteen were regular old collar-marked slaves of the coach, and the other two young and wild, unbroken colts, on which no hand had yet been laid. These young ones, as soon as they saw the horseman approach, began to snort and wheel, and galloped off into the ridges, followed by the old, stiff-shouldered coach horses at a lumbering canter. Anxious to cut off the mob before it should reach the shelter of the thick-growing mulga, Devine set spurs to his mare and raced across a sandhill dotted with quinine bushes. The colts, with heads up, and long tails streaming behind them, went at the top of their speed for the dark line of the timber. After a half-mile gallop the mare began to gain on them, and, catching her by the head, Devine dashed her down the edge of the trees just in time, and with swinging whip wheeled the colts and drove the whole mob westward along the edge of the ridge, towards home and the stock-yard. Still restless, the young horses kept trying to break away, and the rider was kept busy watching them. Suddenly, as though following out a preconcerted plan, they made a determined dash for freedom, and raced at full speed up the ridge; sitting down in his saddle, and driving home his long spurs, Devine went after them, when, without the least warning trip or stumble, the brown mare put her foot in a rabbit-hole, and went down in a heap giving her rider a stunning, crashing fall.

It was fully an hour later when Jack Devine regained consciousness, with a throbbing pain in his head, an aching arm, and an excruciating numbing pain across his back. He was unable to move. His hat was lying twenty feet away from him, and the afternoon sun, though long past its full strength, was still hot enough to give him serious discomfort. He tried to turn over, but the cruel pain in his back at the slightest movement compelled him to desist. He lay still, and tried to collect his scattered senses. He was suddenly aware of an overwhelming thirst, which seemed to clog his tongue and burn his throat. He raised himself cautiously on his elbow, and considered carefully his whereabouts. He was lying on the edge of the mulga ridge about forty yards from the dark line of the shady trees, which he knew that, in his crippled condition, it was impossible for him to reach. The hut was about two miles away; the nearest water — in exactly the opposite direction — was a small gilgai hole in a clump of belar-trees about a quarter of a mile from where he lay. If only he could reach that water, and the shade of the trees beside it, he felt that he might hold out until a search-party came and found him. To lie where he was, even if he should survive the coming night, meant death or madness in the full glare of the next day's sun. And yet — he raised himself an inch or two — the pain of moving was insupportable. He felt that he could never crawl even the few feet necessary for him to recover his hat, much less the four hundred yards which lay between him and the water which was life. The horses had galloped out of sight, his mare with them. Devine knew that they would not go far in the direction of the hut, but, led by the wild colts, would soon wheel into the mulga scrub, and return to the feeding-ground from which they had been disturbed; and, in all likelihood, the mare would go with them, thus taking away the last chance of her being discovered at the hut and an accident suspected. Dreamily the man wondered how long it would be before any one would suggest that he might be lying crippled in the bush. He was such a fine horseman, and had carried through his daily work so long without the slightest mishap, that, even after he had been missed, it was unlikely that those who knew him would suspect that anything untoward had happened to him. Lying there in the dazzling sunlight, in pain that drew from him from time to time groans of agony, he pictured vividly in his mind the arrival of the coach at his little hut. First there would be the crack of the whip down at the watercourse, where Harry, the driver, always signalled his coming, so that Jack might know to fling the traces on to the team in the yard. Then he heard the rumble of the wheels, the creak of the axles and the rattle of the bars as the coach drew up at the yard. Harry would look in vain for the horses and the man who should have been there to greet him. He would coo-ee, and get no answer. Then he would tie his reins to the brake and jump down from his seat and go into the hut, and come out and coo-ee again, listening intently, with his face to the ridges. He would wait for perhaps five minutes, with his watch in his hand, then, muttering to himself, he would climb on to his high seat and whip up his jaded and disappointed horses on the long twenty-mile stage to the next change.

It had always been Jack Devine's pride to serve his company faithfully, and it hurt him now to think that this was the first time he had ever failed them. Harry, the driver, would go on to Hungerford, and report that he had found no horses waiting for him at the Box Hut, and the general opinion would be that he — Jack — had gone to Bourke for a drunken spree, or something of that sort, and that he would return when he had had enough of it. Not one of the many who would discuss his disappearance would be likely to put it down to accident, for so finished a horseman, so clever a backwoodsman, was considered capable of getting out of any trouble which he might get into, even with the wildest of his colts. Yet his only chance, as he well knew, was that some one should organise a search-party without delay, pick up the tracks and follow them to where he fell; and grimly he realised the truth — that if help did not arrive before the blazing sun of the morrow had lighted its scorching fires, he must die like a crippled sheep upon the sand-hill. Meanwhile the sun crept slowly down the western sky, and with the coolness of its waning came a partial cessation of his suffering. His head ceased to throb so acutely, and he found by lying on his right side that his back ached less cruelly. The sun disappeared behind the mulga trees, and the cool dews came down upon his scorched face and hands, and, helpless and suffering as he was, he blessed the friendly night and found some measure of hope in its soothing touch.

As his pain grew less, his racked mind became clearer, and he tried to evolve a plan of escape from the frightful death that threatened him. One thing was certain, he must reach his hat before the sun rose, and he must reach water within a very few hours later, or, failing the arrival of a rescue party, he must reconcile himself to his doom, and die with his face to the sky, as a brave man should. Carefully he moved this way and that, an inch at a time, trying to discover some mode of progress, however slow, unattended by the severest pain. At last he found that by lying partially on his back and partially on his right side, and using his right arm as a lever — his left was useless — he could move over the ground an inch or two at a time without more than intermittent spasms of pain. He now began, with much misgiving, but with a feeble ray of hope to guide him, the long journey towards his cabbage-tree hat which lay but a few feet from him among the pebbles of the ridge. Very gently he drew himself forward — then rested; another inch or two of progress, a keen spasm of pain — another rest. The journey was begun. Slowly, very slowly, the distance shortened. At last he reached the goal. With difficulty he picked up the precious headcovering, and set it on his head. Then, quite exhausted, he sank back upon the ground, as the pain across his loins gripped him with tenfold power.

And now he knew that he must face the long and painful journey to the water, four hundred yards away. What a short distance it seemed to a strong man mounted on a good horse. Just across the crown of the ridge, through that thick patch of mulga, over the open glade, between the two tall belar-trees, and there lay the tiny pool. There would not be much water in it now he reflected, after the heat of the last two days. Still, a mouthful or two would give him his chance — his chance to keep going till the rescue party came. *Was* there a rescue party? Would it come in time? Realising that if he was to attempt the long and painful journey across the ridge, the more of it he managed in the cool of the night the better, Devine set himself at once to his task. Grimly he began his snail-like progress, and slowly, very slowly, he crawled over the brown tufts of wire-grass and dragged his crippled body over the small stones and sticks which strewed the ridge. More than once his path was crossed by a dead mulga-log, and painfully he made a detour round it, losing much valuable time. The moon hung a silver lamp above the ridge and looked down pityingly on his gallant fight with fate. Wallabies sprang past him in the shadows, and kangaroos loped in and out of the timber. Towards morning he had won to the crown of the ridge, and could see below him, over the tops of the intervening mulga scrub, the feathery plumes of the belar-trees which marked the goal which he was seeking. Grey dawn showed in the eastern sky, and a soft wind rose and stirred the mulga leaves. Devine turned aside to a little patch of grass, and licked the dew from the burnt brown herbage. His downhill progress was even slower than his ascent of the ridge. His back pained him more, and the ground had become more stony, and more covered with pointed stumps and dead logs. To make matters worse, the sun rose red and angry, and blazed down upon him. Every half-hour the heat increased, and his progress grew slower. He had still nearly two hundred yards to go, and he was thoroughly exhausted. Dragging himself under the shade of an umbrella-mulga, he lay still and rested. An hour later he resumed his painful progress, with every bone in his body aching. Gradually he wormed his way through the thick mulga, and came out upon the open glade. Here the sun beat down fiercely, blistering his half-protected face. The earth was hot below him. The stones burned like heated iron. His right side and elbow were worn and sore with contact with the ground; but hope was strong within him, for a hundred yards away he could see the tall belars waving their green plumes, and beneath them was water — and life — and his one and only chance!

With extraordinary courage he crawled on, and on, and on. A loathsome iguana rattled past him and climbed a tree-stem close to him, a snake scurried away into the grass, mocking with its crawling progress his own mode of progression. And always the sun blazed down relentlessly. It was high noon when at last he raised himself painfully over the bank of the gilgai hole and looked down. Limp and exhausted, he fell back upon the burning ground, and hope died in his heart, for there below him was not the dark, stagnant pool he had expected to see, but a grey, cracked circle of clay. The heat of the last few days had dried up the water — and his last chance was gone!

Sinking back in a faint, the bushman lay still, just within the shade thrown by one of the plumed branches of the great belar tree. A crow that had been patiently following his progress all the morning flapped down from a dead branch, and sidled cautiously towards the motionless body, and a stream of busy, black ants, whose high road across the clay pan had been blocked by this huge bulk, crowded over him in ever-increasing hundreds and thousands. The cruel, relentless Bush was preparing her sacrifice.

*   *   *

Back on the crown of the mulga ridge a black-boy, leading his horse, was bending low over the indistinct tracks on the stony ground. Behind him a little group of serious-faced bushmen walked, leading their horses.

'Hurry, Billy, hurry!' one of them called impatiently. 'The crows and ants may have him even now.'

The black fellow groaned sympathetically, and strained his eyes to his work; he was doing his noble best. Half an hour later he gave a cry of delight, and dropping his bridle, rushed forward and threw his bronzed arms round the huddled figure under the belar-tree.

Jack Devine was nursed back to health, and a year later took up his old work at the mail-change, and ten years ago he told me with his own lips his thrilling story of the mulga ridge.

The Lifting of Myall King

WE HAD A NUMBER of fine old stock horses on our station, but by far the best of them, by common consent, was Myall King, a ten-year-old son of Cowrie, a handsome dark-brown with a white streak down his face and both hind feet white. Far and wide upon the Queensland border he was known as a horse of extraordinary courage and stamina, and a fast one to boot. Not only was he unsurpassed at a muster or on a cattle camp or in pursuit of wild horses in the bush; he had also won a considerable reputation as a racehorse in fair company, and many travelling owners of fast horses who had taken them up into the bush with a view of sweeping the board at our township meetings had had cause to curse the indomitable courage of the old bush horse, who had on many memorable occasions snatched the prize-money out of their very hands.

On the station the old horse came in for a good deal of hero-worship. Hughie, the stockman, who rode him in his daily labour, as well as in his occasional races, simply idolised him.

No one but Hughie ever rode Myall King, and between man and horse had developed a close understanding and companionship, which grew in intensity as the years went by.

About three weeks after Myall King had won the Squatters' Handicap in Bourke, and covered himself with fresh glory by the deed, he was brought into the horse paddock at the head station to renew his ordinary station work. One morning, as we were all preparing to go out mustering, some delay was caused by the non-appearance of Hughie's horse in the stockyard. The black boy was sent back at once to look for him, but, as he was a careful lad and seldom or never missed any of his horses, and as Myall King was always to be found in front of the mob as they galloped down to the yard in the grey light of dawn, it was at once surmised that the old horse was either ill or had somehow escaped from the paddock.

A careful search revealed no sign of him, and Hughie was obliged to take another horse for the day. Late in the afternoon, when we returned from mustering, we rode carefully through the horse paddock, searching behind every bush and tree, scouring the scrubby banks of the river and examining every foot of the wire fence for a gap or break which might have tempted the old horse away from his pasture.

It was the keen eye of Dave Wilson, our overseer, which discovered a scarcely noticeable bend in a top wire at the extreme east end of the paddock in the centre of a lignum swamp. Getting off his horse, Dave eagerly examined the wires and the ground below them, then he coo-eed to me. I rode over, and together we studied on the hard ground the tracks which told us in so many plain words the solution of the mystery of the disappearance of Myall King. 'Some one on a shod horse', said Dave, 'strapped down the fence, went up and caught old Myall King, led him over here. See, where his saddle strap bent the wire!'

We tied down the fence, led our horses over, and rode along the tracks across the corner of the wool-shed paddock, and so on to the main Bourke road. Here we lost them in the gathering dark. 'Somebody has lifted the old horse, and has taken twenty hours' start of us!' and the curse of the exasperated overseer was purely Australian in character, and not pretty for ladies to hear. Then we galloped up to the station. Dave wrote half-a-dozen wires and sent a stockman racing to the township. 'If the police at Bourke miss him, we'll never see the old horse again', he said to me.

Hughie was heartbroken. 'If they'd a taken any other horse but *him* — that rotten crock I was ridin' to-day, for instance — but the old King, the best horse that ever champed a bit! I'd like to have five minutes with the man that's riding him now.' Then his feelings found relief in pathetically weird blasphemy.

No consolation came from the police. They had watched the approaches to Bourke, and had apprised every trooper in the district, but no horse in the least answering the description of Myall King had been, so far, seen. The inspector at Bourke gave it as his opinion that the clever thief had ridden as far as the Bourke road merely to put the station men off the scent, and had then wheeled round through the scrub and made his escape into Queensland, where he would have a much better chance of evading the law.

Dave Wilson cursed the police collectively, and returned to his work of gathering the Red Ridge calves for branding. The rest of us sorrowed for a little, and then became wrapped in our several interests of sport and toil. But Hughie, poor fellow, nursed a very real grief, and became low-spirited and fretful. Usually of a bright, sunny disposition and a great favourite with us all, he grew morbid and self-centred, and rode often by himself, having little to say to any one, and frequently showing temper towards his horses. At last, one evening, he interviewed the boss in his office and resigned his place.

'What's wrong, Hughie?' said the boss, knowing perfectly well what was wrong.

'I've not been feelin' well lately', said the stockman. 'I guess I want a change to a cooler country.'

The boss paid him his cheque, shook him by the hand with a kindly word of good-bye, and, as the little bushman's spurs jingled down the office steps, he

called after him significantly: 'And mind you bring back Myall King.' Hughie
gave no sign to show that he had heard, but he threw his pack-saddle on
Madam Malone and his saddle on Grey Cloud, and bade us good-bye as we
stood in the store verandah.

It was a farewell marked with much friendliness, for Hughie was always a
favourite with us, and it was an open secret that he was undertaking this journey
with a view to finding and recovering the gallant old horse which he loved. So
we wished him all sorts of good luck, and pressed his hand with the beat of
true hearts behind the pressure. Hughie called back to us, sitting light in the
saddle on the prancing Grey Cloud: 'Good-bye, fellows! You'll never see me
back on the station unless I come with the King!' Then he dropped his heel
and gave the rein to the grey, and, with the race mare pulling forward on her
halter, he cantered away through the horse paddock.

His subsequent adventures we learned that winter at the meetings in the
men's hut.

In two days he reached Bourke, and, though he made every inquiry and left
no stone unturned to gain information, he could find out nothing of interest
regarding the brown horse. So many shearers and travellers rode through Bourke
with one or two horses that but small attention was given to them, and no one
remembered having seen a horse answering the present description. Indeed, a
large number of people in the western town knew the famous stock horse by
sight, but none had seen him in a stranger's hands. Somewhat dispirited by this
lack of news our stockman rode slowly down the country, camping night after
night in the open bush, with his horses hobbled near him. He did not seek for
work, as he had plenty of money to pay for his food as he went along, but he
called at every station and at every bush hotel and township seeking news of
his favourite. Only once did a ray of hope cross his path, when a selector on
the Bogan River, who had evidently a keen eye for horses, told him of the
passing, three weeks before, of a young man with two horses. His attention had
been roused by his reticence regarding the magnificent pack-horse which he
led, and the fact that the brand on this horse had been recently smudged and
crossed with a hot iron.

'It is my opinion', said the selector, 'that he was a stolen horse, but, of
course, it had nothing to do with me. Colour? He was a brown horse, with a
heavy crest, like a stallion's, and he stepped very proudly and walked about six
miles an hour, keeping up easily with the ambling saddle mare.'

'Any white on his face?' asked Hughie, anxiously.

'None at all.'

'White hind feet?'

'No.'

This puzzled Hughie. The most conspicuous thing about his favourite was
the white marking.

'That's nothing', said the selector, 'a pot of brown paint and five minutes would fix that. When I was out on the Barcoo, I remember — ' but Hughie had heard enough, and he swung into his saddle and jogged away on the Southern road. Here and there he met some one who dimly remembered an ambling mare and a good-looking brown pack horse, and slowly he puzzled out the trail right down into Riverina. Then he heard no more of the man he sought. He camped near Wagga, and ran Madam Malone in a mile race for grass-fed horses at the annual race meeting. The mare won, and Hughie sold her well. Then he took work on a station for a time, still making diligent inquiry as to the horse which might, or might not, be Myall King.

At last he made up his mind to leave the place where he was working and ride eastward towards the coast. He saddled Grey Cloud, and tying his blanket and a few necessaries on the saddle in front of him, he took his cheque and departed.

A week later, as he was riding along the dusty high road, looking right and left for a suitable place in which he might make his dinner camp, he was aware of two horses tied up to a pine-tree. He turned off the road, for where horses were tied there would be a man, and where a man had chosen to camp there would be water. As Grey Cloud drew near them one of the horses lifted his head and neighed, and a man sitting on a log, smoking, looked up quickly.

Hughie's pulse beat fast, and something hammered at his temples; his every nerve quivered with excitement, for in the brown horse looking at him over the shoulder of the other, he recognised, in spite of the absence of his white streak, the face of his old favourite — the honest face of Myall King. With assumed carelessness he rode up to the youth on the log. 'Good mornin', mate. Any water about here?'

The man in possession made a motion with his pipe stem towards a stagnant pool below him. 'Lots of it — of a sort!'

Hughie dismounted and tied his horses to a convenient sapling. Then he took a quart-pot from his saddle and dipped it in the pool, and set it on the still-burning fire on which the other man had just boiled his billy-can. 'Come far?' asked the youth on the log.

'A longish way', said Hughie, trying to keep calm. 'That's a fine-looking brown horse you have there. You don't often see such a good stamp. Just like the stock horses you see on the Queensland border. Had him long?' Hughie asked the question carelessly.'

'Oh! a long time', said the youth; 'in fact, I broke him in.'

The stockman strolled over to the subject of their remarks and patted his neck. The old horse whinnied delightedly and laid his muzzle in the bushman's brown hand.

'What's the matter with his brand?'

'D—d if *I* know. He was like that when I got him — bought him a colt out of the Wodonga yards.'

Hughie sniffed. 'What a smell of wet paint! They must be painting gates hereabouts!'

The tall youth looked uneasy, and glanced suspiciously at the stockman. 'I don't smell nothin'!' he said.

'Well, *I* do', said the little stockman. 'I smell some d——d crooked work. Now, look here, young fellow, it would take more than a pot of paint and a faked brand to disguise Myall King from *me*. I know every hair in his coat. I've ridden nearly 900 miles to get him. Now I've found him, and the King goes home with me!

The youth looked Hughie up and down, and doubtless the diminutive size of our station light-weight encouraged him to say, in a slow drawl:

'I dunno what you're givin' me. That's *my* horse, and I'll thank you to clear out and leave him alone!'

This was too much for Hughie, high-strung and nervy from his long quest. 'Don't talk to me, you sneaking thief!' he said.

The other advanced with uplifted hand, but the stockman smashed down his arm with his loaded whip-handle, and springing on him, felled him to the ground. The battle was as furious as it was short. Hughie rained blow after blow upon his adversary, holding him and thrashing him with the strength of a virtuous indignation. 'Can I take him now?' he asked, standing over his prostrate foe.

'Take him, and be d——d! ' said the horse thief.

*   *   *

A cloud of dust showed upon the plain below the station. 'By Gad!, said Dave, 'that's like little Hughie's seat in a saddle.'

'Hughie', I said, 'will keep his word. He'll never come back here again till he finds old Myall King.'

Something in the lift of the head of the led horse attracted our attention and held us fascinated. Then Dave threw his big hat into the air and gave a yell.

'I'll be hanged', he said, 'if that *isn't* old Myall King!'

And it was.

At the Mercy of the Barwon

THE BARWON RIVER flows south-westward from the borders of Queensland, through the north of New South Wales, till at Bourke, the thriving capital of a vast tract of pastoral country, it becomes known as the Darling, and winds away across the western plains to its junction with the Murray and its final rest in the South Australian lakes. For a great part of every year the Barwon and the Darling — really the same river — are slow-moving, muddy streams, with but a moderate volume of water running between their high mud banks; but at certain seasons, when heavy rains have fallen in Queensland, they come roaring down in stupendous flood, carrying with them the debris of town and farm, and writing their scroll of freedom in flood-wrack on the trees. Men still speak with awe and wonder of the great flood in 1890, when the river rose to a height never before witnessed, and when the town of Bourke was swept from end to end by the flood water. Here and there the river is flanked by tall gum trees; in other places the thick pine and gidyea scrubs fringe the banks; the stems of many fallen trees lie athwart the current, making navigation difficult except at certain seasons of the year, when the little river steamers come snorting round the bends on the brown flood water, carrying provisions to the far-out western towns and stations, and returning with high-piled bales of western wool.

For the most part the Barwon runs through silent bush spaces, but here and there a station homestead, a wool-shed, or a lonely selector's house gives token of riparian civilisation, and breaks with shining iron roof the dark monotony of the river-timber; and now and again a boundary rider's hut or the home of some lonely woodcutter stands perched upon the high red bank.

In such a dwelling lived Ned Strickland, with his wife and two little sons. Strickland's only means of living was the supplying of wood to the river steamers, a fairly certain, if not very lucrative, occupation. All summer he toiled with his axe in the clumps of gidyea timber, piling up great stacks of three-foot furnace logs, stacks which rapidly diminished when the steamers began to travel in the winter months behind the Queensland rains. His boys, the eldest only ten years of age, were his willing helpers, hauling home the logs two or three at a time on a rough, home-built sledge, and helping to slide them down the steep bank when a steamer called for fuel.

By the dwellers on the western rivers every change in the height of the water is strictly watched; and one evening in June — which is mid-winter in Australia — Ned Strickland noticed that the river was rising rapidly. Next morning a horseman passing on the river road brought the news of recent heavy rains across the Border, and of a river coming down in raging flood. Strickland's hut stood on a high bluff, or bank, and during the fifteen years which he had lived on the Barwon the safety of his home had never seriously been threatened; but on this occasion the reports were ominous, and the wood-cutter watched anxiously the water which hour by hour crept higher on the crumbling red bank. He secured the boat by pulling it, with the help of the boys, into a small creek, and then dragging it up the bank and fastening it securely with double ropes to a tree which, so far, had been always well above flood-mark. Late that night Strickland looked again at the river. It was now level with the banks, a wide sheet of racing, red-brown water. Huge trees were plunging down in the central current; a dead bullock drifted by in the moonlight, then a barrel, then two dead sheep. The Barwon was taking his toll.

Strickland was anxious. Though he knew that no flood could possibly reach his dwelling, he was aware that if the water rose much more his pile of wood would be in danger, and there was also the possibility that the water, backing up in the creeks and runners, might cut them off from the road and communication with the outside world — for the state of the river would prevent any steamers from coming up or down for some time.

Early next morning the wood-cutter was up and about. Round him, like a sea, spread the swollen river. It spread out through the river timber in every direction, brown and threatening. Half the pile of cut wood had already drifted away — setting at naught the labour of many weeks. No spot of dry ground could be seen except the high red bluff upon which the hut stood. Strickland's first care was for his boat. Without it, he saw at a glance, all communication with the outside world would be cut off, and he hastened to reassure himself that the ropes were secure. The little creek was full of water; the boat, high and dry but a few hours before, was rocking on the brown breast of it, but the ropes still held, and Strickland gave a sigh of relief.

The boys came down and joined him, looking with wondering eyes on their friend the river, which they had known all their lives and which they had seen in drought and in flood, but never in such flood as this. And still the water rose. At noon Strickland took counsel with his wife, and determined to row in his little boat along the creek, or backwater, which was now a seething river itself, and so to make his way across the flooded plain to the little hotel which was perched on the river-bank a mile below his hut. He realised at once that it would be the height of folly to try and pilot his little cockle-shell — a cast-off pleasure-boat from Bourke — down the river, but across the plain he had a chance: a chance to get some men and a larger boat to aid him in removing his family and his household goods to a safer spot till the flood went down.

Accordingly, he went with the boys to where the frail boat lay pitching at her moorings in the fast-rising backwater. As he was untying the ropes a shout from one of the children made him turn.

He followed the direction in which the boy was pointing, and saw some animal struggling in the river. It was one of the five goats which comprised the whole of the live stock owned by him; evidently it had been washed away from some point of refuge higher up the river. It was bleating piteously as it struggled hopelessly with the rushing torrent which was rapidly carrying it past the watchers on the bank. If a rescue was to be attempted there was not a moment to lose.

Strickland sprang into the boat, calling to the elder boy, who followed him, and, unshipping the oars, pulled out of the comparatively still water into the whirl of the current. As he approached the struggling goat he gave the oars to the boy to hold, and, picking up the coiled rope, tried to fling a loop of it over the floating horned head. He missed his aim and the inevitable stumble which he made set the frail craft rocking dangerously. The rope caught on one of the oars. 'Lift your oar!' called Strickland. 'Lift your oar, d—n ye, look sharp!' he repeated, as the bewildered boy began to pull desperately to keep the boat's head up-stream.

The boy jerked the oar from the row-lock; the next moment it was snatched from his hand by the racing tide. As he leaned over to try and recover it the boat heeled almost to filling, and the man steadied himself with difficulty and cursed the youngster's clumsiness. Now thoroughly unnerved, the child dropped the oar, and in a moment they were whirling down steam in the raging brown torrent, oarless, and helpless save for ten feet or so of light clothes-line.

'*Now* you've done it!' said Strickland, and for the life of him could say no more as he watched the frightened boy cower down in the stern, white-faced and wild-eyed.

The position was, indeed, a desperate one. Not only was the swiftness of the current a menace to the frail boat, but the stream was now full of floating logs, fence-rails, and heavy flood-wrack, which threatened to upset the little craft at every moment. Once in the middle of the stream the boat kept closer to it than the finest steersman could have held her. The trees upon the banks were much too far away for any use to be made of the limited length of rope, and even had they been closer the pace was so swift that to attempt to throw a line would have been to court disaster.

There was nothing for father and son to do but to sit close together in the centre of their rocking craft and to pray that some variation of the current should alter their course towards the bank, or some eddy or backwater draw them into safety.

They whirled past the little bush hotel, unseen by any of the people connected with it, who were probably at the moment occupied in securing safety for themselves. Strickland stood up in the boat and shouted but his voice was carried away in the roar of the gathering waters, and even had he been noticed, no help could have been given him except, perhaps, the sending to a point lower down the river the news of his desperate plight, where some organised attempt at rescue might have been made.

Past woolshed, station wharf, and lonely hut the little brown cockleshell hurried with its crouching human freight. From a cottage on a high bank a man saw them as they drifted past, but he was isolated from the world by a waste of spreading water, and could only wave sympathetically as he guessed their plight.

They travelled swiftly onward on a wide sea of open water. The river banks were now to be seen only here and there on a high red sandhill, for the most part their pathway was merely defined by the tall gum-trees on the submerged margins, and the boat drifted on in the guiding arms of the central current. Once, at a sharp bend in the river, it seemed as though the stream would toss them into still water and safety, but the racing tide caught them again at the critical moment, and once more the tiny craft was flung like a straw upon the central current.

The sun went down in a blaze of crimson, lighting up the weird waters with fire. The boy had fallen asleep in the bow, and the man sat moodily watching the brown swirl as it raced beside the boat, and calculating the chances of rescue as they came abreast of the town of Bourke. So far, fortune had favoured him, for, though they had drifted many miles at the absolute mercy of the stream, they had encountered no heavy logs or trees to bring about a collision and upset the tiny craft which swung and tossed, now side-on, now stern-first, in its wild, ungoverned race.

In the last of the fading sunlight Strickland saw the glitter of the silver roofs of Bourke, and knew that now, or never, must be the hour of rescue. A mile above the town the white-railed approaches of the Darling bridge showed up in the dim evening light, but the man could see that over the central portion of it the brown river was racing unchecked.

In mid-stream even the high side-rails were submerged. Nervously he fingered his light ten-foot rope. If only there might be some jagged point of broken railing over which he might throw a loop! But as he came nearer he saw that the woodwork was forty yards clear of him on either side, and with a roar of malicious triumph the river hurled its light burden over the buried bridge and down the starlit waterway to Bourke.

The town was a glitter of golden lights, coming rapidly nearer and nearer. In a flash the boat was level with the Chinese gardens that lie on the river bank, but the main stream carried them past full a hundred yards from the land.

Strickland stood up and coo'eed loudly, making a trumpet of his hands. Figures moved about the Chinese huts, and he could see some one waving. The boy woke, and merged his voice with his father's.

A little lower down a river-steamer, lighted stem and stern, was moored among some trees. Again the boy and man shouted at the tops of their voices, and an answering shout came back from the steamer's deck. 'They will try and pick us up', said Strickland, hoarsely, 'but they've no steam up, and by the time they're ready to come we may be at the bottom of the river. But it's our only chance!'

Swiftly they slid past on the oily tide. The moon rose red above the tree-tops, and lit the vast plains with flame. The lights of Bourke dwindled and faded behind them. For another mile they raced along; the water became more turbulent, the boat rocked and swung, and threatened to capsize every moment. The lights of a homestead fluttered and went by. Suddenly Strickland, who was sitting in the bow, gave a warning shout. The next moment the boat crashed sideways into a huge floating tree, half submerged in the flood. The boat's side crashed in like paper, and she filled rapidly. 'Jump!' yelled Strickland. The boy scrambled as best he could, and the man put an arm round him as the frail cockleshell went to pieces under them. Next moment both were clinging to the slippery, wave-washed trunk.

Strickland hooked his arm round the upright knob of a broken branch, and clung for his life; with his other hand he supported his son, who lay with his breast across the slippery tree.

The brown water tugged and tore at them, their sodden clothes dragged them down; not long could they cling to their dangerous perch. The end seemed near indeed.

Strickland was a strong man, but his strength was gradually slipping from him. The horror of the situation gripped his soul; the shock of the sudden wreck of the boat had unnerved him. 'What is the use?' he asked himself. 'It can only be a few minutes longer!'

A far-off hail rang over the water, and the lights of the little river-steamer came round the bend above them. She was steaming full speed ahead man with the racing current, and in her bows stood a man with a coiled rope in his hand. Strickland used all his remaining strength in one desperate shout, and the rest was darkness and a dream.

A little later he and his boy stood on the deck as the gallant little steamer threshed her way back to Bourke against the stream, snatched but just in time from the very jaws of death.

The Rebel

THE REBEL had never been treated fairly. Even as a foal he had been considered a dangerous horse, and bullied and beaten accordingly. Once, when the mares and foals — he and his mother among them — had been mustered from the Wilga Paddock to the stock-yard he had lost his head in the noise and excitement of the drafting, and, more from fear than vice, had lifted his tiny heels to the head stockman, and had received in return a cruel, biting blow from the ten-foot stock-whip. That blow he never forgot, and from that moment onwards he treated all men as things to avoid or to fight, according to the circumstances in which he found himself placed. He fought savagely when he was branded, and more savagely still when he was roped for breaking-in. He had to be blindfolded before Red Mick, the breaker, could mount him; then he bucked furiously and long, and when he found that no effort of his could loosen the iron grip of the man who rode him, he threw himself down and tried to crush the life out of his rider. Red Mick thrashed him to his feet, mounted him again, and flogged him round the sandhill till he was too tired to offer any resistance. After that, his conqueror rode him regularly, but the station men who had seen him buck as they had never seen any horse buck before, would not have anything to do with him; and, indeed, The Rebel would let no stranger approach him.

When Red Mick left the station The Rebel was turned out in the Back Paddock and wore no saddle for three years. Then came a rough-rider from Queensland, anxious to try conclusions with this colt, whose fame as a buckjumper had travelled far beyond the Border. He yarded The Rebel and roped him, but the bridle was never fastened on his head, for with one blow of his forefoot the outlaw smashed the man's skull. After that, the horse was turned out again, and might have ended his days peacefully in the Back Paddock had not a teamster, who was looking for a lost horse, seen him and been struck by his strength and beauty. This man made an offer for the horse, and the Boss, glad to be rid of such a useless brute at any price, willingly accepted it.

And so it came to pass that after an interval of twelve months The Rebel was once more in the stockyard, awaiting the arrival of his new owner's team, when he would be roped, blindfolded, and dragged to a place in the chains, where, starved and beaten into subjection, he would learn, like his comrades, to pull his heart out in the blacksoil swamps of the river road.

The Boss's wife had been ill for many weeks, it had been found impossible in the state of her health to move her to the nearest town, which was forty miles away. The Boss himself, his two young daughters, and an old trusted housekeeper had nursed her with loving care, but, do what they would, she remained in a state which gave them constant anxiety. The doctor's visits were of necessity few and far between, and the household were dependent to a great extent upon themselves in tending the sick lady.

Early in the afternoon of the day of which I write the Boss and all his men had been called away to a bush-fire at the back of the run. Not a soul remained at the head-station except the Chinese cook, the housekeeper, the sick woman, and her two daughters. Towards evening the patient took a sudden turn for the worse. The women were in despair. There were no telephones; the doctor was forty miles away, and, worst of all, there was no messenger to send for him, or for any help.

The girls were brave, as bush-girls are, but as they flitted distractedly from sick-room to verandah they realised the hopelessness of the position which chance had thrust upon them. Their father, with any of the men who might have helped them, was thirty miles away, fighting the flames upon the eastern boundary fence. Every horse was gone, as they knew, for some of the hands had been obliged to drive, owing to a shortage of saddle-horses. 'But there's surely one horse standing in the stock-yard!' said fifteen-year-old Maisie, who, though two years younger than her sister, usually took the lead in a difficulty. 'That horse is The Rebel', her sister answered; 'Dad has sold him to a teamster, and he is to be taken away to-morrow; just the one horse that is no use to us. Maisie's face fell. Had it been any of the stock-horses, or even a wild colt, she would willingly have tried to ride it for her mother's sake — but The Rebel! She buried her face in her hands, and cried softly to herself. Her sister went back to the sick-room.

In a few moments Maisie pulled herself together. 'There's always the chance', she said. Her mind was reverting to something her father had been saying only the day before about intractable horses going more kindly under a woman's hand, and how if you could combine a woman's voice and hands with a man's firm seat and determination you would have indeed the model horseman.

'There's just a chance. She hurried to her room and changed her dress for a suit of knickerbockers in which she was used to ride astride when going out with the musterers. Then, pinning on her cap securely and picking up a light riding switch as she ran, she darted across the garden and down among the darkening buddah-bushes to the stockyard.

*   *   *

The big-boned chestnut horse stood in the yard with his head down. He had been confined within these forbidding rail fences for many hours, and he was hungry and ill-humoured. In a dim way he realised that it was man, his arch-enemy, who had shut him up here without food or water; and he feared, and was ready to resent with tooth or heel, further indignities. He heard a light step approaching the yard; immediately he was on the alert. When he saw in the dim light a slight figure, bridle in hand, stoop and come under the slip-rails, he was uncertain whether to be frightened or angry. The figure approached him rapidly without any sign of fear and held the bridle up to him. Now, The Rebel had only once in his lifetime been approached without fear or indecision, and that was in the days when Red Mick, who feared nothing in heaven or earth, had given him his first harsh lessons in obedience. This figure which approached him now was not the figure of Red Mick, but it had Red Mick's confident and almost careless way of coming up to him. He was surprised, and he forgot to be angry. Maisie was a brave girl, and of the ordinary station horse she had no fear; but none knew better than she the risks she was taking when, bridle in hand, she walked up to The Rebel in the open yard. She knew that the last time he had been thus approached he had killed his man with a blow of his quick fore-foot; so, though she was apparently careless, in reality she was watchful and wary to a degree. Surprised into obedience, and with memories of Red Mick before him, The Rebel bent his head for the bit, snorting a little as the forehead-band slipped over his nose. Then Maisie began to speak softly to him, more softly than any human being had ever spoken to him before, and the horse stood quietly while she slipped the bit in place and buckled the throat-lash.

Although she had won one move in the game, the girl knew that the contest was scarcely begun. She felt strangely small and helpless beside the great bulk of the chestnut as he stood above her in the failing light; but nothing would now turn her from her task. If he let himself be so easily bridled by her, this notorious outlaw, why should he not let himself be ridden as well? With a firm step, but a hand that trembled a little on the reins, Maisie led the big horse to the fence. She was determined to saddle him inside the yard for fear that when he felt the first pinch of the girth he should plunge and pull away from her, and so jeopardise her last chance of bringing the doctor to her mother. Holding the bridle with one hand, she lifted from the fence her frail little saddle, a specially constructed soft-seated little pad of doeskin, with the lightest of girths and leathers, a hopeless piece of tackling to put on anything but the quietest of horses; but Maisie knew that if she could ride The Rebel at all she could ride him as well bareback as any other way, for if he bucked she would be powerless on his back in the best saddle in the world. As she placed the saddle on his back she crooned to him in her soft musical voice, and the horse stood perfectly still, with his head turned towards her. Evidently he did not connect in his mind this fairy-light toy with the huge unwieldy knee-padded saddle which the breaker had been wont to buckle on his back with trebled girths and a ring surcingle which cut him nearly in two. Even the pulling-up of the light girths did not disturb his equanimity. He neither shrank nor plunged, mesmerised, as it seemed, by that sweet, low voice. Encouraged by his quietness, Maisie pulled down the sliprails and led the horse out of the yard; and now it required all her nerve and all the urgency of the occasion to brace her for the crucial test. Would he let her mount, or, mad when he felt her weight upon his back, would he buck and fling her from him on that iron ground — perhaps cripple or kill her? She shuddered to think that she might be caught up in the stirrup and kicked to death by those savage hoofs; and there was no one to help her; and her mother lay ill — perhaps dying. This last thought nerved her to her final effort. Her mother was in danger, and what was her own danger in comparison?

Letting down her near-side stirrup to a convenient height for mounting, she climbed cautiously into the saddle. The chestnut stood like a rock while she pulled up the stirrup again to its proper height, then, handling his mouth as lightly as though it were a butterfly's wings, she urged him to walk forward. On the lighted verandah of the house she could see figures moving, and could hear her name called — 'Maisie! Mai—s—ie!' The horse paddock gate was open, the men galloping to the bush-fire had left it so to save time, as all the horses were away. She walked The Rebel through, and then, speaking soothingly to him, she raised herself in her stirrups and started him into a canter. She remembered that Red Mick, the breaker, had told her four years ago that The Rebel was a determined puller and bad to hold, but to-night he went as gently as a lady's hack, arching his strong neck to her hand. Mile after mile he cantered steadily on, scarcely aware, as it seemed, of the light weight on his back, bound by the spell of the soft voice and the caress of the light hand as it lay upon his neck. Soon the white foam began to show upon his shoulder. The Rebel was fat and soft and in no condition for hard work, and the black sweat ran in channels down his forearm. Foam gathered on his snaffle, and he tossed his head uneasily; but always he went on with tireless stride.

'You beauty — you beauty!' She crooned to him as she felt the strong muscles beneath her and heard the rhythmic beat of his bare hoofs upon the road. How he cut down the miles — and so easily! She had never ridden any horse half so good before. They reached the ten-mile gate, and The Rebel wheeled round to the latch of it as cleverly as a boy's pony; he had not forgotten Red Mick's teaching. The moon came up, red and splendid above the myall trees, and Maisie's spirits rose with it. She was already nearly half-way on her journey, the horse was quiet and docile, and covering the miles with a determined stride. She would reach the town and send the doctor on his errand, and all would yet be well. How glad she was that she had found courage to mount the notorious outlaw. Even at this hour of her mother's danger she could take pride in the feat that she had accomplished — the riding of a noted buckjumper that even the finest riders of the back country dared not mount.

With renewed confidence she drew her whip smartly down the shoulder of the sweating chestnut. A few more miles at this pace and he would have forgotten all about bucking; she would conquer him as Red Mick had conquered.

Game horse as he was, the long canter was beginning to tell on him in his soft condition, and when the girl felt his heart beginning to thump under her knee she drew him into a walk. After a couple of hundred yards at this pace her fear for her mother's safety made her urge him again to a quicker speed, and The Rebel, though breathing heavily, gathered himself into a canter as she touched him with her heel.

A mile further on a little mob of sheep that had been camped near the road started up and went rustling through the long grass. The Rebel, nervous and high-strung, plunged to one side; as he did so, the girl, taken unawares, lurched awkwardly, on to his withers. With a snort and a squeal of rage the great horse came out of the trance into which her courage and soft voice had thrown him, and only remembered that one of his hated enemies was on his back, and must be thrown from it if he was to recover his freedom. Snatching the reins from the girl's slender hands he dropped his head between his forelegs and gave one stupendous buck — such a buck as had tried even the superb skill of Red Mick, the champion horseman. It was enough, and more than enough, for poor Maisie; with a little scream she was hurled roughly from the saddle, and thrown heavily upon her back in the road.

And now the horse, partially tired though he was, became like a mad thing. Turning off the road he went bucking and plunging through the darkness, the little white saddle flashing ghostily above him. Maisie, lying hurt and frightened in the road, could hear the myall boughs cracking as he dashed through them; then the beat of his hoofs grew fainter, and the bush became strangely, weirdly still. The girl tried to get up, but one of her shoulders was hurt and she soon realised that she could not move. She was suffering excruciating pain; but even this became as nothing before the thought that she had failed in her object, and that the last chance of bringing help to her mother was gone. She shouted and coo-eed, but the silent bush seemed to have no help to give her.

*   *   *

The fire on the boundary was subdued long before midnight, and the tired bushmen were riding slowly homeward. Just where the bush-track joined the main road Albert pulled up his mare. 'There's a coo-ee, Boss!' The Boss and the others pulled up. 'It *is*, by Gad! Someone in trouble!' And putting spurs to Witchery he galloped up the road in the direction of the sound.

It took poor Maisie but a few moments to sob out her story to her father; and in a few more one man was riding hot-foot to town for the doctor, while another raced on to the station to tell of Maisie's rescue and to harness his horse to a light trap to bring her home.

The girl soon recovered from her injuries; the timely arrival of the doctor crowned her brave deed with success, and the happenings of that daring night became little more than the memory of a fevered dream. The little white saddle was found torn and broken in the myall scrub, and The Rebel tangled in a six-wire fence — into which he had dashed in the dark — hopelessly crippled and dangerous no more.

The Derelict

WE WERE GATHERED in front of the store at Mulga Plains, one Sunday evening, smoking our pipes and talking of our horses, when Hammond, the book-keeper, who was leaning against a verandah post cutting up tobacco, with a lazy eye turned towards the horse paddock gate, said suddenly, in a quiet tone of voice, 'Whom have we here?' We looked in the direction of his amused glance and saw a swagman shambling up the track towards us; yet not an ordinary looking swagman, or Hammond's remark would have been superfluous, for this was precisely the hour when the usual 'sundowner' might be expected to put in an appearance and ask for rations and a night's lodging. The figure which approached us was grotesque in the extreme. It was covered with fluttering rags and looked more like a scarecrow than anything else; the long hair flowing from under a small straw hat with a faded double-coloured ribbon; the thin legs, like pipe-stems, faltering in and out of the deep waggon ruts as though in imminent danger of snapping at any moment; the dirty blanket tied in a loose bundle with a strap, instead of the usual neatly-rolled swag, all showed our visitor to be somewhat different from the ordinary swagman. Out of a pocket hidden somewhere in his disreputable rags the neck of a bottle protruded accusingly, and bleared eye and drink-reddened face proved the accusation no more than just.

This apparition approached us unsteadily, threw down his badly tied bundle in front of him, and with a neat kick that would not have disgraced K. G. McLeod, he landed it cleverly on the top of the meat-block. Then he raised his battered straw hat in courteous salutation. 'Good evening, gentlemen!' he said, in the easy conversational tone of the well-bred and well-educated man, a tone which contrasted strangely with his grimy face and greasy rags. 'May I ask for a night's lodging and a little flour and meat?'

It was an ordinary request. Every sundowner who passed Mulga Plains knew that he might claim the usual hospitality of the Bush. It was the manner of asking that surprised us.

'You can camp in that old shed yonder', said Hammond, who, as storekeeper, took charge of these matters; 'and if you come here, I'll give you some rations.' He took out his keys and opened the store door.

The swagman untied his bundle and produced from it a rather dirty tucker-bag; then he followed the storekeeper.

'That's a rum-looking fish!' I said, in a low tone, to Dave Wilson, as the scarecrow disappeared into the store. Dave's good-humoured eyes twinkled.

'He's no Australian, that fellow', he answered; 'that's one of your English 'Varsity wrecks, Billy. Dear old Hingland!'

Presently Hammond appeared again, driving the old scarecrow in front of him; and the greasy tucker-bag was full to overflowing. 'Now', said the storekeeper rather gruffly, 'go down to the cook at the hut and tell him I sent you to get some meat from him.'

'I am much obliged to you', said the wreck, politely, raising his faded straw hat with a purely mechanical motion. 'May I ask if there is any employment to be obtained on this station?'

'There's the boss', said Hammond, indicating Dave with a sweep of his pipe-stem; he seemed relieved to be able to pass this bundle of rags with the soft voice and precise speech on to somebody else.

The nomad looked inquiringly at our overseer. I expected to see the usual shake of the head from Dave, but to my astonishment he asked: 'Can you cut burrs?'

A light gleamed in the bleared eyes of our visitor. 'I have already served an apprenticeship in that line', he said, seemingly proud to be able to present himself as skilled labour.

'Then take your swag to the men's hut', said Dave, 'and tomorrow morning I will show you where I want you to begin work.'

'I am indeed much indebted' began the rag-bag, but Dave cut him short.

'What's your name?' he asked.

The crouching figure stood suddenly erect. 'Arthur Mountjoy De Crepney Villiers!' he said; and every syllable was a challenge to democracy.

I burst out in a sudden snort of uncontrollable laughter, and was immediately ashamed of it. The strange figure drew itself up and looked at me out of its bloodshot eyes with a certain sorrowful dignity.

Perhaps Dave, like myself, was considering the effect this lean and ragged apparition would have on the men at the hut, for he said, a little diffidently, 'If you care to take them from me I can give you an old pair of trousers rather better than those you're wearing!'

'Thank you!' said the wreck, simply, and in two minutes he came out of the overseer's room arrayed in an old patched pair of clean white moleskins. Dave appeared behind him carrying something on the end of a walking stick, something that he threw on to the rubbish-heap where the ashes of an old fire still smouldered.

The tramp was retiring to the hut, when Dave called him back. 'Now, remember', he said, severely, touching the bottle which swung in the ragged coat-tail, 'none of *this* while you work on Mulga Plains. Understand me?'

'I assure you, my dear sir' began the derelict, but Dave stopped him with a wave of his hand towards the men's hut; and he stumbled awkwardly away on his lean shanks.

The next morning he was set to work cutting burrs in the Woolshed Paddock. There is no art required in cutting burrs; you simply hook them up with a broad hoe made for the purpose; but it is hard work on a hot day with the thermometer at 116 degrees in the shade — and there is no shade on the Woolshed Plain — and it requires a good deal of stamina and determination to put in ten hours of honest work in the blazing sun. But when Dave and I rode through the paddock in the evening, the overseer expressed himself as well satisfied with his new hand's progress.

'Can't beat these hard-drinking 'Varsity men of yours for work, Billy; drink hard, work hard, always holds good in the Bush.'

I looked at the wide acreage of uprooted burrs, already white and withered in the sun, and agreed that Arthur De Crepney Villiers had not been idle. Dave rode up to the worker, who was just gathering the ribboned rags that served him as a coat, preparatory to going home. 'Gettin' 'em down, Arthur?' he said, pleasantly.

'Yes, sir; not the Persians at Marathon fell faster.'

I noticed for the first time that the faded colours on his straw hat were those of a world-famous English Public School.

The Derelict, as we called him among ourselves, fully earned his wages, and the tale of his day's work belied his slender physique. On the third day he shambled up to the store and purchased a Crimean shirt and a pound of tobacco, but soap was not in the list of his purchases. The name 'Crimean' seemed to suggest to him a picture of British trenches and Russian guns, for he said suddenly to Hammond: 'Have you noticed, sir, that in Kinglake's very spirited account of Cardigan's — ' but the storekeeper broke in rather sharply, as he tossed him a red shirt out of the pile:

'Five and sixpence. I'll charge it against your wages.'

Hammond read very little, and knew nothing of Kinglake, and did not wish to expose his ignorance before this battered relic of other days.

'There is not the least doubt' began the man in the tattered coat, but Hammond drove him tactfully towards the door, and escaped without further conversation, with the cardboard walls of his Redan of literary reputation still intact.

Towards the end of the week De Crepney Villiers began to get restless, and on Saturday at noon he declared to Dave his intention of leaving, as he had business in Hillston. The overseer took him up to the office and wrote him a cheque for twelve shillings and sixpence, which represented his 'pound a week' wage with the price of his shirt and tobacco deducted. The tramp looked at it with a whimsical expression, counted it carefully over, and slipped it into the pocket of Dave's patched moleskins, lifting with a quaint flirt the tails of the tattered coat to do so. Then he fluttered off to the hut to get his swag. The men were glad to see him go. His grimy personality and dirty habits, as well as his superior education, formed a barrier between him and them; and though at times they found him amusing, as a house fellow he was less than desirable.

But from the first he had appealed to the cook's keen sense of humour, and that official was grateful for a week of entertainment in strange contrasts of classical allusion and fluttering rag. It amused the cook to see a gentleman and a scholar alternating with a down-at-heel loafer, though probably the pathos had escaped him. Anyway, he busied himself now with finding a second strap for the dirty blanket and tying it into a more respectable bundle. Arthur Mountjoy De Crepney Villiers looked on with a comical air of critical aloofness, and when the work was completed shouldered the swag with a word of courteous thanks. The cook bid him a cordial good-bye and held out his fire-reddened hand. The scarecrow slipped a shilling into it with the air of one who wishes to be generous, while aware of his condescension.

'Gor' bli'me!' said the cook afterwards, when telling us of it, 'you could 'ave knocked me down with a sheep's liver!' But Villiers, like a man proud in the consciousness of having done the right thing, tottered away up the Hillston track.

Later on, in the same afternoon, as Dave Wilson and I rode through the town, we caught sight of a familiar figure in white moleskins, red shirt, and tattered coat, waving a glass of beer on the verandah of one of the principal hotels.

His face was still unwashed, his long locks still unshorn. He hailed us with a bony arm like a rag-covered semaphore. As we reined our horses in front of the hotel he introduced us to a beery-looking loafer who stood at his elbow, 'My late commander-in-chief and his aide-de-camp! Pray join me in a (hic) glass, gentlemen!' Bush etiquette allows of no refusal in such cases. We tied up our horses and followed him into the bar. He watched the white foam settling on his flagon with a dreamy smile. 'Gentlemen', he said, holding it up with a regal arm-sweep, 'here is: Prosperity to Australia, and death to all her enemies, including the Bathurst burr, with which I have just waged long and honourable battle!' He drained his glass at a gulp.

'And what about Old England?' I said, trying to wake some chord of cleaner memory.

'Damn England!' said the wreck, with a full and hearty emphasis.

We put down our half-emptied glasses and went out to our horses. As we mounted and rode away, we could hear his voice raised in protest, 'I tell you, sir, it was at (hic!) Hurlingham in '85!' We looked back. Arthur Mountjoy De Crepney Villiers, his rags fluttering in the wind, stood with one hand on the shoulder of the bar-room loafer; in the other he held a glass. It was full to the brim.

The Last Straw

THE NEW CHUM stood on the verandah of the Squatter's Hotel in Bourke, and argued with the coach-driver about his luggage. He had four portmanteaux and boxes and one huge, overland, iron-bound trunk which it required three able-bodied men to lift. 'I can only take the three smallest', said the mailman, who already had a considerable complement of luggage aboard, 'the other two must come by bullock team.'

The new chum looked regretfully at his trunk. 'O, very well; of course, if you can't take them, you can't. When may I expect them at Mingabba?'

'Depends on the roads', said the driver, buckling a dusty strap round a brand-new Gladstone bag, 'maybe a week, maybe three months, if the river comes down.'

The new chum's face fell, but he was beginning to get used to Australian methods, and, reluctantly giving instructions for the remainder of his luggage to be sent on in the way suggested, he mounted to his seat and was whirled away over white and dusty plains and red and dusty sandhills to the station which was to be his home in the near future.

His father's friends gave him a cheery bush welcome, but the kindly old squatter smiled when he heard that, in addition to the ample baggage which the driver was unstrapping from the rear of the coach, two large boxes were to follow by bullock team.

'You see, we travel light in this country, my boy!' he said, by way of apology for the smile.

There were heavy rains in Queensland about the time of the new chum's arrival at Mingabba; the river came down in flood, and the great table-top waggon with its load of miscellaneous station stores and a huge, iron-bound trunk and a large black box bearing the bold initials 'J.B.F.', was obliged to camp for three weeks beyond the swamps, twelve miles from the station. The new chum fretted at the delay. Not that he was inconvenienced for want of clothes; his wardrobe, even in its crippled state, was larger than that of any other man on the station. It was simply that he was longing to handle and to show to his friends the treasures which the great trunk contained — treasures which his parents had bought him, with much deliberation and heart-searching, at the London Stores.

The new chum was a little lonely and homesick in his new surroundings. He enjoyed the station work, and the manager and his family were kindness itself. But he was thrown a great deal into the company of the boundary riders and stockmen, and he shrank a little from their full-blooded, boisterous carelessness over the little etiquette of dress and manners which meant so much to him. They jarred upon him in many ways, and, discovering this, they made fun of him, laughed at his finicky neatness, swore with exaggerated cheerfulness to shock him, and in fact, made rather a butt of the well-meaning but misguided jackeroo.

However, he found a good friend in the overseer, a manly, kindhearted fellow, who did his best to help the new chum over some of the difficulties that beset the Englishman in those trying first few weeks of station life, and to the overseer he confided more of his feelings than to anyone else.

So, when at last the boxes did arrive, in a cloud of dust and whipthunder and blasphemy, as the slow bullocks pulled up in front of the store, it was the overseer who was invited to attend on the following Sunday morning to assist at the unveiling of the treasures.

At the appointed time he arrived in the new chum's bedroom, and, taking a seat on the edge of the bed, tucked his spurred feet under it, and leaned forward expectantly, while the new chum turned the shining key in the burnished lock of the overland trunk which nearly filled the little floor-space of the room from window to door. The first thing to come to light was a gun in its case. This was unwrapped and admired. 'Of course', said the overseer, who had been asked to comment freely on the treasures, and give his opinion of their usefulness, 'of course, it's a devil of a long way to bring a gun when you can buy just as good a one in Sydney; but sometimes a man has an old favourite —.' And the new chum did not think it worth while to explain that this gun was brand-new, and that he had never owned one before.

A very light and beautifully mounted half-hunting, half-racing saddle was next produced, with bridle in keeping.

'Whe-e-ew!' said the overseer, 'what a beauty!'

He handled it lovingly, and the new chum glowed with pleasure and pride. 'That was worth fetching', said the overseer, 'you can't get leather and workmanship here as good as the British. By Jove! that's a dandy little turn-out!'

The new chum dived further into the cavernous depths of the great trunk, and produced a pair of brown riding-boots. The overseer handled them with a smile. 'Pretty swagger', he said. 'I've two pairs of black ones', said the new chum, proudly; 'my people thought the brown ones would do for riding to church on Sundays.' He pulled out the two pairs of black ones, and shewed them.

The overseer was trying not to laugh. 'We don't ride to church here to any great extent', he said. 'You see, the nearest church is at Bourke, seventy-five miles away; but they're nice boots. Only you see we ride mostly in leggings or moleskin trousers here; these are a bit too swagger for anybody but the boss. — Holy smoke! what's *that?*' The exclamation was prompted by the bringing to light of a gorgeous brown helmet, surrounded by a resplendent puggaree of blue and gold Indian silk.

'It's a helmet', said the new chum.

'It's a poem', said the overseer, 'no one but the boss could wear that without being shot. Far too swagger, you know!'

'Oh! I'll burn the beastly thing', said the new chum, anxious to please. 'I never really liked it, it's far too splendid for me. In fact, I tried to leave it behind in Sydney. I kicked it under the bed in my hotel, but the chambermaid pulled it out, and brought it to the door just as I was getting into my cab to come to the station. I offered it to the cabby, but he wouldn't have it; so there it is.'

'Put it in the river next flood', advised the overseer. 'Golly, what a bundle of silk handkerchiefs!'

'Pretty, aren't they?' said the owner. 'You can have that pink one if you like!'

'Thanks!' said the overseer, pocketing it and thinking of a certain girl in the township whose weakness was silk pocket handkerchiefs.

At this stage the keen eye of the critic had lighted upon a leather box reposing in a corner of the trunk, the shape of which was not to be mistaken. 'You don't mean to tell me — ', he began.

The new chum began to apologise hastily. 'Well, my people thought, you know; for Sundays, you know.'

The overseer showed signs of merriment. 'With the brown top boots, I suppose!' He rocked with mirth.

'D—n the thing!' said the new chum pulling it out with a recklessness that would have shocked Lincoln and Bennet, had they been present. With a weak man's ludicrous bravado he banged his fist through the top of it.

'Serves it right!' said the overseer.

The new chum flung the despised badge of civilisation under his bed, and dived into the trunk again. He tossed out a huge bundle of underclothing of a texture more suited to the South Pole than the Queensland Border, and drew out a flat green bottle or flask, with a shoulder strap attached to it. This he handed to the overseer, who was drumming his heels on the battered Lincoln and Bennet, and chuckling softly to himself. The bushman took it in his hand, and examined it carefully. 'It's a water-bottle', the new chum explained 'kept cool by evaporation; the hotter the day the cooler the water.'

'Wouldn't hold enough to satisfy the thirst of a fly', said the overseer, 'and it's a godless colour. A touchy colt would never let you mount him if he saw it coming. What next?'

The new chum tossed a dress-suit aside, and began to struggle with something at the bottom of the trunk. As it came to the surface a hot flush overspread his face, but whether as a result of his diving exertions, or for other reasons, it was impossible to say. The article in his hand was — an umbrella! a huge white gamp, lined with green.

The overseer burst into uncontrollable fits of laughter. 'What the devil — ? O, Lord! O, my mother-in-law! What in the name of all that's ridiculous have you got there?'

The new chum rather resented his friend's levity. 'An umbrella' he said seriously, 'nothing funny about that! I've seen old generals carrying umbrellas when the sun was hot.'

'Well, it's pretty hot here sometimes', said the overseer, trying to pull himself together, 'but I wouldn't let the boys see you carrying it, if I were you.' Here he went off into fits of extravagant laughter, clasping his knees in an abandon of mirth. He was just beginning to recover, when unfortunately his foot came in contact with the discarded silk hat, and he fell back upon the bed, with aching sides, helpless and unashamed.

The new chum turned from him in disgust, and began rattling some tin-ware which he lifted from the bottom of the trunk. The overseer sat up, sobbed at a recollection, stared for a moment, and then with a shriek that suggested incipient insanity rolled from the bed to the floor, and lay trembling — an occasional sobbing snort the only sound which betrayed that he was still alive and suffering.

The new chum held in his hand a brand-new shining piece of tin-ware. The overseer pointing at it, mumbled, 'A Billy-can — a Billy-can — O, Lord!' and fell limply on the bed. It was the last straw.

Langa

LANGA WAS ONLY a sheep-dog, but he was worth his weight in gold. He belonged to Bertie Maiden, the drover, and no amount of money would have tempted his master to sell him. Maiden earned a living by taking flocks of sheep across Australia, north, south, east, or west, as their owners decreed, and always Langa went with him, a comrade in labour, and a trusted friend. Maiden changed his shepherds very often, for Australians are independent, and droving is a trying and monotonous profession; he also changed his other dogs from time to time as opportunity arose of selling them and buying others, or of giving them in advantageous exchange; but Langa was as a brother to him, and these two were inseparable.

Sometimes Bert Maiden had men with him whom he could not trust, and dogs on which he could not depend, but always he had Langa, and Langa never failed him. Langa was what is called in Australia a Barb. The Barbs are a breed of black sheep-dogs, strong, broad-headed, prick-eared fellows, supposed to be descended from the dingoes, or native dogs; they are famed for their intelligence, and Langa was the finest of his breed. Every drover on the road between Rockhampton and Wodonga, and between Broken Hill and Homebush, knew him, or had heard of his prowess. Many would have liked to possess him, and some would not have scrupled to steal him, but his master knew this, and kept jealous guard over him when strangers paid him attention.

There were many who had tried to buy him. One man, asking his price, was told by Maiden that he would take a hundred guineas for him. Maiden merely said a hundred guineas because he meant to name a prohibitive sum, but a week later the man came again, and said he was prepared to give that amount. Maiden was taken aback; he flushed to the roots of his fair hair; then he turned pale beneath his tan. What had he done? He felt a traitor to his comrade. In stammering accents he explained that he had changed his mind, and that no money in the world would buy Langa. The man went away grumbling and talking of 'fools' and 'madmen', but Maiden gave a great sigh of relief, and Langa slept on his blue blanket that night with a fond black muzzle pushed into his master's hand.

There was no finer working dog on all the great North Road. He was swift as a speeding arrow, tireless, patient, and determined, and he obeyed his master's signals like a machine. You could send Langa round a mob of fifteen thousand wethers, and he would go right to the head of them, though the leaders were a mile away. You could send him round a mob of ewes and lambs in thick scrub and he would leave nothing behind, pushing the tired lambs on with his nose and shouldering up the cunning old ewes when they lay down. He could work three sheep as well as he could work three hundred, and one sheep as well as three. He had one peculiarity — he never by any chance barked. There are quite a number of sheep dogs in the Australian Bush who are known as silent workers; but, noiseless as a rule, they will bark when a sheep turns and faces them. But Langa never gave tongue under any provocation whatever. You might have thought him dumb if you had never heard his little yelps of delight when his master took off his muzzle or freed him from his chain.

Maiden's one great fear for Langa was that he might be poisoned. On the great sheep runs of New South Wales and Queensland it is customary for the squatters and managers to scatter poisoned baits for dingoes, and sometimes these baits are thrown upon the great drove-roads or stock-routes on which the drovers travel. For this reason his master, when he was in strange country, invariably worked Langa in a muzzle. Sheep-dogs hate muzzles. Perhaps they look upon them as an insinuation that they have not brains enough to discriminate as to when to bite sheep and when not to bite them. Anyway, they hate them.

Maiden was coming down the Macquarie River with seven thousand old ewes from Deloraine, when he lost Langa. The sheep were travelling in two mobs some miles above the town of Warren. Two shepherds were with the leading mob, and Maiden himself, with a black boy to assist him, was driving the second lot, which consisted of about three thousand sheep. It was easy droving country, fairly open, with some timber down by the river. There had been rain a couple of days before, and the flats were covered with a faint shading of green grass, which made the hungry sheep run and spread in every direction. The black boy had no dog, so Langa was kept busy, but he was too clever, too well versed in his business, to run about needlessly and get hot and excited, as some dogs would have done in similar circumstances.

He slipped quietly round his sheep, keeping a nice distance from them, and letting them know he was there, without fretting or disturbing them. Had the sheep been wild and timid he would have kept even further away, but long weeks upon the road had accustomed them to dogs, and they took but little notice of him, turning in as he passed, but turning out again as soon as he had gone forward to another point. Langa wore his muzzle, for there was danger of poison having been laid in the paddock through which they were passing. Perhaps that was why the sheep were extra bold with him; they knew that when he was muzzled he could not nip them if they misbehaved. Sheep are pretty stupid animals in some ways, but they know a muzzle when they see one.

Maiden rode slowly on the right-hand side of the mob; the black boy rode behind and kept up the laggards; and Langa, wise and alert, worked the wing next the river without aid or advice from his master, who rode with his head busy with his thoughts and threshing out the problems of a grassless track. When at last he looked across and saw that Langa's wing was spreading much too widely — in fact, was steadily drawing away into the river timber — Bert Maiden was surprised, for he knew that Langa understood just as well as he did how far to let the sheep spread, and when to check them.

He stood up in his stirrups, looking across for the dog, but could not see him. Then he gave two shrill whistles, the signal for Langa to stand still and be alert for orders. He peered into the belt of gum trees; the sheep were still running towards the river; no dog was to be seen. The black boy called out, 'Mebbe he got down longa creek, boss, get 'em drink!'

Maiden scoffed at the idea. He knew well that Langa would rather die than desert his post without leave. Again he whistled; and still the sheep kept running into the timber unchecked.

'Whip round that wing, Jackie, and turn 'em in', shouted the drover, 'and see if you can see that dog anywhere. Where the blazes has he got to?'

Jackie galloped on and put the sheep together; came back, and said he had not seen Langa.

Bert Maiden began to get uneasy. Perhaps the dog had scratched off his muzzle — which he detested — and had picked up a poisoned bait, and was even now writhing in mortal agony behind one of those great gum trees. The thought was maddening. He left his side of the mob to take care of itself and galloped round to the river. He whistled and called, but there was no sign of the dog. He had disappeared as completely as though the ground had swallowed him up.

There was no one to be seen in the river bend except a respectable-looking old swagman who was sitting on a fallen gum-tree eating his lunch. No! he had seen no dog. He had seen the sheep running through the trees, but he had not seen any dog.

'What kind of a dog was it, mister?'

Maiden described his favourite, but the swagman could throw no light on the subject. He did not look like a man who would steal a dog; besides, Langa was shy with strangers, and would never leave his sheep to make friends with him; furthermore, if the man had stolen the dog there was no place where he could have hidden him.

The sheep came pattering down through the dry gum leaves, and the drover put them back with his whip.

'Well, that's most damnably mysterious', he said.

Again he whistled and called, but only the echoes answered him as they travelled through the tall stems and died away across the river.

Bert Maiden took his sheep on to camp that night with a heavy heart. It was a clear, moonlight night; and after supper he took the black boy with him and rode back to the bend where he had lost Langa. Carefully they scoured every bit of the river-bank and the weed-grown gum flat, expecting every moment to come on the dog's dead body. Maiden knew that Langa would not follow a stranger, that if he had strayed he would have found his way back to camp before this. The only conclusion he could come to was that the dog had rubbed off his muzzle against a tree and had then picked up a poison bait; but, if so, where was his body?

At last Maiden, full of sorrow for his favourite, gave up the fruitless search, and the next morning passed on down the river with his sheep, to mourn for many a day the loss of the best dog a drover ever owned.

*   *   *

Langa always revelled in his work, and to-day he enjoyed to the full his responsibility, as, with one eye always on his master, he trotted up and down along the spreading wing of sheep, turning them back and turning them back continuously. One or two adventurous ewes in the very front of the flock gave him considerable trouble. Every time his back was turned they rushed towards the gum-trees, and tiring of their stubborn persistence, Langa dashed angrily at them to frighten them.

In his eagerness he sprang through the rough bushes which grew among the gum trees without taking heed of his steps. Before he could realise what had happened he suddenly found the ground give way under his feet and he fell down — down — down, turning over and over in his helplessness, till he struck with a thud what seemed to be the bottom of a deep well. With a little yelp of pain he scrambled to his feet. It was very dark and damp, and only a tiny patch of light showed, a long, long way above him. His ribs were very sore, one of his paws was hurt, and he was dreadfully frightened. He began to scratch at the walls of his prison. Then he fought to try and get his muzzle off. Then he raised his head and howled.

*   *   *

Three days later John Laffan, the hawker, drew his sturdy mares off the road and pulled up the van under a gum tree. It was almost sundown, and time to make a camp for the night.

'Get a fire made', he said to the boy who was with him, 'and fill the buckets at the river while I take out the horses!'

The boy went away whistling and swinging his buckets. Presently Laffan heard him calling.

'What's wrong wi' you?' shouted the hawker, as he tied a bell round the neck of one of the brown mares. He walked towards the river and found the boy kneeling down and peering into a queer-looking round hole, whose top was level with the surface of the ground. It was an unusual sort of hole, unlike the entrance to a well or to a mining shaft; it was mathematically a correct circle, and it dropped away into the bowels of the earth without any mound or heap of material which could have been taken from it. The boy was nonplussed.

'Look at this rummy-lookin' hole', he said.

John Laffan smiled. 'Did you never see that kind of a thing before, lad? Well, I'll tell you what it is. All along the flats of this Macquarie River the sand is silted up, blown in from the plains, sometimes as deep as thirty feet of it. You'd think these gum trees was growing on the top o' the ground. They ain't. Some o' their roots is down thirty feet below where we're standin'. Well, along comes a bush fire, or a man campin' sets a light to a dead gum; down she comes. The stem buried in the sand goes on burnin', down and down and down, the ashes drops down, o' course, and that queer round hole is left, big enough to swallow a man. Many's the drover loses a sheep down one of these places, and never knows what became of it.'

The boy was leaning over, peering into the dark recess beneath him. 'I believe there's a sheep down this one, dad!' he said. 'Listen!'

A faint moan sounded in the stillness. 'There is something there', said the man. 'Cut away and bring the rope from the van — and a lantern!'

When he returned, John Laffan said, 'Will ye go down and see what it is?'

'Al' right!' said the boy, always ready for adventure.

Laffan tied the rope round the lad's waist and lowered him with the lantern in his hand. 'It's a dog', the boy called.

'All right, fetch him up if ye can lift him. Mind he don't bite you!'

'He's muzzled', came the faint voice from far away.

A minute later rescuer and rescued lay on the grass. 'A Barb sheep-dog, and a beauty; but, by heavens, he's wasted to a skeleton! Wonder how long he's been down there. Run and get some water Ted!' The hawker stroked Langa's wise black head, and the dog licked his hand gratefully; then tried to stand up, but staggered from weakness and fell. When Ted came with a bucket of water the hawker put some in the crown of his hat, and Langa lapped it greedily.

They carried him over to the waggon and fed him; then they slung a sort of hammock under the van and put him in it, and Langa curled up and slept. The next day the hawker yoked up his horses and continued his journey towards Queensland, putting every day twenty miles more between the Barb dog and his master, slow travelling towards Sydney in the dust of his seven thousand sheep. Langa fretted, and would not be comforted. He followed the waggon quietly enough, and took his daily food from the hands of the kindly hawker and his son, but his eyes had always a fixed look of sadness, and he looked inquiringly into the face of every stranger who came near the waggon. Especially was he excited when a mob of travelling sheep passed them. Langa would trot round the wing, turning the sheep solemnly back, and searching the faces of the sun-browned drovers for the face of one he loved. Many men were kind to him and praised him; but his master never came, and Langa never forgot.

John Laffan travelled to many of the Border sheds, sold out his goods, and turned southward again.

One night a drover rode over to his camp to ask about feed and water on the stock-route ahead. This man was interested in Langa, for he was a great lover of all sheep-dogs, and a particular admirer of the Barbs.

'That's a nice dog', he said, jerking his head towards where Langa lay under the van, 'too good to be following a hawker's cart. He ought to be working sheep, that fellow. Do you know he's the living image of Bert Maiden's Langa — the champion of the road? 'Langa heard his name for the first time for many weeks, and he came forward at once and laid his wise head in the speaker's hand. 'He knows I'm speaking about him', said the drover.

When he mounted his horse to ride away, Langa followed him, and Ted was obliged to go after him and fetch him. They tied him up to the wheel of the van, and he whined drearily all night. Dimly he realised that this man who knew his name was some link between him and his lost master. For three or four days after that they had to keep him chained. Then he began to follow the van obediently as before. It was many months afterwards when Langa again heard his master's whistle, and from a poor dispirited, broken hearted creature changed suddenly into a keenly alert comrade, and took his old place as champion of the road.

*   *   *

Bert Maiden was bringing four thousand wethers down the Macquarie River. He was riding, sad at heart, behind his spreading sheep. The feed was good, and there was plenty of water, but Maiden was in low spirits, for he remembered that it was at this very bend of the river where eighteen months ago he had lost Langa, the pride of his heart. He had a yellow dog with him now, but it was plain to any observer that it was only a dog, not a trusted comrade. It worked without system, ran in on the sheep and hustled them, and was constantly being sworn at by the drover. There was a van with two brown mares coming up the middle of the road, and Maiden turned the sheep outwards from the river to avoid it. As he did so, he saw a mob of station sheep beyond his own lot, and feared that the two mobs would mix. He sent the yellow dog round to block his own.

The yellow dog ran cheerily, but he was only a tyro at the game. He ran much too close to his sheep and cut off about two hundred which scampered away towards the station sheep. Bert Maiden yelled an oath at him, and whistled him to 'Go on and head 'em!'

The yellow dog stood and stared, then followed the sheep undecidedly, chasing them further away. 'Confound your useless yellow hide!' Desperately he gave the sharp, shrill whistle that means, 'Get forward — quick!' The yellow dog stopped, just as a black streak hurled itself from under the hawker's waggon and flew round the sheep like an arrow.

'Ah! if only I had Langa here', moaned the drover, who had not seen the black streak.

Just then he caught a glimpse of a dog beyond his runaway sheep, a Barb dog, crouching, alert, watchful. He stared. Was he going mad, or was that Langa, his own Langa, who was standing there with lolling tongue, waiting for orders. He gave the double whistle that means, 'Bring 'em on, slowly!' and the Barb crept in upon the wethers, crept, cat-like, as only Langa crept.

With a rush the runaway wethers came back into the travelling mob. The station sheep galloped away across the paddock. The situation was saved. Maiden gave the slow whistle that means 'Come up to me!' and then, flinging himself from his horse, he was borne almost to the ground by a hurricane of black dog that threw itself upon him.

And so Langa and his master met.

The Parson's Mare

THE LANDLORD of the Royal Hotel, having finished his breakfast, strolled out on to the verandah and cast a careless eye down the deserted street. It was only nine by the clock in the bar, but already the sun was high and hot, and everything gave promise of another scorching day. The red dust lay in ripples on the boards, and the drifted white plumes of the umbrella-grass lay heaped against the verandah posts — debris of yesterday's dust-storm. The iron roofs crackled in the heat, and a blue haze shimmered on the mulga trees at the edge of the scrub; but the landlord was not unpleased, for hot weather means thirsty weather, and thirsty weather means custom at a Bush hotel. He had a good supply of beer on hand, and all that he asked for was an equally good supply of customers.

His eye was arrested by a solitary approaching figure that seemed to dance on the dancing heat haze. Perhaps a customer, he thought, some shearer or tank-sinker come early to town to quench an already aggressive thirst. He shaded his eyes with his hand and peered earnestly into the sunlight, then a shadow of disappointment crossed his face as he recognised in the approaching figure that of the local clergyman, the Rev. Arthur Ellis.

The reverend gentleman was slight and small, and walked with a quick, nervous step; he carried a Gladstone bag in his hand, and he said 'Good morning, Mr Tysam', very hastily, like one who is anxious to conciliate before his intentions can be misconstrued.

'Good morning, sir', said the hotel-keeper, with a somewhat forced cordiality, disguising his disappointment as well as he could.

'I've come, Mr Tysam, to see if you can — er — hire me out horse and — er — trap to drive to Mulgatown?'

'Certainly, sir', said the publican politely — a man who hired a horse was as welcome as a man who drank beer — 'when would you want it, sir?'

'At once, please. I have my — er — bag here. A quiet horse, please.'

'Certainly, sir. You can 'ave the old brown mare and the Abbott buggy. ('Ere, Billy, sling the 'arness on old Judy an' shove 'er in the light trap.) 'Ow far would you be going to-night, sir?'

'Well, I thought I would — er — drive as far as Gidyea Plains to-night, Mr Tysam, then on to Maroombah to-morrow, and then I could — er — get to Mulgatown the next night, perhaps?'

At this stage Billy appeared from the stables, driving the old dust-covered buggy with a lazy-looking brown mare between the shafts. The Rev. Arthur put his bag in at the back, and Billy officiously busied himself strapping it in place.

'That's a grand mare for a long journey', said the hotel-keeper, slapping the old brown hypocrite on her dusty flank. 'Don't be afraid to give her the whip, Mr Ellis, if she tries to loaf on you. Well, good-bye, sir. Good-bye. See you back on Tuesday or Wednesday at the latest, I suppose. Good-bye.'

The clergyman surreptitiously conveyed a sixpence to Billy, whose sour expression suggested that he had appraised his intentions to the Gladstone at a somewhat higher sum, and took a rein carefully in each hand. A red-headed girl with her hair in curl-papers looked out of the bar-door and grinned.

'Well, she won't bolt with 'im, anyway', said Mr Tysam with conviction as the mare moved unwillingly down the street at a foot pace, after having made a half-hearted attempt to turn into the stable-yard.

The dust rolled up in a smothering cloud from the slow-revolving wheels as they dragged across the myall plain. The clergyman made play as well as he could with the broken whip, but the mare took very little notice of him, merely switching her long tail lazily and biting back at the flies. A slow jog-trot was her only pace, and the Rev. Arthur soon gave up trying to make her improve it, and very sensibly devoted his time to fighting the flies on his own account.

It was a long, wearisome journey, and it is questionable whether the Rev. Arthur or the irreverent Judy was most relieved when at last the welcome roofs of Gidyea Plains homestead reflected the red light of the setting sun.

After a good night's rest he started cheerfully at nine o'clock next morning for another dusty day.

Judy travelled somewhat better on the firm red sand of the mulga ridges, and it was still early in the afternoon when Ellis reached the big cattle-yards of Maroombah. David Scott, the manager, welcomed him warmly and entertained him for the remainder of the afternoon at the stockyard, where the horsebreaker was putting a couple of colts through their paces. After dinner the traveller impressed upon his host the absolute necessity of his making an early start in the morning, so as to overtake the long stage yet before him.

'All right', said Scott. 'What time?'

'About six o'clock, I think', said Ellis.

The manager laughed good-naturedly. 'That may be early for *you*', he said, 'but every man on the place will be away mustering by half-past four to-morrow morning. You can have breakfast when you want it, though. Your mare will be in the yard. Can you harness her yourself? I'm sorry the groom will be away; for my overseer, Cuthbert, is up at Mulgatown trucking bulls, and I'm shorthanded.'

'Oh, yes, I'll manage all right', said the little clergyman cheerily. 'I once put in a horse all by myself at Baroona Station — at least — er — only — one of the — er — young ladies was there to help me.'

'All right, then, I'll bid you good-bye to-night, for I'm off with the men at half-past four in the morning. Good-night. Good-bye, and safe journey to you.'

He tramped off to his room, and the Rev. Arthur Ellis turned in to sleep the sleep of the just.

The next morning he was wakened before daylight by the sound of trampling hoofs as the horses were driven to the stockyard. An hour later he got up, bathed, dressed, and went across to the dining-room, where breakfast awaited him. Having finished his meal and packed his bag and stowed it into the buggy, he took the driving-bridle and went over to the yard to catch Judy. In the centre of a small yard she stood waiting for him, and she whinnied impatiently as she heard him approach.

However, when he had climbed through the rails and tumbled into her presence in rather undignified and unclerical fashion, she seemed disinclined to let herself be caught, and began to race round the small yard, and once, when he got rather too close to her, she deliberately threw up her heels at him. After five minutes of this kind of thing, he began to lose his temper, and scrambling out of the yard he went across to the buggy and returned with his whip. Next time the mare tried to dodge past him he gave her a smart cut across the rump. At last she was captured, and, taking down the slip-rails, Arthur Ellis led, or rather dragged, her over to the stable to put the harness on her. As the breaching-straps fell jingling over her quarters, she jumped forward, and nearly upset the little man; when the collar was put on, she blew through her nostrils like a frightened colt; and when he reached up to pull the hame straps she trod heavily on his toe. All this was most disconcerting, but she behaved even worse when he stood her up, and tried to drop the shafts in place. The moment his hand left the bridle, she turned completely round, and stared at him in a frightened sort of way. In the end he had to go and get the Chinaman cook to come and hold her while he yoked her up.

Between them they finished the job, after long semi-clerical, semi-culinary discussions as to whether the breeching was fastened to the saddle-band or to the shaft, and whether the reins should run under the collar or over it. At last everything seemed right, a shilling found its way into the Chinaman's yellow hand, and the Reverend Arthur gathered his reins and climbed into his seat. He was hot and dusty and covered with grease from the harness, and his toe was aching where Judy had stepped on it. His usual pulpit calm had deserted him. He took up the broken whip, and leaning well forward with a 'Now, you cunning old thief, you!' he let Judy have a real hot one with the whalebone handle along the ribs. The result was amazing. Instead of the dispirited forward shuffle which his two days' experience of her might have led him to expect, the mare treated him to a performance worthy of the arena of Buffalo Bill's show. She made one mighty spring into the air, pulling her driver well out over the dashboard; then with both forelegs sparring like a boxer's arms, she stood squealing; then she dropped to earth, and letting out with both hind feet she knocked the dashboard into smithereens, and shot the astonished clergyman into the bottom of the trap. Then she broke out into a lather of sweat, and stood trembling with what seemed to be fear.

'She no likee', said the Chinaman moving away to a safe distance.

'She's *got* to likee!' said the clergyman hotly; his blood was up, the fighting blood of the Ellises; he might be a duffer with wild bush horses, but if he couldn't drive an old besom of a mare like that his name wasn't Arthur Ellis.

Whack! Whack! Whack! went the whalebone along the well-lined ribs, and rattle! bang! rattle! came the hoofs in answer on the underwork of the buggy. Then suddenly the mare launched herself forward, and swinging over the sandhill took the track to Mulgatown.

The Reverend Arthur leaned back, braced his feet against whatever woodwork was still unshattered, and hauled at the flying mare. As well try to stop the wind. The four-mile horse paddock was crossed like a flash. By some chance in a million the gate at the top was open; through it they went on the top of their speed, with the hub of the wheel not an inch from the post.

The clergyman turned white as he noted the narrow escape; his hat had gone, his arms ached with pulling at the reins; before him the track ran into thick timber; he was frightened now, and would have been the first to confess it. He closed his eyes as the dark line of timber rushed upon them, and swallowed them up; but the maddened beast kept to the wheel tracks — indeed, she could not very well leave them — and two miles further on she dropped into a lobbing canter, into a trot, into a walk, and Arthur pulled her up just as the road once more emerged upon the open plain.

Shaken and unnerved, the little man climbed out of the vehicle and sat down on a fallen tree with the reins in his hand. Presently he stood up and shook himself; then he looked at the foam-covered beast in the shafts; the sweat was literally dropping from it, and every now and then it started as a strap or trace touched it.

He sat down again with his head in his hands. To a man unaccustomed to horses it had been a trying experience, and Arthur Ellis, no coward in the larger trials of life, had been a good deal frightened in this one.

Presently he looked up, and saw some horsemen approaching on the Mulgatown road. As they came nearer he recognised the leader as Cuthbert, the overseer from Maroombah; behind him rode one of the station men, leading a pack horse.

Ellis stood up, dusty and dishevelled, to greet them. His hand was bleeding where a splinter of wood had struck it, and his eyes were wild from his late adventure.

'Hulloa! What s up?' called Cuthbert, his keen eye taking in at a glance the broken buggy and the trembling, exhausted horse.

'She — er — she bolted!' said Ellis, simply. The bushman looked at the horse again, and his usually impassive face showed its amazement.

'Who did?'

'Why, Mr Tysam's old mare', said Arthur.

'Mr Tysam's old grandmother!' said the overseer rudely, 'Why, man, that's our brown colt out of Passion Flower; we only began to break him last week, and he's only been once in harness in his life! How the devil — '

The clergyman held up his hand in protest. 'The men were all away, Mr Cuthbert; I saw a horse in the yard, and I thought it was mine'.

'But yours was a mare', said the bushman drily, 'wasn't she?'

The Laggard

A GREAT MOB of Queensland cattle was travelling down the river road. There were eight hundred of them — eight hundred and fifteen, to be precise — and they made a gallant show as they moved slowly through the lignum bushes, tugging at the golden barley grass, with the sun flashing on the lifted horns of the leaders as they picked out the path for the rest. From wing to wing the mob spread over fully half-a-mile of country, and from the cock-horned, wild-eyed red and white that led them, to the lean-ribbed roan that stalked gauntly in the rear, they must have covered a mile at least.

Most of the bullocks were in good condition, and some were quite fat, but a few of the laggards showed signs of their long journey, and one — the roan bullock aforesaid — was little more than a skeleton. None of the drovers knew what was the matter with him; one said he had been crushed in the yards and suffered from some internal injury; another said that his teeth were troubling him; while a third averred that he was merely sulking, and starving himself to death out of sheer obstinacy. However that might be, the roan bullock would scarcely feed at all. When the mob was on good grass, and the shaggy frontlets were all lowered to the feast, this beast stood apart, with his head high and a far-away look in his eyes, as though he were too weary or too proud to feed. Sometimes he merely lay down, as though tired to death. On very rare occasions he might have been seen picking in a half-hearted way at salt-bush or blue-grass. And each day he grew thinner.

The other bullocks changed places continually in the course of the long day's march; but the roan steer was always the last, dragging wearily on behind the mob, over close-bitten ridges or well-grassed flats, stopping under every shady tree, only to be pushed forward again as one or other of the riders caught sight of him.

There were three men generally at the tail of the mob, and each one had a different method of dealing with the laggard. One was a loud-voiced, dissipated-looking youth of eighteen or so, with a pair of long-necked spurs on his heels, and a bright red handkerchief knotted loosely round his neck Whenever he caught sight of the roan bullock lagging behind he galloped after him, and, flogging him unmercifully, drove him well up among the others. The whip-blows were severe, and left great crossed weals along the back and ribs of the victim; but as soon as the boy had gone the weary beast dropped back to his customary place again. One of the men was a smart, neatly-dressed little stockman, who rode superbly on a long tailed brown mare of which he was very proud. When he found the laggard far behind the rest he would ride up to him and flick him below the hocks with his whip and call out, not unkindly — 'Get up, Roanie; you've a long way to go yet, old son!'

The third man, who was a tall, handsome fellow with a suntanned face and kindly brown eyes, never even uncoiled his whip from the saddle-dees, but walking his grey horse close up behind the laggard would move him gently forward, saying, 'Come on, poor old chap!'

The lagging bullock took little notice of any of them. He was very, very sick indeed.

Of course, the drover in charge might have left him behind. His value could not have been great, and the chances of his ever making satisfactory beef were slender indeed; but it is a point of honour on the Overland Trail to carry on with you every beast that can be induced to walk, however sick or lame it may be; and owners grow impatient with the drovers who arrive at their destination with their number short and the excuse 'Had to leave 'em; they couldn't travel!' On the Queensland roads everything with four legs is *bound* to travel.

One day the cattle were moving slowly off the noonday camp. In half-an-hour's time they had achieved their usual half-mile spread and the leaders stepped out smartly, for there had been but little feed in the morning and now the long barley grass on the flat before them was up to the girths of the horses. The rear-guard trailed slowly off camp. At last one beast only remained. It was the roan bullock, and he was lying down. The three men who usually rode at the tail of the mob were standing by their horses under a wilga tree, smoking their pipes and watching the cattle trail slowly past. 'Look at that lazy bag of bones!' called the young fellow with the red handkerchief round his neck; 'I'll shift him!'

Standing up in his stirrups he caught his mare by the head and raced across the flat. The sick steer saw him coming but did not try to rise. His limbs were like lead; his eyes were heavy and dim; the other cattle went past him in a streaky, spotted mist; a great weakness overpowered him and stifled effort. The drover reined his mare within striking distance and dropped his heavy whip along the bony ribs. It left a long, red ribbon where it fell. The roan bullock did not even turn his head. He was past caring for blows. The man changed the position of his horse, and facing the recumbent beast brought the heavy doubled thong down with all his force across its nose. 'Get up, you lazy blighter!' he shouted, angrily.

The tall man rode up. 'Here, drop that Fred! You won't get him up that way!'

He dismounted, and with the unwilling aid of the younger man pushed the unresisting steer to one side until it got its legs under it; then with one man lifting at its haunch and the other pulling at the horns at was at last induced to make an effort, and staggered to its feet. After stumbling forward for a few yards it fell again. 'No good', said the tall stockman; 'put up that whip and go and tell Wilson that we can't get the roan chap to travel any further!'

The youth galloped off and presently returned with the head drover, who said, 'Done up, is he? Well, I'll leave word at Allan's place as we pass; and if Allan can get him home he can have him. Come on, it's no use wasting time over him!'

They rode off together and left the sick beast to the mercy of the plains. Scarcely had they gone a hundred yards when first one crow, then a second, then a third, dropped apparently from nowhere and, cawing harshly, sidled along the sand to take stock of a possible banquet.

The tall man half-turned in his saddle and looked back. He saw the ominous black specks gathering from every side. 'Poor old Roanie', he said, 'I've dogged him along for nearly four hundred miles, and I've a soft spot in my heart for that steer. I'll go back with my knife and save him from the crows.'

'Leave him alone', said Wilson, shortly — 'Allen will get him along all right to-night. I owe Jim Allan a good turn for letting me put my horses into his cattle paddock last trip.'

'The crows will have his eyes out before night', said Jack Drysdale.

'Not they — not as long as he can swing his head!' Drysdale said no more, but there was a sad look in his eyes as he rode on after the cattle.

In the cool of the evening Allan, the selector, cantered up the stock route on his old grey Arab. He found the sick bullock standing, gaunt and huge in the evening light, under a kurrajong tree by the river.

'Well', said the selector, surveying the lean ribs and hollow flanks through a lifted stirrup-iron, humorously, 'you're a handsome gift to be presented with! Kept your eyes intact, though, I notice — good chap! What do you say to coming home with me, eh? I hope you'll be quite polite with those spiky horns!'

The roan bullock swung his head slowly round and gazed with limpid, brown eyes at the newcomer. He had had nearly five hours' rest and the cool evening wind had refreshed him a little.

At a very slow pace he travelled down the road in front of the selector, who turned him through the slip-rails into his cattle paddock and left him.

Rest seemed to be the main thing that he required, and in three weeks time he had lost his skeleton appearance, there was a new spring in his walk, and he could be seen feeding contentedly among the other cattle on the rich frontage grass. In three months he was mud-fat, kicking up his heels and tossing his wide-horned head wantonly, as he raced up and down the river bank with the young steers.

Allan, riding through the cattle paddock to make calculations about a draft of fats for market, took note of his altered condition and smiled.

'The Queenslander's as ready as any of 'em. He'll go, too!'

*   *   *

Jack Drysdale was taking over his first mob as head drover. He and his men were helping Jim Allan to cut out the fats on the plain behind the selection house. A mob of about a hundred-and-fifty good-conditioned cattle were rounded up on the open ground, and circled restlessly while Allan and Drysdale, moving their clever stockhorses among them, shouldered out the fattest and compelled them to leave their companions and join the small mob — only about a dozen or so as yet — of the chosen ones.

'*There's* a heavy one — that roan behind the spotted chap!' said Drysdale, pointing with the handle of his whip. 'Yes, I want that fellow', Allan said, moving his grey horse into the mob. — Ever see him before, Jack?'

'Don't remember him', was the answer — 'why?'

The roan bullock, annoyed by the shouldering attentions of the little grey Arab, thundered past at a gallop, stopped short, and wheeled, but the nippy little horse followed his every movement like a shadow, cut him out fairly and squarely from his companions, and drove him away, wide-horned head in air, to join the mob of fats.

Drysdale stared after the lumbering bullock. 'Those horns look familiar', he said.

'Do you remember a sick — ?'

'Roanie, by Gad!' exclaimed the drover. 'So the crows didn't get him after all! I wonder if Fred Keen will know him. He ought to, for I see the marks of his whip are on him yet!'

But Fred, who was shepherding the fats, received the newcomer without any sign of recognition.

After cutting out the cattle the drovers took them to the stockyard to put a tar-mark on them. Huddled in the large yard, a heaving mass of tossing heads and flashing horns, they were driven, a few at a time, into the branding race which opened from it.

'Mind that Queenslander!' Jim Allan called out from his seat on the rails — 'I don't like the way he shakes his head at you!'

Fred Keen and another man were on foot in the yard, forcing up the cattle to the gate of the branding-race. Fred, as usual, was more than free with his whip.

The roan bullock was just in front of him and was being crushed back upon him by the frightened steers in front. With a savage blow he brought the double of his thong across the bullock's quarter. 'Get up, you lazy blighter!' he roared.

At the voice and tone some old chord of memory seemed to waken in the roan bullock. Wheeling suddenly, he lowered his head and charged.

'Look out, Fred!' called half-a-dozen men at once, but the well-meant warning came too late. With a roar of rage the beast was on him; one of the great spiked horns thrust cruelly; and then the huge bulk swayed above the hapless man, stamping, kneeling, crushing the life out of him.

Before the watchers of the grim tragedy could strike a blow in rescue, a tattered, trampled thing was tossed high in the air and flung fiercely at their feet.

The roan bullock's vengeance was complete.

A Rider of the Rabbit-Proof

JIM WINTERTON set his hut door on the latch. There was no need to lock it, for it was a rare occurrence indeed for any one to pass his humble dwelling, which was forty miles from the nearest human habitation, save only the next hut on the fence, which was twenty-five miles west of his, and the next one on the other side, which was twenty-five miles east. And if anybody should chance to arrive at his lonely home in the owner's absence Jim knew that it could only be some poor traveller or stockman who had lost his way in the big scrub to the north, and who would be glad enough to have free access to the water-bag and the provisions. Therefore, in accepted Bush fashion, Jim Winterton left his door unlocked.

He mounted the bumble-footed old black mare which the Queensland Government provided for his use, and ambled away on the well-trodden path which led along the netted fence. In the bluegrass swamp by the tank the tinkle of bells marked the presence of two other horses, his own private property — a game-looking old grey hack and a dark brown speedy-looking mare. When Winterton, for personal reasons, had resigned his position as book-keeper on Owen Downs Station and buried himself in the silent scrubs along the Rabbitproof Fence he had brought with him his two favourite horses and the old Barb sheepdog which now ran at the black mare's heels. With these for his constant companions he seemed to suffer but little from the enforced solitude of the remote, unpeopled Bush.

His position was a humble and sub-ordinate one, differing in no way from that of his next neighbours — the unwashed and ignorant Mick Flynn on one side of him, and the morose and ill-tempered Peter Barrett on the other. Like these men, he rode his portion of the Rabbit-proof Fence day after day and month after month, mending broken wires and broken netting, filling in rabbit burrows and scrapes that threatened the undermining of the barrier, and beating back the bush fires that approached it; like them he took his orders from Harvey, the Fence Superintendent, who passed along the line of huts about once in three months. Harvey was an educated man, and to Winterton his visits meant much, for the lonely man had little or nothing in common with the stupid and ambitionless fellows who shared his labour.

The fence rider glanced across at his horses feeding contentedly in the knee-deep bluegrass, then he bent himself mechanically to the work which had become second nature to him. His thoughts wandered chainless down the wide aisles of the years, but his eyes were never lifted from the shimmering line of wire and netting that slid slowly past him as he rode. Thousands of rabbits on the New South Wales side of the fence made the sandhill seem in constant motion. The ground was fouled by them, and all along the cleared line of the barrier not a blade of grass was to be seen, and not a bush or tree but was barked by their ravenous teeth; making the Queensland side look lush and tangled in comparison. On the south side a beaten track — hammered by millions of tiny feet — ran alongside the netting, telling eloquently of the strenuous endeavour of the marching armies to win their way northward to cleaner ground.

The black mare plodded steadily along the bridle path which ran parallel with the fence. She was a quick walker, in spite of her deformed foot, and, like her master, was intent only on the business of the hour. Even when a black snake glided stealthily out of the path in front of her she merely laid one ear back for a moment to show that she had seen it, and then paddled on as before. Iguanas scuttled away through the dry grass, bright-hued parrots chattered in the low bushes, and once a mob of kangaroos, disturbed at their feeding, loped away into the scrub, but these everyday companions of the lonely ride distracted neither the man nor his horse. A single emu turned on to the fence in front of them, and ran along for a hundred yards or so in the path before turning aside again; but still the rider kept his eyes on the fence, and the mare kept her glance on the ground.

The sun was fairly high above the mulga trees when the fence rider's nag stopped of her own accord in front of a large box-tree, on which was a broad 'blaze', or axe mark, with beneath it a shortshafted arrow cut in the grey bark.

Winterton threw one leg over the pommel of his saddle and, sitting sideways, faced the fence and pulled out his tobacco pouch and proceeded to cut up a pipeful of strong black tobacco. As he rolled the weed between his hands the mare threw up her head and whinnied. Winterton did not trouble to look up, although he heard quite plainly the pad-pad of horsehoofs in the sand, which betokened the arrival of his fellow boundary rider.

Jim was a sociable fellow, or at least had always been considered so in the days when he moved among men of his own education and tastes, but he had no liking for Peter Barrett, the sullen, dark-browed companion in exile who met him at this point on every alternate day.

As a rule, they scarcely accorded each other decent civility. Barrett was sulky, and the book-keeper reticent. They would have quarrelled long ago had there been anything to quarrel about, but as each man's work was wholly independent of the other's there was no possible excuse for them to do so.

'G'day!' said the newcomer, grudgingly, as usual; and 'Ger'rout ye cur!' he growled, as he generally did when the Barb sheepdog showed his teeth at the blue cattle dog which followed him. Every second day for the last ten months Peter Barrett had given his grudging welcome, and the two dogs had met as enemies and parted as comparative friends.' 'Day!' said the book-keeper, without looking up. He took his pipe leisurely from his pocket, and as leisurely filled it, after tapping it thoughtfully on the pommel of his saddle.

'Give us a fill!' said the other man rudely, holding out his hand. Winterton offered his pouch without enthusiasm. You cannot refuse a man tobacco in the Bush, however much you would like to.

Barrett produced a short-stemmed blackened clay and filled it, and both men smoked silently for a minute or so. The dogs lay down in the shade with lolling tongues and noisy breathing. Flies hovered around the horses' ears in dense black clouds.

Suddenly Barrett's chestnut cocked an ear and lifted its head, and immediately afterwards the black mare did the same.

'Horseman comin'!' mumbled Barrett, with his pipe between his teeth.

'Brumbies more likely', said Winterton. 'There can't be a horseman within twenty-five miles of us!'

But as he spoke a horse emerged from the myall trees in the direction from which Peter Barrett had just come, and on its back was certainly a man. The two fence riders scrutinised with interest this horseman, who had discovered their remote solitude and penetrated into this vast desert which knew no human beings but themselves and Harvey, their superintendent. They saw at a glance that he was spent and famished, and his eyes had an unnatural glassy stare in them as he raised them from the path where he had been following Barrett's horse tracks with feverish intentness. His horse was lean and tucked up, and very leg-weary, stumbling as it walked. When the rider saw the two men sitting in front of him on their horses he gave a gurgling sound, half-sob, half-cry, slipped from his saddle to the ground, and rushed to the water-bag which was hung on the neck of Winterton's horse; tilting up the collar-shaped canvas, he drank greedily. It was pathetic to see the furtive, fearful haste in the simple action, and to see the thin hand raised as though to ward off all possible interference. At last he seemed for the moment satisfied, and looked up with a great sigh of relief. The starved horse had walked forward with bridle trailing, and was nosing at the water-bag which hung on Barrett's saddle. The dark, sullen-looking boundary rider dismounted, and setting his broad-brimmed hat upon the ground filled the crown of it with water. The horse put its head down and sucked noisily at the tiny pool. Again and again the make-shift bucket was filled, and as quickly emptied.

The newcomer was talking to Winterton — 'Thank God! Thank God! Thank God!' he was repeating in hysterical sobs — and then recovering himself a little, he asked, 'Do you live near here?'

'Twelve and a half miles to the west along that fence — and he', pointing to Barrett, 'same distance down it to the east. This is the Queensland Rabbit-proof. Lost yourself?'

'Two days and a night', said the man, 'two days I've played a lone hand with Death. I missed the track a mile or two below Donnelly's on Back Creek. I must have ridden a hundred miles since then, and never seen water, and never struck a fence till now. My horse is just about done in. Look at him!'

The tired beast had tucked his weary limbs under him and sunk down on the little bridle path between the high fringes of golden-yellow barley grass. 'I spurred him rottenly, poor beggar', the man went on; 'I was mad. Look here!' Winterton looked at the spurs and boot-heels, which were purple with clotted blood — and did not dare to look at the poor tortured flanks half-hidden in the kindly grass.

'You've had a devil of a time', he said. 'Come home with me. The mare will carry us both, if that poor beast can carry its hide!'

Barrett kicked the cattle-dog, which was sniffing at the knocked-up horse, and then climbed into his saddle. His water-bag was empty, but for once he had played the man. With a careless 'So long, then!' for the others to share between them, he shook up the chestnut and faded away down the line of the fence.

The man who had been rescued was back again at Winterton's water-bag. This time he finished it to the last drop. Then he leaned against the blazed tree and laughed hysterically.

'Come', said Jim, 'the sooner you get out of this sun and get something to eat the better for yourself. Get up on the mare. I'll walk for a mile or two and lead your beast. Come!'

And so they went in single file along the little pathway that followed the netting fence over sandhill and flat and swamp. The sun beat fiercely down upon them, and of necessity they travelled slowly, the tired horse dragging wearily on Winterton's arm; and the twelve miles seemed like twenty-four. But at last the tinkling bells on the book-keeper's horses gave them welcome, and they emerged on the plain where his hut stood.

Winterton conducted his unexpected guest into his humble dwelling, and busied himself in finding food for the famished man. Ten minutes later the rescued bushman was sleeping soundly in Winterton's bunk; the tired horse was lying in the shade of a wilga tree within easy reach of the water at the dam; and Winterton himself was boiling meat at the open fireplace outside the hut.

The sun was low in the west when the stranger awoke, mightily refreshed, and once more — shadowed by some former fear — drank greedily from the water-bag hanging in the verandah.

In the stillness of evening, when the summer lightning played on the edge of the plain and the bullfrogs croaked in the dam, Winterton listened to the lost man's tale. With a certain nervousness, which seemed to be a natural outcome of his recent experiences, the tall, lean bushman, who looked like a shearer or drover, began —

'I'll never forget what I went through in that scrub; if I live to be a hundred. It was God's mercy that I hit the Rabbit-proof and your mate's track going along it. Another hour and I'd have been done. I was nearer death this morning than ever I've been before and I've been feeling pretty mean about a trick I played a fellow back on Owen Downs a year ago.' Winterton winced a little at the well-known name, but forbore to interrupt; and the man, speaking rapidly, went on; evidently so grateful for his recent deliverance that he felt himself bound to make atonement for his fault by detailing it to this new-found friend.

It was last summer. I was riding out to Windorah, and I was camped on the Creek below Owen Downs, when a fellow rode up to my tent one evening; a short, dark chap, with a heavy brown moustache — a jackeroo, I found he was, afterwards. Well he tied up his horse, and had a drink of tea with me, and we began to chat about one thing and another. He told me that he belonged to the station, and when he found out in conversation that I was pretty hard up he offered me a job — offered me a tenner if I'd do a bit of work for him on the following night. I was to ask no questions, do what I was told, and swear on my life not to tell a word of the matter to any living soul. I promised readily, for I was dead broke, and ready for anything short of murder if I got a tenner for it. I promised — but I've broken my promise to-night, mate, for I've looked in Death's face and I'm scared, and I want to tell some one of the mean thing I did, but I trust you not to tell what I'm going to tell you. Is it a promise?'

'It's a promise', said Winterton, without hesitation. He was leaning forward listening intently. Somehow he felt he was on the verge of a discovery that should make or mar his life.

'Well, this was what the dark chap wanted me to do. It appeared that he was in love with the manager's daughter, and so was the bookkeeper, and, so far as I could make out, the bookkeeper had the inside running.'

Winterton shifted uneasily on his upturned soap box, but said nothing.

'Now, the dark chap had hatched a plot to disgrace the other man, and to get the girl for himself, and he wanted me to help him. For two reasons, mate, he wanted me. One was that I was a stranger and could be forty miles away from the place by next morning, if necessary; and the other was that he had seen me at the station store and had noticed that I was very like the bookkeeper in height and build, and something like him in face as well.'

Here Winterton for the first time took a close look at the speaker, but the other, without noticing the scrutiny, went on with his story.

'Well, when he had explained his plan, I thought it was a mean kind of business; but a tenner was a tenner to me last summer, so I agreed to help him and to hold my tongue.'

Winterton's brown hand clenched and unclenched on his knee, but by no other sign did he show the tenseness of his feeling as he listened for what was to follow — the events of a year ago, which were branded on his very soul.

'I put myself in his hands', the bushman was saying, 'and the jackeroo returned to the station. Early the next evening he came to my camp on foot with a suit of the bookkeeper's clothes. Under his direction I dressed in these. They were rather unusual clothes for the bush. A light grey coat and light grey corduroy trousers, with a hat, or rather helmet, of brown cloth, wrapped round with one of those blue and gold puggarees, a rich-looking top piece it was, and I was told to wear it tilted over my face, as that was the way the bookkeeper always wore it.'

Winterton involuntarily pushed his cabbage-tree hat back from his sun-burnt nose, but the man, with eyes fixed on the far horizon, where the lightning was dancing on the purple edge of the world, took no notice of him.

'At dark', he went on, 'we stole up to the homestead, and, according to directions previously given me, I crept unobserved into the manager's private room, and proceeded to take from his desk, which was open, a roll of bank-notes. I thrust them into my pocket, and as I turned round I was confronted by the manager and the man who was paying me. I looked confused, and hurried to the door. 'Winterton! — Jim! — what are you doing?' called the manager, but I knew my instructions, and, rushing headlong through the dark, I reached my camp, where my horses stood packed and saddled. Stuffing the bookkeeper's clothes into a hollow log — as instructed — I hastily dressed in my own, and in half an hour was ten miles away on the northern road. Whether the plot succeeded or not I don't know, but if a half-blind manager, a false-swearing jackeroo, and an easily-duped girl, together with the finding of the missing notes in the suspected man's pocket, could make it do so, there is every reason to believe that it did.

'I swore to tell no man about it, mate, and I've broken my oath; but I've been too near death to-day to go about any longer with that bit of mean work on my conscience, and just feel bound to tell somebody.'

Jim Winterton sat for a moment or two with his head in his hands, then he sprang to his feet, and faced the man he had rescued.

'I too, promised not to repeat what you've told me; but I'm going to break my promise also. I, too, have been face to face with death once or twice in these last months of torture. I'm the bookkeeper from Owen Downs. Look at the man you've disgraced!'

The bushman shrank away. Dishonoured, friendless, an exile as he was, there was something in Winterton's face that made the other cringe before him.

'In three days', said the one-time bookkeeper, speaking slowly, 'you will leave here. I'll give you five pounds to take you out of Western Queensland, and look to it that I never see you again!'

In three weeks a new rider had come to Winterton's hut, and the bookkeeper had gone back to civilisation with knowledge that he valued more than life.

Confronted with the man who had learned his perfidy, the jackeroo made full confession. Winterton was reinstated in his office; and the girl, in the manner of true hearts, made loving reparation to the man she had never really doubted.

The Wild Man

ON THE DARK edge of a pine scrub, far away in the heart of the Never-Never country, stood a tumbledown bark hut. From one end of its roof rose a battered tin chimney, the loose sheets rattling weirdly whenever the wind blew. This old hut had once belonged to a party of sandalwood-cutters, but the precious clump of priceless timber which had grown on the ridge behind it had long since been cut down and carted away, and the adventurous explorers who had found it had carried their axes and camp-fittings to further fields. The old hut was far from any road or river, and a world away from any house or town; scarcely a foot, save those of the wild things of the bush, had disturbed the silence of its surroundings in for more than thirty years.

One night, as it stood in the white moonlight, pathetically deserted and alone, like some human thing crying for companionship, a strange creature glided gibbering out of the shadow of the pine trees, and stood in an attitude of wondering amazement before it. This fearsome apparition would have seemed to the onlooker, had any such been present, an extraordinary mixture of man and beast. It displayed what was apparently the figure of a man, and it walked erect; but the long matted hair that covered its head and chin and breast, the curved talons on hand and foot, the wild, hunted, yet rapacious eyes, were the attributes of the brute creation. Round its loins clung a belt of skins, and in one hand it carried a knotted vinestick, on which from time to time it leaned and gibbered. White foam-flecks clustered on its lips, and as it walked it turned its head rapidly from side to side as one fearful of attack.

Two wallabies that had been playing in the open space in front of the hut saw it and fled terrified into the dark line of the trees; a night bird cried overhead, then flew away on silent wings. The evil thing crept stealthily forward, glancing furtively this way and that, and then glided through the broken doorway of the hut. Silence fell upon the bush. Suddenly there was a rattle as of tinware falling, a wild unearthly yell cut the night with terror, and the weird creature rushed headlong from the hut, and, loping like a kangaroo at speed, fled away into the shadows.

Three nights later it came again, detaching its grey and horrid form from the dull grey of the tree-trunks, and again moving like a spectre into the deserted hut. Then for many nights it came, crept into the deserted dwelling, and stole away like a ghost at the first white gleam of the dawn.

*   *   *

Down on the river road a cloud of dust rose and hung heavily in the still hot air of noon. Through it rang the clink of chain and the drone of deep-tyred wheels. Twelve bullocks emerged slowly, two by two, from the murky cloud. Beside them a tall man rode doggedly, grunting at them now and then behind his beard as their slow step grew slower and well-nigh ceased altogether. The wagon which they drew was loaded high with bags and tents and camp utensils, and under an awning in the fore-part of it two women crouched silently. Grey dust lay on the folded canvas of the tents, on the yellow awning under which the women sat, and on the rails of the wagon. A black boy, dozing in his saddle, rode behind on a starved white horse, and under the wagon, in the scanty shade it threw, a blue cattle-dog moved slowly with blistered feet and lolling tongue. Presently the crawl of the footsore bullocks altogether ceased. At a word from the driver the women climbed down from their perch, and began to make a small fire with twigs. The black boy took a billy-can from the wagon, and rode off to the river for water. The bullocks scraped the hot sand with their feet and then lay down; and over all the noon sun blazed relentlessly.

'I'll go no further to-day', said the tall man, wiping the sweat and dust from his forehead with a red-brown hand; 'the bullocks are done up. Come here, Jacky, and we'll take the yokes off 'em.' The black boy tied his horse to a sapling and came over to obey. The tall man turned to the younger of the women, a big, red-lipped, full-breasted girl of seventeen. 'Here, Kate, you jump on my horse and see if you can get a pound or two of flour from old McNiven, his house is about two miles from here. There's the track crossing the road; you follow it up, and it'll bring you right to his slip-rails. Tell him you're a daughter of mine, and he'll give you the flour all right. Many a time I've obliged him on the road. Come on; I'll give you a leg up!'

The girl settled herself in the saddle, and, kicking her heels into the lean brown horse, forced him into a shambling trot, and, crossing the main road, was soon swallowed up in the line of timber which flanked it.

For more than a mile she rode, then suddenly came to a place where the track she was following divided into two. The one to the right seemed the more likely, though both were but little marked with traffic; she followed it through a thick pine-scrub, and on across a black-soil plain, and found herself once more in a thicket of tangled vine and gum saplings; riding on absent-mindedly, she was suddenly aware that the track she had been following had altogether ceased. Pulling her horse round she tried to recover it, but could not. Forcing her way through the twining branches she got into even thicker scrub. Now she could not even see the sun, and she realised with a creeping shudder of fear that she was lost. Up and down she rode, and round and round — really frightened now, but no sign of the path was apparent, and the bitter truth came home to her. She had followed a wrong turning, had taken some old wood-carter's track instead of the road to the selection, and had now little chance of regaining her sense of direction. Pulling up her horse she coo-eed and coo-eed again, loudly, reverberantly, as only a bush-girl can; but the great awesome scrub returned no answer, and the echoes died away in the ridges. Stirring up her lagging horse she rode hurriedly on.

Hour after hour she travelled. Once she came upon her own horse's tracks, and knew that she had been riding in a circle. Then the sun sank slowly over the tree-tops, the dusk gathered, the cicadas shrilled in the branches; it grew darker and darker. The girl dismounted and tied her horse to a sapling. Then she sat down at the foot of a twisted vine and began to doze. Every few moments she woke with a start as a night-bird called at her shoulder, or a wallaby stirred the scrub beside her. She was frightened and lonely, but also she was very tired. She could hear the click-click of the brown horse's bit as he tugged at a branch above him. He had had nothing to eat since early morning. How long she slept she could not have told, but she woke with a start in the cold grey of dawn. Bewildered, she leapt to her feet, then remembered her plight. She glanced to where she had left her horse. He was gone. Only some straps of the broken bridle hung on the sapling. Something must have frightened him in the night. Utterly unnerved, the girl bent her head in her hands and cried bitterly. With the horse she had a chance of finding her way out of this labyrinth of trees; without him she had none. Aimlessly she walked on through the wakening bush. The magpies shrilled joyously, singing glad paeans to the rose-crowned morning. The spider-webs glistened in the dew like fairy shields. Then the sun rose hot and angry, and burned down on the ridges. The girl's feet sank into the sand, the branches tore her arms, the cloudless sky mocked at her. She was lost in the bush — lost — lost! How long would it be, she wondered, before they came after her! Jacky was a rare tracker; he would soon find the hoofmarks and follow them. Perhaps the brown horse would gallop home and warn them at the wagon. Even now they might be close to her. She took courage from the thought, pulled some berries and ate them, and found a little pool of water under a gum-tree. It was bitter with the syrup of purple gum-leaves, but it cooled her parched lips. Noon came, and she rested. In the afternoon she plodded on. Again the sun sank, again the cicadas woke to life. The scrub suddenly ended, and as she came out on a bit of open plain she saw with a great joy a bark hut just in front of her. The door was off its hinges, the lintel was bent, the bark was rotten and gapped with age. The hut had been long deserted. Still it was refuge for the night.

Inside all was neglect and decay. A pile of old kerosene tins lay in one corner, a tattered kangaroo-skin was on the floor, a heap of grey ashes lay in the huge fireplace, and a battered tin billy-can stood at one side of it. In one corner was a rough bush table, a shelf above it held a couple of empty tins. Two bunks, with the remains of a few tattered sacks mouldy with age, had been built against the wall. Into one of these the tired girl crept and pulled the torn bags over her. She would rest here till morning. If they followed her tracks they would find her as easily here as anywhere; if not, well, it would soon be too late, and nothing would matter.

*   *   *

The new moon hung like a silver wisp above the pine-trees. The night was so silent you could hear the tap-tap of the wallabies as they crossed from the scrub to the plain. The little flat was rich with grass, and all the wild things of the woods came there at night to feed.

A mopoke called through the star-mist: 'Mopoke! Mopoke! Mopoke!'

Then a tall grey figure came stealthily, ghostily out of the pinestems — a figure half-man, half-beast.

*   *   *

The girl woke with a start and that indefinable sense of a near presence that no darkness or silence can deny. In the dim light conveyed by the stars from the wide chimney she was aware of someone bending over her — a nightmare phantom of misshapen humanity. She sprang up from her rude couch and tried to cross the floor of the hut. A long hairy arm was stretched forth to bar her way. With a loud scream of terror, repeated again and yet again, she fell fainting at the creature's feet.

The wild man stood looking at her in the dim light. He did not attempt to molest her, nor was there either anger or mischief in his gaze; only wonder, and a deep and human pity. Slowly the soul in him awoke as he looked again, for the first time in thirty long years, upon the face of a fellow human being.

In those thirty years, or the greater part of them, no picture like this one so dimly lighted by the stars had ever arisen to give him disquietude or to give him hope. For nearly thirty years he had lived as a wild beast of the bush. To-night he was a man again.

Again! Back came the more recent scenes of his manhood, like biograph pictures thrown wildly by a drunken hand. The clang of the axes in the sandalwood clump, the crash of the falling trees, the roar of the bullock-driver to his patient beasts, the ring of the taut chains, the slather of the great trunks in the sand as the team hauled them through the pines, the blazing fire in this very hut, the laughter and the songs, the dreams of home and fortune. Ah! how it all came back to him. He crouched-over the prostrate form of the girl and the one word 'woman' crossed his lips.

'Wo-man!' He said it again very softly. He bent gently down and touched her lips with his hand. The girl shivered and opened her eyes. With superhuman power she rose and flung him from her, then with shriek after shriek that pierced the quivering night she dashed through the broken doorway and fled like a wraith into the darkness.

The wild man stood discomfited, and a tear, a human tear, glistened a moment in the starlight. A wave of feeling surged over his awakening heart. Dimly he recognised the fact that through this woman, and only through her, lay his chance of regaining his kingdom of manhood. He groped his way to the door and stepped out into the starlight. He had entered the bark hut as a beast, a wild beast of the woods; he left it regenerated by a voice and a glance and a memory, once more a man.

Flinging away his vine-stick, he drew himself to his full height and walked rapidly away across the ridges in the direction which the girl had taken.

                *   *   *

The sun was well up above the mulga trees to the eastward when a white man and a black boy dashed up to the hut on horseback. The black was in front, and he leaned low from his saddle as he followed with a keen eye the light tracks in the sand, that meant so much to one who could read them aright.

'Bin gone out again', he said shortly to the man following, 'bin gone out early — early this mornin'!' The man saw at a glance that he was right. The fresh tracks of a woman's foot pointed away towards the ranges. Suddenly the black boy checked his horse.

His eyes bulged with astonishment and then with fear. He pointed to a strange new track upon the sand, the track apparently of a naked human foot, adorned with prodigious talons. 'What *that* fellow?' he asked, in awed tones. The white man bent down from his saddle, and his bronzed face grew pale beneath its tan. 'Don't you know an emu track yet, Jacky?' he said, with an affectation of contempt, but in a tone that did not deceive the black fellow. 'Come along, hurry up!' They dismounted and peered into the hut. It was empty, as they had expected. They remounted their horses and galloped away on the tracks they were following, though Jacky looked back with a scared face at the great bird tracks that he could not understand.

                *   *   *

The wild man walked rapidly in the direction which the girl had taken. It may have been only some instinct of the woods which guided him, or he may indeed have followed the footprints with the human intelligence which was fast returning to him; but in any case scarcely a mile had been traversed before he came upon the object of his search huddled up at the foot of a great gum-tree.

A little distance from her the man stopped, and, squatting on his heels, sat watching her with an absorbing curiosity that was something less than human. At last the woman looked up, and saw him; with a shriek that rang through the Bush she leapt to her feet, but, almost immediately slipped to the ground in a faint. The wild man began to gibber to himself, but had anyone else been present he might have caught amid the jargon of strange sounds here and there a familiar English word. In the shock of this strange meeting with one of his own kind the wild man was slowly coming back to his kingdom. Much agitated, he bent over the fainting girl; then, as reason gradually reasserted itself, he rose, and, running to a little pool of water in the gum trees, dipped his hand in it, and carried what he could of the precious liquid, and dashed it on the lips of the unconscious object of his concern. The woman stirred, moaned, and sat up. With a cry of joy the wild man leapt to his feet just as the teamster, dashing up, sprang from his horse and began to fumble in his belt. The newly awakened intellect of the naked man in the tattered loin-skin was keen as a knife; he saw the gesture and dropped on his knees, dumbly asking for his life. It was too late the revolver spoke, and he reeled and went down with the old beast-cry on his lips.

One Man's Wages

It was in the middle of a sixty-mile dry stage in the burning heart of the Northern Territory.

The great mob of travelling cattle drew slowly on through the stunted saltbush; during the extreme heat of the noon hours they had camped in scattered companies of three or four under the trees at the edge of the ridge, but now, with the sun sloping steadily towards the Western horizon and the breeze of late afternoon tempering its furnace heat, the great beasts plodded on across the plain, weary and foot-sore and in desperate need of water, but grateful for the comparative coolness of the waning day. Behind them and beside them the drovers rode, bent low upon the necks of their tired and thirsty nags. The whole picture gave an impression of failure and despondency, and suggested a baffled army in defeat. The drovers were all black fellows, with the exception of one, the swarthy gaunt Australian who was in charge of the cattle. He rode stooping over his horse's withers, and his face was lined and wrinkled with care, but his eyes were keen as a mountain hawk's as his glance strayed hither and thither over the bullocks and the black boys and the little mob of pack and spare horses that with jingling bells walked with the rearguard of the cattle.

A man of from fifty-five to sixty years of age, bronzed and hardened in the bondage of the Bush, Harry Scrivener was well known on the outside tracks as a clever and successful drover. His only fault was a violent temper which blazed out on the smallest provocation, and on this account he was feared and hated by most of the men who worked for him. So fierce and morose had he become with increasing years that he found it almost impossible to get white men to accompany him on his longer overland journeys, and on this particular occasion — with two thousand miles of desert to cross — he had been obliged to employ an outfit composed entirely of black fellows, who were capable, if not wholly reliable, assistants. Scrivener had always got on well with the blacks; a silent and dignified man when his temper was not roused, he appealed very much to these children of nature; and it is a well-known fact that they work more willingly and more faithfully for a white man whom they fear than for one who is merely just to them. This stern disciplinarian and fearless backwoodsman had shot down their countrymen like dogs for an insolent answer or an order disobeyed, and they knew it and respected him accordingly.

The present trip was one of more than usual difficulty. A long spell of dry weather had made the distances between the waterholes further than ever, and a less dauntless drover than Scrivener would have turned back ere half the journey had been covered; but it was this man's boast that he had never turned back on any trip that he had undertaken, and he meant to push on to the South Australian border in the teeth of whatever difficulties might be in store for him.

Several times during the journey he had congratulated himself that he had only black fellows in his camp, for assuredly white men would have deserted him in those first dry stages, when the heat was almost intolerable, when the cattle were dropping from thirst, the horses dying, and the men themselves put to the utmost straits to carry enough of the precious liquid for their needs. The worst that can befall any drover is that his men should leave him in such a crisis as this. A strike of workmen in any form and in any surroundings of commercial life is a serious thing; but picture the position of a man left single-handed in the desert with a thousand head of cattle to control! Before him looms inevitable failure to carry out his contract, the loss of the valuable stock in his charge, and, worse than all, the loss of his reputation as an overlander. To avoid this final and irreparable disgrace men have carried their shoes in their hands — so to speak — on many occasions, and have rendered all sorts of concessions to those under them to prevent their desertion and all that it entails. To a man of Scrivener's temper and masterfulness such an experience would have been galling in the extreme. With his riggers he had felt safe enough; a man of stern measures at all times, he would unhesitatingly have shot dead any one of his boys who had talked of deserting him. The life of a black fellow is held but a little thing on the outposts or civilisation when weighed in the balance against the reputation or ambition of a white man.

On this particular day a feeling of uneasiness assailed the leader. The cattle were restless and stubborn; the black boys sullen and suspiciously intimate with one another. Had they been white men Scrivener would have been alarmed, but they had come so far with him and had stood so many hardships cheerily that he never dreamed of their wishing to desert him; nor did he think that they would dare to do so, in any case.

At last the scorching sun sank below the ridges in a ball of fire; a crimson glow reddened the stony surface of the salt-bush plain, and the tiny flame of the camp fire shot up in a clump of timber in front of them. Slowly the footsore cattle drew in to camp. Scrivener set two of the black boys to watch the cattle, and, with the others, rode over to the camp fire. The horses were belled and hobbled, and turned out to feed, the packs were unfastened, the blankets spread, and the white man and the four blacks who were off duty took their simple supper of beef and damper and tea. A quarter of a mile away the cattle, rounded up on the edge of the sandhills, moaned and muttered in their restless thirst. The two black boys on watch rode slowly round them, their squat figures silhouetted against the glow of the sun-set. And then came down the dark.

Scrivener was oppressed with a strange presentiment of approaching trouble. He noted the black boys whispering together, and swore at them in the rough oaths of the overland. They drew apart, muttering. He sent two of them to relieve those on watch and then about ten o'clock he turned in, dead tired, and slept. All the night before he had been in the saddle, riding forward to inspect the country over which his cattle would have to travel in the next few days, and — strong man as he was — he was overcome with fatigue. He slept heavily, and woke at last with a start. The sun was already up, the fire had burned low, not a black fellow was in sight, where the cattle had camped not a beast was to be seen. Scrivener sprang to his feet with an oath. It took him some moments to realise the position: the blacks had deserted him, the cattle were spread far and wide across the fenceless desert; the horses had been driven away; he was helpless, ruined! As he stumbled across to the fire, with eyes searching the far-off horizon, his foot struck something. He looked down, and saw, laid against his now useless saddle, a quantity of food and water, perhaps enough for two days, or three at the most, if used with the utmost economy. It might take him as far as the Redwood waterholes, forty miles on; it would take him no further.

With clenched fists and staring eyes, Scrivener stood, and cursed the men who had played him false. If he had had a horse he would have ridden on the tracks of the deserters day and night till he had overtaken them, and then he would have shot them down one by one without compunction. Thank heaven, he still had his revolver! But the cunning natives had taken care to leave no such means of vengeance within his power. Deeply and fervently he swore that if he ever reached Queensland again he would hunt down those dark-skinned traitors, and send each one of them to his just doom, for the scurvy trick they had played him. The more he thought of it the more his anger grew. He, Scrivener, the shrewd, clever man of resource, to be hoodwinked and outwitted so simply by a parcel of slab-headed niggers! How the Queensland cattle men would laugh at him! And his brother drovers — they would say he should have stuck to white men, he who was always so sure of his d—d niggers! On such thoughts he fed till his anger nearly choked him; then, practical bushman that he was, he pulled himself together, and considered what was best for him to do. His cattle were gone, his horses, and his men; there remained for him nothing but to roll up his blankets and his few provisions, and with the water-bag the blacks had left him set out on his long tramp to the Redwood waterholes, where possibly there might be some drover camped who would lend him a horse. As to his recovering his cattle, he knew that his only possible chance in that direction was that he might in the next couple of days fall in with a party of drovers returning with an idle plant, who might be prevailed upon to accept a wage from him, help him to recover his cattle, and return with him as far as the South Australian border, where he might pick up men and horses and resume his journey; but this chance he knew was a very slender one. Unless the cattle were gathered within forty-eight hours or so they would be hopelessly scattered throughout the desert, many would have perished from want of water, and the recovery of the others might be the work of many weeks.

Resigning himself to his fate, Scrivener breakfasted sparingly from his slender store of rations, and shouldering his load, started off westward on his long tramp. When the noon heat became oppressive he camped in the sparse shade of a cottonbush, and in the afternoon he toiled on again, cursing the heat and the flies and the fate that had robbed him of his horse. Like all horsemen, he found walking difficult, his light riding boots were no protection from the burning ground; and the unaccustomed effort tired him quickly. Long before sundown he had chosen his camp, and determined to go no further that day, but his slender water supply caused him apprehension, and when the moon rose he picked up his bundle and resumed his march — made easier by the coolness of the night.

At last, too weary and foot-sore to go further, he lay down and went to sleep. In an hour he was awake again, the slave of custom, listening for his horse bells; with a curse he realised that he had no horses, no cattle, no men — that he was without reputation and without hope. The loneliness of the great plains covered him like a shroud, and in his impotent wretchedness he turned his face against his folded coat and cried like a child — this strong, hard man, who had been as iron to his comrades and his subordinates, and who had not wept since a certain terrible night, nearly thirty years before, when his young life had been marred by a traitorous friend. To-night, in his pitiful self-commiseration, the scenes of that drama rose before him again with living power; the quarrel with his young wife; the intercession on her behalf of the man he had thought was his friend; the subsequent flight of the lovers. Again he lived through the lonely, dragging hours of uncertainty; the search for her; the discovery of her letter explaining her flight; and the days of bitter remorse when he found that she had left him for ever, and left no trace behind.

All this came back to him as he lay staring up at the burning white stars, with the moonlit cotton bush swaying at his shoulder. The silence and the loneliness had woke again those ghosts of the past that had thought were laid for ever. Instinctively his fingers closed on the cold steel of his revolver — at least he had one friend left! He did not care now. His life and reputation were wrecked; he had tried to live down his sorrows like a man, but now even his outpost life was blasted. If he were rescued he would go back to Queensland, track down those cowardly niggers and shoot them one by one, and then — he would go South to Sydney on the renewal of the quest he had long abandoned, careless of anything but revenge, he would track out the scoundrel who had wrecked his life — if he were still above ground — and would shoot him too, like the dog that he was! And then — well, then — he might turn his weapon on himself for aught that any one would care!

From his desperate thoughts he was suddenly aroused by the sound of hoofs and the clink of muffled bells. At first he thought it only a trick of his disordered imagination, but, raising himself on his elbow, he saw four men riding across the plain, driving pack horses in front of them. He knew at once that they were drovers going out to Queensland with a cattle plant, travelling in the cool of the moonlight over this long, waterless stage. Leaping to his feet, he coo-eed loudly.

The men reined up their horses and looked curiously at the lonely, haggard figure which sprang out of the stunted bushes to greet them. It was hardly the spot at which they might have expected to meet a traveller on foot on that lonely, deserted track. 'Good Heavens!' said the leader of the party, when Scrivener in a few words had blurted out his story, 'Niggers cleared out? Lucky they left you some water, old chap! They aren't always so considerate in these cases! Only last night, you say? Why, the cattle won't have much spread on 'em yet, and they'll be all drawing on towards the water. We could gather 'em in a day. If you'll pay us droving wages I and my mates'll turn back and give you a hand as far as the Border with 'em. You'll get riggers at Ardmooka, and horses, too. Cheer up, mate, we won't see you stranded!'

Scrivener's heart leapt at the words. He would live; he would save his reputation, he would wreak his vengeance. He came forward and held out his hand in grateful recognition of the proffered help.

'I'm Harry Scrivener', he said simply; 'everybody west of Charleville knows me, and knows that I always remember a good turn, and by the same token', he added fiercely, as the bitter thoughts of five minutes before crowded to his mind again 'I never forget a bad one'.

The stranger's hand seemed to tremble in the swarthy fingers that clasped it, and the stranger's eyes wandered past Scrivener across the shining sea of moonlit saltbush and into the shadows of the years that the locust had eaten.

Scrivener noticed the tremor, and set it down to the usual cause — a spree after the delivery of the cattle. Ten months upon the droughtbound road, ten days in the Adelaide bars — it was the accepted programme of the Territory drovers.

At dawn they started out to round up the scattered bullocks, and Scrivener rode a horse lent him by his rescuer. To skilled cattlemen and to trackers of experience the mustering was easy, the main body of the herd was found together, still moving onwards towards the water with a wonderful instinct, and the stragglers and laggards were soon gathered in. At sundown the cattle were counted on the camp, and Scrivener found that only forty were missing. These he chose to abandon rather than risk the safety of the larger number by delay; so with his self-elected assistants he pushed the cattle on at dawn, and within forty-eight hours was safely camped at the Redwood waterholes.

Hitherto he had been too much occupied with the work in hand to pay much attention to the personnel of the little band of men which had lent him assistance so opportunely; but here, with the thirsty cattle watered and restfully camped, with the red fire blazing merrily and the horse bells jingling in the grass, Scrivener turned with renewed interest to his kindly benefactors, and especially to their leader. He was a short, dark-bearded man with a silent, rather nervous manner, and the usual reserve of men who make their living in the wilds. The manner, and something in the tone of his voice, seemed familiar to Scrivener, but the face recalled nothing to him, and the name — Wilgarn — given by the stranger, was one which to the best of his knowledge Scrivener had never heard before. Yet that voice and manner puzzled him exceedingly; for they were as familiar as the face was strange.

Two nights later a glint of gold in the camp firelight revealed the secret On the third finger of the stranger's left hand glittered the coils of a gold snake ring that had once belonged to Scrivener's wife. In a moment he saw behind the disguise of the full dark beard and the tan of the scorching West, the crafty, cunning features of the traitor who had ruined his home. Involuntarily Scrivener's hand tightened on the handle of his revolver, but with an effort he restrained himself. They were still two days from the Border; he had a reputation to save; this vile coward should save it for him before he died.

Meanwhile, the stranger — once the friend, later the betrayer, and now the rescuer — confident that Scrivener had not recognised him, had determined to carry through the rescue which he had promised before hearing the name of the man he had offered to assist. He trusted to his disguise, and the forgetfulness born of thirty strenuous Western years, but he trusted in vain.

Once he had discovered who his benefactor was, all feelings of gratitude faded from Scrivener's heart, and in their place rose the dark promptings of vengeance. He became again the silent, watchful man of iron; and he spoke but little to the other drover, fearful lest he should betray himself and the stranger cheat him of his revenge.

At last the long line of the South Australian fence cut the shimmering vastness of the plain in two, and some hours later the silver roofs of Ardmooka caught the setting sun. Scrivener made arrangements for men and horses for the rest of the journey, and that night for the last time he camped with the little band of overlanders who had pulled him out of his tightest corner.

After supper he drew from his pocket-book a thick bundle of bank notes, and proceeded to pay the men their well-earned wages. To each of the stockmen he gave, in addition to the wage already promised, a gift of a pound. Then he turned to Arkles — or Wilgarn, as he called himself — holding out the money which he had promised to him if he lent his aid as far as the Border.

As the man bent forward to take the proffered notes, Scrivener whipped his revolver from his belt. 'And this as a gift from Marion's husband!' he said, in stern, even tones, shooting the traitor through the heart.

The Master Horseman

AUSTRALIA HAS BRED many famous horsemen, but it was the proud boast of Mooculta Station, on the Moonee River, that there in the stockmen's hut was to be found the finest rider in the world. No buckjumper had ever thrown him, and he had ridden the worst that Queensland could produce; no man could ride faster through the river-scrub, and he had tried conclusions with the most noted stockmen of the cattle-country; no man had ever lighter hands or a firmer seat; no one could get more out of a racehorse or could better handle a stubborn colt. As a driver he had no equal; four horses or six he could swing at speed among the bristling stumps of the half-cleared bush roads or wheel through the branching scrub. Wherever horsemanship was valued or discussed Bob Champion's name was known. Moreover, unlike many famous horsemen, he was modest in the extreme, and seldom or never spoke of his distinguished deeds in the saddle or behind a team. A gallant and a useful member of bush society was Bob Champion, second stockman on Mooculta.

The Redgards of Mooculta were an old and much-respected family. Their homestead, far removed as it was from the refining influence of the cities and their civilisation, reflected culture and content. There for three-fourths of the year, the little family was satisfied to bury itself apart from town society, and to busy itself with the somewhat monotonous labour of the household and the sometimes strenuous toil of the paddocks. Old Mr Redgard acted as his own manager and supervisor; his son Ted was overseer and leader of the two white stockmen and the army of blackfellows who rode the fences and worked the cattle; and Mrs Redgard and her young daughter Claire, with the head stockman's wife to help them, found ample occupation in the care of their dainty, well-furnished house.

To the quiet homestead on the Moonee River came Rachel Warburton, Clare's cousin, on a month's visit. Rachel was twenty, six years older than Claire, bright, vivacious, and fond of company, and to her the sleepy little white-roofed home seemed dull and prison-like after the endless life and movement of Brisbane. At first the novelty of the Bush appealed to her, the picturesque beauty of the river-bend, the garden, and the tall windmill, the blacks' camp, the Chinaman's quarters, the bullock-team, the stockyard full of its restless mob of horses. She loved the wild flowers the cockatoos and parrots that wheeled and chattered overhead, the white cranes that sat like brooding river-spirits upon the dead limbs of the gum trees, and the silence of the weird Bush nights appealed at first to her romantic soul.

But soon the Bush and its bizarre beauty began to pall in a week she had exhausted these new sensations, the silence set her nerves quivering, and she longed for excitement — for the rush and gaiety of the streets, for women to prattle to and for men to flirt with, for picnics up the Brisbane River, and moonlit dances with the friends that understood her. She found the Redgards kind, but slow-going and methodical and content, while every pulse of her thrilled in yearning for the wider life.

At first she was content to take a novel to the river, and, with cushions piled about her in the old flat-bottomed station boat, to read for a little while and then to lie back looking idly at the burnished blue of the glorious Queensland sky — to dream of her many conquests and of the thrilling, rapturous life which already she had tasted in its fulness; for Rachel was fair to look upon and had gained more homage and attention than fall to the lot of most girls.

Very soon she learned to hate the river, with its monotonous, stifling silence, its slow-moving, muddy current, its slimy backwaters, and myriad mosquitoes. Then it was that she found out the stockyard and its attractions. Horses, although she was afraid of them unless with the stout gum rails to protect her, fascinated her strangely. She loved to watch them racing wildly round the yard when the stockmen and the blackfellows went in to bridle their nags for work. She loved to watch a yearling colt roped and thrown for branding, and, most of all, she delighted in seeing a buckjumper — a real Queensland outlaw — blindfolded and saddled and ridden by one of these men who seemed to know not what fear meant. Bob Champion was her hero, from the first. She soon heard of his great reputation, and, indeed, fine horsemen as were Ted and Jack, the head-stockman, and one or two of the blackfellows, it was soon evident, even to her unaccustomed eyes, that Champion was the master horseman of the ranche.

Apart from his skill in the saddle she found herself fascinated by the man himself. He was so brave, so skilful, so alert, so modest, and yet so masterful. Here was a man indeed. She found herself worshipping this handsome bronzed son of the bush who forced the wild untamed creatures to do his bidding. Mentally she compared him in his physical perfection with the narrow-shouldered dancing men of her acquaintance — this brown-faced, lithe-limbed Apollo.

At this time Champion was busy breaking a mob of three-year-olds. The other men were away all day upon the run, attending to fences, and rounding up the cattle to water. Champion's work lay in the stock-yard at the head station, and here he was to be found, day by day, catching and handling the young stock, riding them in the round yard, and sometimes out upon the sandhill, dust-covered but happy; always smiling, patient, resourceful. For hours at a time Rachel Warburton would sit upon the stock-yard fence and watch him.

Soon she found herself, though loath to admit it, craving for a word from this prince of horsemen. The first time she addressed him he was fully engaged in reaching for the dangling girth of a plunging, wheeling filly, and he deigned no answer to her gentle remark. But when the critical moment had passed and the girth had been captured and secured he turned to her with kindly blue eyes and said, 'Yes, Miss! I'm very fond of horses and workin' among 'em. You see, I've always been used to it, since I was a kid. No, I never was frightened of 'em, as I can remember.'

'O, yes', he went on, as she plied him with questions, 'I've often got kicked; you see, a man gets careless sometimes; being so used to 'em like, he takes 'em cheap; then he gets kicked, and then he keeps a better look out for a time or two.'

She watched him, fascinated, as he walked round the filly, picking up her feet one by one, stroking her here and there, and slapping the big buckjump saddle with his hand.

'Is that a wild on?' she asked.

'Lor' bless you, no, Miss! Quiet as a sheep! This one's out of the old grey buggy mare. A kid could ride this one. Some o' them's a bit nasty, though, right enough. That's a bad chap standing in the little yard. He'll buck all right. His mother was a bad one!'

For several days Rachel spent most of her time at the stockyard. She and the stockman became firm friends and Champion looked eagerly for her coming, and felt that his work had lost some of its interest when she had gone. Sometimes, in a pause of his labours, he would come and stand by the fence where she sat, and talk to her of the Bush, of the cattle, of the droughts and floods, and fires, which they of the back country never ceased to fight; and she would listen enthralled, but most she loved to hear him speak of himself, of his triumphs over outlawed horses and old rebels that no other horseman could master. His modesty appealed to her, and she knew that, however humble his position might be, he was one of the world's great men in achievement and modest wearing of his laurels. She found herself thinking of him even when away from the yard. In the drawing-room, in the garden, at the riverside, he seemed to be beside her — handsome, reckless, debonair, a prince of rope and bridle.

One day she made him promise to give her riding lessons, and, after obtaining leave from her host and hostess, she went out often with him on an old quiet pony of Claire's. Champion taught her how to hold the rains, how to mount, how to treat her pony's mouth as though it were delicate and breakable as a butterfly's wing, how to straighten him when he swerved, how to hold him when he pulled, and Rachel listened gladly for love of the kind blue eyes of the man and his masterful voice, and his brown hand clasped over hers upon the rain.

After one such ride she came home a little flushed and uncertain of herself, and that night she admitted to her own heart that she loved him, loved this great bronze giant of a working-man, this servant, this underling, her Apollo and her prince. She admitted the fact to herself with shame, yet deep down in her inner consciousness she knew that she was proud to own this love — whatever the world might think.

For his part Bob Champion was becoming thoughtful. Her hand's touch that was almost a caress disturbed his honest mind. He felt that here lay danger, perhaps tragedy; and this man who feared no tangible thing that earth could bring against him looked on love and was afraid. 'She's not for the likes of me', he said, burying his brown face in the cool mane of the colt he was handling, 'and I guess I'll pull out'.

From that time till the end of Rachel's visit she saw very little of him, except on the rare occasions when it was impossible for him to refuse to act as her escort. She noticed the change in his manner, but never guessed the reason, putting it down to the likelihood of her having been too importunate in interfering in his business hours, and she tried to make amends by treating him with more kindness than ever.

At last came the day when Rachel was to leave for Brisbane. This entailed an eighty-five mile drive to the nearest point of the railway. She hardly knew whether to be pleased or annoyed when she learned that Bob Champion had been chosen to drive her. It was a busy week of mustering, none of the other three white men could be spared for the two days which the journey to and fro entailed. Champion, being already off the working strength of the station by reason of a wounded knee which a restive colt had jammed against a post of the stockyard, was the obvious one who could be spared, and to Champion's care the girl was entrusted. They were to do the eighty-five miles in one day and part of a night, relays of fresh horses having been sent on with black boys to different parts of the route. The plains were heavy after a week of rain, and Champion was to drive the light wagonette with four horses, which he would change every twenty or twenty-five miles.

Rachel had been dreading this day of parting; this day on which she felt she must leave behind, to his horses and his cattle and his bondage, the one man who had ever made her pulses quicken by his touch. She felt that she would never see him again, that she must put his handsome brown face and lithe strong figure out of her heart for evermore, and she felt that she could better have bidden farewell to this disturbing incident in her young life had the chief actor in it not been told off to escort her on this final journey from the scene of its happening.

As to Champion, he, too, looked forward to the drive with misgiving. He had honestly done his best to avoid this woman whom he knew now that he loved better than his life, whose sweet bewitching face came between him and his work, and haunted him in the long sleepless silence of the night. He feared himself, feared that he would be unable to disguise from her the love that he felt, the love that his sense of honour forbade him to disclose. And so, fearing yet greatly loving, these two set forth upon the long, grey river-road.

For the first few miles Bob Champion was busy with his horses, which were fresh and lively, and though he drove with consummate mastery and generally with absolute confidence, this morning he was extra careful, and instead of springing his team along for a mile or so to 'warm them up and steady 'em down', as he would have done in the ordinary routine of a drive across the station with rations or camping outfit, he pulled them well together and compelled his reefing leaders to trot at a pace so slow that they tossed their lean heads up and down in haughty disdain.

Champion was generally gay and communicative, but to-day he was extremely silent, only occasionally speaking to his horses. Soon the silence began to set Rachel's nerves dancing. She felt she must speak.

'How well they go along!' she said, and was angry because for some reason her voice had a tremor in it.

'Yes, Miss!' said the stockman.

'Is that grey one the mother of the one you were breaking?' asked Rachel.

'O, no, Miss — that's old Billy Blue.'

Rachel gave up the horses and was silent for a while.

'How far is it to Birnam Station, where you change horses?'

Bob Champion pointed with his whip to a silver roof in the river-timber. 'That's it', he said, 'about three miles from here.'

A black boy was ready with fresh horses. The change was quickly made, and they bowled gaily along over a hard red sandhill with feathery pine trees leaning above them. The silence between them was oppressive. Rachel felt angry with herself; her time with the man she loved was all too short, and she was throwing precious moments away. Ah! Why would he not be friendly and courteous as he had been but two short weeks ago? He was breaking her heart, this great silent, handsome bushman, with his quiet scorn!

The miles rolled steadily by, and still they never spoke of the things so near the hearts of both. At noon they reached Warrington Downs and their second change. Here Rachel lunched with the squatter's family, whom she knew slightly, and Champion refreshed himself in the stockman's hut. At two o'clock they started again. The road now left the river and climbed the stony ranges, and the bare-footed horses made slow progress, limping painfully over the flints.

'Should have had them shod for this stage', said the stockman, and it was the first time he had made a remark without being called upon.

The westering sun blazed down upon them, and it grew hotter instead of cooler as the day went on. The reserve that had been so marked between them in the morning seemed to melt away as the miles went by, and Bob Champion began to chat in something like his old cheery way. He thought the girl was beginning to grow tired, and he felt it incumbent upon him to make the journey as pleasant as possible for her. At five o'clock they reached a little bush hotel, their last changing place, and here Rachel found tea prepared for her. At six o'clock they were ready to start again.

'This is my best team', said Bob Champion, as he took an all-round pull at the four eager chestnuts, 'and we'll be in Larrastown by half-past eight'. The sun went down behind the myall trees, and red and splendid came up the winter moon.

Once more silence fell upon the lovers, and the weird hush of the Bush wrapped them round. Only the crop, crop, of the bare hoofs, the jingle of the harness, and the creak of the lead-bars sounded under the moon. Champion spoke first — 'Will you try holding them, Miss?' Mechanically Rachel stretched out her hands for the reins, and the stockman's fingers closed over hers as she took them. 'This way', he said, setting them between her fingers in approved fashion, 'leaders here, wheelers there!'

With the thrill of their touching hands came the sudden leaping together of their hearts. There was a moment of splendid silence when all the angels of heaven stood listening together, then Champion put his arm round the girl — 'God forgive me', he said reverently, 'I can't help it, Miss — Miss Rachel — can't you see I love you?' The moon reeled above the tree-tops, the grey bush spun before her eyes. At last, at last! Her heart had not betrayed her, then! Her gallant horseman loved her as she loved him.

Monotonously the hoofs of the chestnuts rang forward through the night. They rang on the river bridge, and they clanged up the wide paved street, and two hearts gave back the music of their rhythmic beat.

And when the night train pulled out for Brisbane the tall, fair society girl and the bronzed bushman stood hand-in-hand looking back into the moonlit bush, and the world was all their own

Notes

Part I: Introduction
1. *Life*, Melbourne, April, 1904.

Chapter One: Youth!
1. George Ogilvie, *Balladist of Borders and Bush*, 1994.
2. Ibid.

Chapter Two: The Belalie Jackeroo
1. William Cameron, *History of Bourke*, not dated.
2. Mary Durack, *Kings in Grass Castles*, 1959.
3. George Ogilvie, *Balladist of Borders and Bush*, 1994.
4. Will H. Ogilvie, *My Life in the Open*, 1908.
5. William Cameron, op.cit.
6. Ibid.
7. George Ogilvie, op. cit.
8. Ibid.

Chapter Three: Bound for South Australia
1. *The Bulletin*, 9 February 1963.
2. Will H. Ogilvie, *My Life in the Open*, 1908.
3. Letters in possession of Catherine Jeffries, Edinburgh.
4. Margaret Muller, *Dreamers and Singers*, 1994.

Chapter Four: On the Lachlan Side
1. Will H. Ogilvie, *My Life in the Open*, 1908.
2. Ibid.
3. Miles Franklin, *My Brilliant Career*, 1901
4. Ogilvie, Will H., Letter to Alexander Irvine, in possession of David Irvine, Toowoomba, Qld.

Chapter Five: The Bogan Gate Polo Club
1. *Champion Post*, Parkes, 9 December 1964, from a MS in possession of the Beuzeville family.
2. J. Watts and C. Wright, *The Story of Trundle*, 1987.

Chapter Six: Breaker's Mate
1. Mitchell Library of N.S.W., ML.MS.CY2096A. Quoted by M.Carnegie and F. Shields, *In Search of Breaker Morant*, 1979, but not sighted by author.
2. Mitchell Library of N.S.W., ML.DOC. 1809.
3. Ibid. P1/O. Quoted by Carnegie and Shields, op. cit. but not sighted by author at this location. Later found at ML AL/29/36 (Lawson Letters).

Chapter Seven: A Tarnished Hero?
1. W. Stone, 'The Puzzle of Breaker Morant', *Biblio-news*, 1953
2. M. Carnegie and F. Shields, *In Search of Breaker Morant*, 1979
3. Mitchell Library, A. G. Stephens Papers, ML.MSS. 4937/2, No. 429
4. Cutlack, Frederick Morley, *Breaker Morant*, 1962
5. ibid.
6. James Gibney and Desmond, *The Gatton Mystery*, 1977
7. Merv Lilley, *Gatton Man*, 1994
8. Cutlack, op. cit.
9. ibid.

Chapter Eight: The Boer War Ballads
1. Mitchell Library of N.S.W., A. G. Stephens Papers, ML.MSS. 4937/2 25 Jan. 1900, No .813–816.
2. Ibid, 3 February 1900; No. 817–818.
3. Mitchell Library of N.S.W. ML.MSS. CY2096A.

Chapter Nine: Ben Hall Legends
1. Will H. Ogilvie, Annotation in his personal copy of *Fair Girls and Gray Horses*, cited in a thesis by Geoffrey Cains, Mittagong, N.S.W.
2. Untitled and undated newspaper cutting in possession of Miss Nell Beuzeville, Parkes, N.S.W.
3. Will H. Ogilvie, Letter to Alex Irvine, in possession of David Irvine, Toowoomba, Qld.
4. See note 2.
5. Mitchell Library of N.S.W., A. G. Stephens Papers, ML.MSS. 4937/2, Aug. 1898; No. 529.

Chapter Ten: Going Home
1. Mitchell Library of N.S.W., A. G. Stephens Papers, ML.MSS. 4937/2, 5 Nov. 1900; No. 881.
2. George Ogilvie, *Balladist of Borders and Bush*, 1994.
3. ibid.

Chapter Eleven: An American Sojourn
1. Mitchell Library of N.S.W., A. G. Stephens Papers, ML.MSS 4937/2, 5 November 1900, No. 881.
2. ibid.
3. Archives of Iowa State University, U.S.A.
4. Mitchell Library of N.S.W., Op. cit.; 27 June 1905; No. 431/432.
5. ibid, 15 September 1905; No. 467.
6. ibid, 15 January 1906; No. 507–509.

Chapter Twelve: In Double Harness
1. George Ogilvie, *Balladist of Borders and Bush*, 1994.
2. Will H. Ogilvie, Letter to Alex Irvine, 1910, in possession of David Irvine, Toowoomba, Qld.

Chapter Thirteen: Pilgrims and Critics
1. *The Bulletin*, Red Page 25 February 1953.
2. MS unpublished, but author received 20 shillings for the article.
3. *The Bulletin*, Red Page cutting, not dated

Part II: Introduction
1. Will H. Ogilvie, Letter to Alex Irvine 3 April 1907. In possession of David Irvine, Toowoomba, Qld.

Part III: Introduction
1. Mitchell Library of N.S.W. A. G. Stephens Papers, ML.MSS. 4937/3, 7 January 1905, No. 319–320

Select Bibliography

• Will H. Ogilvie

The Bulletin, various, 1894–1912
CAMERON, WILLIAM, *History of Bourke*, not dated.
DURACK, MARY, *Kings in Grass Castles*, 1959.
Life, Melbourne, April 1904
The Lone Hand, 1907–21
MULLER, MARGARET, *Dreamers and Singers*, 1994.
OGILVIE, GEORGE, *Balladist of Borders and Bush*, 1994.
OGILVIE, WILL H., *Fair Girls and Gray Horses*, 1898.
— *Hearts of Gold*, 1903.
— *My Life in the Open*, 1908
— *The Honour of the Station*, 1914
— *The Australian and Other Verses*, 1916.
WATTS, J. & WRIGHT, C., The Story of Trundle, 1987.

• Harry H. ('Breaker') Morant

CARNEGIE, MARGARET AND SHIELDS, FRANK, *In Search of Breaker Morant*, 1979
CUTLACK, FREDERICK MORLEY, *Breaker Morant*, 1962.
DENTON, KIT, *The Breaker*, 1973.
FITZHENRY, W. E .F., 'Breaker's Contributions to *The Bulletin*', *Biblio-News*, 1953.
FOX, FRANK ('Frank Renard'), *Bushman and Buccaneer*, 1902.
Jenkins, Graham, *Songs of The Breaker*, 1980.
MORANT H. *The Poetry of Breaker Morant*, Golden Press, 1980.
ROSS, DAWN, *Pro Hart's Breaker Morant*, 1981.
STONE, WALTER, 'The Puzzle of Breaker Morant', *Biblio-News*, 1953.

• The Gatton Murders, and Criminology

'BOWYANG BILL', 'The Gatton Tragedy', *Australian Bush Recitations* No. 6.
GIBNEY, JAMES AND DESMOND, *The Gatton Mystery*, 1977.
LILLEY, MERV, *Gatton Man*, 1994.
MASTERS, BRIAN, *Killing for Company*, 1985
— *On Murder*, 1985.
SCOTT, ALAN, 'The Gatton Tragedy', (song) *A Collector's Notebook*, 1970.

Index of Poems

Index